Destroying Their God

Destroying Their God

How I Fought My Evil Half-Brother to Save My Children

Wallace Jeffs

With Shauna Packer and Sherry Taylor

Provo, Utah

Copyright © 2018 by Wallace Jeffs, Shauna Packer, and Sherry Taylor

All rights reserved, including the right to reproduce this book, or portions thereof, in any form. No part of this book may be used or reproduced in any manner whatsoever without written permission from the publisher, except in the case of brief quotations embodied in critical articles and reviews.

The views expressed herein are the responsibility of the author and do not necessarily represent the position of the publisher. The events herein are portrayed to the best of the author's memory. While all the stories in this book are true, some names and identifying details have been changed to protect the privacy of the people involved.

Cover design by Jason Robinson
Interior design by Marny K. Parkin

Published by Zarahemla Books, Provo, Utah, U.S.A.
info@zarahemlabooks.com
ZarahemlaBooks.com

ISBN 978-0-9993472-1-8 (paperback)
ISBN 978-0-9993472-2-5 (eBook)

*I dedicate this book to all my children, for whom I would do anything.
Being a parent isn't easy.
Sometimes it takes courage to make a stand to protect the ones you love,
because that's what parents do.
—Wallace Jeffs*

*For Mom and Dad.
Forever grateful for your legacy of love, encouragement, and unfailing devotion.
—Shauna Packer*

*To my family, who are my biggest cheerleaders
and who continually encourage me to never stop reaching for the stars.
Love you guys!
—Sherry Taylor*

Contents

Deadly Retribution	9
The Time to Tell	15
Creating Their God	21
Plyg Kid	29
A Living Hell on Earth	37
"I Will Not Tolerate Rebellion"	51
Tomorrow Is the End of the Earth	65
Brotherly Love	79
Father-Prophet	85
Blood Atonement	93
Marriage Middleman	97
Lifted Up	107
Exodus to Short Creek	117
Eliminating an Obstacle	125
He's Just in the Other Room	129
Marrying My Mothers	137
Yearning for Zion	141

Mission	151
Sadist's Game	161
Heavenly Sessions	169
On the Lam	175
The Fullness of the Law of Sarah	179
Ripping Away Innocence	183
Returned to the Fold	189
YFZ Raid	195
Forever Banished	201
False Prophet	209
"I Am Smiling. Are You?"	215
Moving Against Evil	221
Betrayal	227
My Children Begin to Escape	235
True Love	241
It's Not Over Yet	249
Acknowledgements	253
About the Authors	255

Chapter One

Deadly Retribution

I NEVER BELIEVED MY OWN BROTHER WOULD TRY TO KILL ME.

Boy, was I wrong.

My half-brother is Warren Jeffs, the self-proclaimed prophet of the Fundamentalist Church of Jesus Christ of Latter-Day Saints, or FLDS Church. In 2004, Warren announced a troubling revelation: some FLDS Church members must be separated from their children. Even a remote chance of losing any of my children scared me more than anything. At the time, I had two wives and twenty children. I was prepared to do anything to protect them.

I knew Warren's prophecy to be a convenient, self-serving lie. God doesn't want families torn apart, but few were immune—even infants and toddlers were seized from their mothers' arms. Throughout time, despots and dictators have tried to reduce parental influence on the youth. For Warren, this accomplished two vital objectives. First, it provided a continual pool of FLDS boys as slave labor for construction projects. Second, it allowed him unrestricted reign over young, impressionable girls, so he could use them as chattel in a political game of polygamist marriages to much older men.

Within the FLDS, any utterance from the prophet is deemed the word of God. Most families blindly complied with Warren's edicts. However, I was not like most heads of families. I became the first person to openly challenge this practice and refuse him access to my children.

After my rebellion against the prophet, other families began to question, and some stopped complying as well. Obviously, this didn't sit well with Warren. I had become a threat. As a result, I was kicked out of the church, forced from my home, and stripped of my profession. My children were kidnapped and hidden away throughout the United States under the direction of my half-brother Lyle, Warren's full brother.

Feeling terrified and without recourse, seven years after the revelation I filed a lawsuit, not only against Warren but also against the FLDS Church and its other leaders—they were all in on it. Because Warren's crimes crossed state lines, the sheriff's office and FBI became involved.

Now, because of my actions, FLDS Church secrets were open to public consumption by the hated and feared Gentiles.

It was a balmy Sunday afternoon, October 23, 2011. Though three nail-biting months had passed since I filed the lawsuit, things were starting to go well. I drove the forty miles from my home in Mesquite, Nevada, to St. George, Utah, located on the northwest edge of the Utah-Arizona border, to meet friends for dinner at Olive Garden. This area is known for its breathtaking redrock hills and mesas.

One mile before I reached the St. George Boulevard exit, a major accident occurred in the southbound I-15 lanes. A semitrailer carrying a load of bees overturned, releasing black, pulsating clouds of drones. As I zoomed past, a landscape of bugs splattered across my windshield.

Little did I know, within just a few hours the bees and I would have something in common.

"To the future!"

Nine friends clinked their various glasses of sodas and spirits against my beer bottle. These people

Dinner at the Oliver Garden in St. George, Utah (I'm on the left). This picture was taken about thirty minutes before my "accident."

had gathered to celebrate the return of my daughters, who I'd recently reclaimed from Lyle Jeffs with the FBI's help. But all I could think about was getting home to them. One of my older sons had stayed behind at my house with the girls. Though the months since our reunion had been rocky, I wanted nothing more than to spend every available minute with them. After a couple of hours, I left the restaurant around 7:30 to travel back to Mesquite.

The streets were quiet and dark, the temperature dropping—typical for a desert evening. As I drove, my mind kept wandering back and forth between my girls and the friends I'd just left. What a great day! Not even a red light to stop me. I punched up a classic rock station on the radio. Although things couldn't get much better, catching a Journey or Moody Blues song would only boost the awesome needle. I cranked up the volume, reveling in the freedom of something as basic as listening to a great tune—a simple pleasure forbidden to faithful FLDS members.

All thoughts of the previous incident on the freeway had left my mind.

I cruised down the extended, curving I-15 onramp. When I'd fully accelerated to sixty-five, I noticed a landscape of red lights in front of me. I stomped down on my brakes, but the car did not respond, keeping its momentum toward a semi with crimson brake lights.

Motionless cars crowded the left-hand lanes. To the right was a steeply declining embankment with no guardrail. With only seconds left before impact, there was nothing to be done. I realized in horror that the ramp's downward slope caused the Suburban to actually gain momentum. Pumping frantically on the unresponsive brakes, I plowed full on into the back of the semi.

I lost consciousness at the same moment the car burst into flames. Even before the final crunch of steel, the engine sat lodged in my lap. The exhaust manifold and steering wheel propelled through the wall of my stomach, creating a mass of torn internal organs and burned flesh.

The driver of the semi jumped out of his cab with a fire extinguisher. First responders and Life Flight arrived immediately—I can't imagine how they landed a helicopter in that chaos. Intertwined in my intestines, the steering wheel was only two inches away from the front of the driver's seat. Once they began extrication, they estimated I had ninety seconds to live. During the one-minute flight to Dixie Regional Hospital, I bled out twenty units of blood and my stomach swelled up to the size of two basketballs.

I was crushed in my Suburban on October 23, 2011, in St. George, Utah.

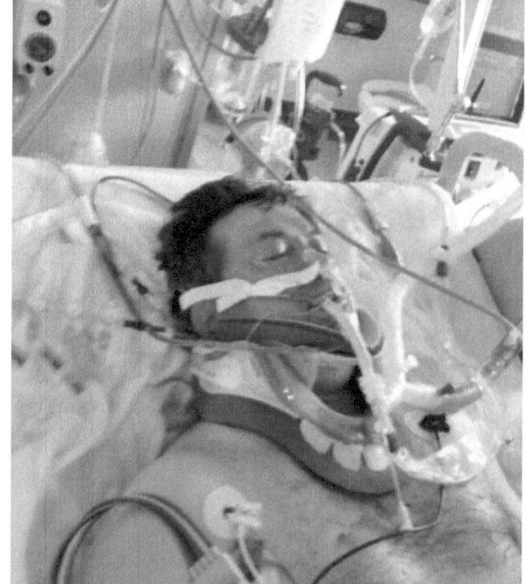

Two days after my "accident," I was still in a coma.

Emergency physicians gave me a five percent chance of survival. They operated throughout the night, including three separate surgeries to stop internal bleeding. The hospital had just installed a brand-new blood pump machine, and I became the first patient to use it. This external mechanical heart pumped blood back in as fast as I lost it, keeping me alive during the operation.

Many questions have been asked about my state of mind at the time of the accident. Could it have been my fault? The facts speak the truth. My phone: found in my pocket. Blood alcohol level: zero. Health: impeccable. Car: in perfect working order. Mentally: sound. I was beginning to get my children back, and I had supportive friends. I had absolutely no reason to want to cause myself or anyone else harm.

Because my vehicle had been destroyed by fire, police investigators found little or no physical evidence. They did note that no skid marks or any other sign existed that my car had slowed. Yet, when they pulled me out of the car, my right ankle was broken and pressed down on the brake pedal.

No concrete evidence exists that the Suburban had been meddled with. I am certain, however, that my brother, Warren Jeffs, from a holding cell in Kingman, Arizona, ordered one of Lyle's many God Squad enforcers to disable my car. I've seen such things happen before. On numerous occasions, I've witnessed Warren's impersonal, droning orders of punishment for an FLDS Church member who dared go against his word.

After the accident, a private investigator went to the Olive Garden parking lot. In the spot where my car had been parked, he found a large oil spill, potentially indicating that the car had been tampered with.

If Warren had tried to kill me, he nearly succeeded.

Chapter Two

The Time to Tell

I AWOKE IN AN INCOHERENT DAZE. I ATTEMPTED TO SIT UP, BUT MY body seemed incapable of following the commands screaming through my mind. *Get up! GET UP!* A middle-aged blond woman hovered over me. She looked like a teacher. Why was this teacher dressed all in white? Her appearance seemed an awful lot like Mother's before a shift at the hospital. As panic flooded my system with adrenaline, I tried to speak, but there was something horrible in my throat that no amount of gagging dislodged. When I tried to raise my hands to investigate, I found they were bound to my sides.

With an authoritative hand on my chest, the woman said, "It's okay. You're in the hospital. You've been in a coma for the past forty-five days."

She offered this information in a matter-of-fact tone, as if this news wouldn't rock my whole world.

"You're intubated, so you need to be calm and go back to sleep."

She must have given me a powerful tranquilizer because, despite my intense desire to flee, I felt my eyes grow heavy. Before I drifted back into the comforting no-man's-land of sleep, my unexpressed thoughts were: *Where are my children?*

IT SEEMED DAYS, IF NOT WEEKS, BEFORE I WOKE AGAIN, BUT IT WAS most likely just a few hours. Feeling more aware of my circumstances, I now fully grasped the frightening fact that I was in the hospital. FLDS members are wary of doctors and public health institutions—in fact, FLDS are wary of all Gentiles and their institutions. Although I had visited a few hospitals in my life, I had never been a patient, except for a brief visit to the emergency room when, as a young man, I shot a nail into my foot.

The room echoed with loneliness, except for one nurse, busy at her duties. I attempted to sit up again, but I found my wrists and left ankle were bound. The cast on my right ankle might as well have been an anvil.

Soon, the friends who I had dined with all those days ago rushed into the room. Incapable of communication, I still felt encouraged to see them, even if the looks of worry and pity on their faces were less than comforting.

But where was my family?

Two more weeks passed before I could utter my first words since crashing into the semi: "Where are my children?"

The nurse said, "Two of your sons were here a few weeks ago."

Weeks? Did she really say weeks? I took a deep breath. *Okay, so two of my boys came, but where are they now?*

Then I asked, "Where is Mother?"

Surely, she was close by.

"No one else from your family has been here," the nurse replied.

Where was everyone?

As difficult as it was for me to mentally grasp what had happened to my body, it was almost more challenging to fathom why not one member of my family was there and why so few had visited. I have a very large family. While I was in the FLDS Church, I had been legally married to one wife and spiritually married to another. With my two wives, I had twenty amazing children. I also had thirty-two half-brothers, thirty half-sisters, one full sister, and my mother.

The sense of lonely abandonment I felt was indescribable, far eclipsing the physical pain from my many life-threatening injuries.

Much later, I found out that Warren and Lyle had ordered the previous visit by my two boys. My sons had come to tell me that because of the prayers of the faithful in the church, my punishment had been meted out through a judgment by God. I had committed the unpardonable sin of speaking out against the prophet. The FLDS people, my people, had prayed for my demise, and it appeared to them that soon the judgment would come to pass.

Warren and Lyle ordered my sons that after saying good-bye to me—even though I was in a coma—they were to go and pick up my daughters, just recently freed from captivity, as well as my possessions, including three of my four cars, and take them all back to Colorado City, Arizona. They seized everything I owned, including a cell phone that contained incriminating information against Warren and Lyle.

My two half-brothers were forcing my family to desert me, a disobedient outcast, to protect their own salvation. Warren just wanted me to go away—he was going to do everything in his power to make that happen.

Not if I had anything to do about it.

As I began my painstakingly slow recovery, my half-brother David started visiting me every day for a few minutes. I would have given anything—everything—to sleep. Though I was on multiple pain medications, I could fall into only a few fitful naps throughout the day. David's visits broke up the monotonous time, and I relished those moments with someone I knew.

After David left each day, I stared at the door, willing it to open and reveal other faces I loved, but my hope was in vain. I've always been an independent individual; some might even call me a loner. But having this much alone time affected me in ways I never thought possible. The ache for my family, even my siblings, felt profound and debilitating.

I've never felt like I actually needed my mother. She was rarely around for me to form a close bond with; after all, since I was two years old, Warren's mother or the communal family had raised me. But through those long, dismal days, how I longed for her comfort and companionship. More than anything, I desired some small words of expert advice from my registered-nurse mother as to my condition. All I had to rely on were the hospital staff, but they didn't have the time to linger on my many questions, and I honestly felt afraid to ask them. I knew I'd lost my spleen and gallbladder, but when nurses came in to change the stomach dressing, they looked at the wound with undisguised horror, as if they didn't know what to do. Their behavior made me nervous and left me with the sense that perhaps I was better off not inquiring too much.

Over time I learned that my stomach was basically a large, unhealing hole. Doctors suggested that they operate to close it together so I wouldn't live my life with a gaping wound in my abdomen. With the tissue cauterization caused by the burning car wreckage, they could not guarantee that my flesh would ever knit together again, but they had to try.

As I went under the general anesthesia, I thought about Warren's desire for me to go away, how easy it would be to just let go.

But I knew I could not give up.

My stomach healed well; however, my foreboding about the safety of my family increased. What were Lyle and Warren doing to them? A friend had come to visit, and I told him I needed to get out of the hospital now, and he had to help me get released immediately. A nurse informed us that they had no right to keep me, but if I left, I would die. I didn't care. I felt so agitated and afraid that Warren had my children that I demanded to be released. They put me in a wheelchair, but I passed out before I reached the hospital doors and ended up waking in ICU.

As the winter holidays inched past, my muscles atrophied due to lack of use. Occupational therapists worked with me, but I could not move even my pinkie finger. The idea of feeding myself again seemed an impossible task. Discouragement threatened to take over. If I couldn't manage to move my fingers, how could I possibly ever walk again?

A few days later, an orthopedic doctor from Salt Lake City came to the unit and said that a bone in my leg had not healed correctly. If I had surgery on it, the procedure would most likely help me become more mobile.

He said, "I am qualified to perform the surgery. However, I won't operate until you answer some questions."

"Okay."

"You're Warren Jeffs's brother, right?"

"Yes," I answered, dumbfounded. I expected the standard questions about my health and past operations. What did Warren have to do with my leg?

"Well, have you ever raped little girls or had sex with a young girl?"

I can only imagine the expression on my face.

"I'm not going to operate on you if you have. I need to know that you are not like Warren and that you don't support him."

That's when I realized the damage Warren had done to me, just by my connection to him. With the doctor looming over my bed, I explained that I had previously been a member of the FLDS Church, but I had never participated in, nor had I condoned, any such behavior.

He replied, "Because you said that, I'll have to take your word for it, but I don't believe you."

This sneering man was someone I had to trust to cut open my leg and fix it?

Weeks later, one of my half-brothers arrived unexpectedly at the hospital. I was excited to see him, as he was the brother I felt closest to while growing up. However, interpreting the expression on his face, I knew something was wrong. My sense of elation plummeted.

With no emotion in his voice, my brother stated that he had come to deliver a message. The accident happened because I had turned traitor and this was my punishment. I needed to repent, accept Warren as the prophet, do his will, and return to the FLDS fold. This I must accomplish soon because Warren foretold that, after suffering enough agony, I would die. Even if I somehow miraculously lived, I would be disowned.

My heart sank as my brother turned and left without another word.

Strangely, after he had gone, an incredible sense of peace overcame me. I fell into a blessed, sound sleep and immediately stopped breathing.

I woke once again in the dreaded ICU—they never did find a medical reason why I stopped breathing. While looking at the results of a heart test, one doctor said that he could not believe how I healed. Willpower alone had to be the only reason behind the miracle.

Eventually, my healing progressed to the point where I moved to a rehabilitation center across town. There, one of the rehab doctors said the same thing to me as the orthopedic surgeon had said—that he would refuse to treat me if I was anything like Warren. Once again, by association with my brother, who I believed had just tried to kill me, I needed to defend myself against something I had never done.

February 7, 2012, was a great day—a miracle. I was deemed well enough to be released from medical care. I walked out of the rehabilitation center on my own. One hundred and seven days had passed since I drove away from that dinner at Olive Garden.

A good friend was kind enough to take me into his home because I had nowhere else to go. Within thirty days of being released, I suffered through an excruciating kidney stone and a severe pulmonary embolism, which almost took my life again. But after that, I never looked back.

Finally, I was to the point where I could begin reassembling the pieces of my life, which had fallen apart over the last four months. The accident basically bankrupted me. I had no insurance, and the hospital bill was over seven hundred and fifty thousand dollars. My last car was repossessed. Because my credit cards had not been paid while I lay comatose, my credit was destroyed. A business I'd begun to develop with a partner was now lost to me—he, of course, had to move on and continue to grow the enterprise while I recovered. Worst of all, my children were gone again.

I had lost everything.

But I had gained something: resolve. I was over the shame and hurt. I had nothing left to fear. My worst nightmare had already been realized when my family deserted me for my half-brothers Warren and Lyle. I had to prove to the world that I was not like them. It was time to help those trapped by the mysticism of Warren Jeffs and the FLDS Church to see the reality. I believe that Warren Jeffs is the evilest human being currently on the face of the planet. However, the good, kind people of the FLDS Church, blind in their obedience, have no way to know how Warren rose to his place of power and the truth behind his monstrous acts.

The time has come to tell. This is my story of sacrificing everything I held dear, not only to show my love but to protect my family from a narcissistic, evil man I once called prophet and brother.

Chapter Three

Creating Their God

My earliest memory remains cemented in my mind because it was an experience rooted in fear.

Most kids eagerly await their birthday. As a soon-to-be-minted four-year-old, I felt no different, even though the people in my church rarely acknowledged special days because celebrating was considered a worldly, Gentile tradition.

Unless you happened to be the prophet; then everyone celebrated with you.

Still, I anticipated something nice from Mother—a book from the thrift shop or even a birthday card. As I sat on the ragged living-room couch trying to figure out what a surprise might be, a blast of February air filled our tiny house as the door burst open.

"Sharon?!" The gruff voice thundered through our normally quiet home. I caught the sharp scent of recent snow.

Heart slamming, I stared at the enormous man. No man had ever invaded the sanctity of our little home before—I had never really even seen a man close up. I dove behind the couch and curled into a ball, hoping he wouldn't see me.

"Oh, Rulon, you're here," my mother said, clattering a spoon into the sink.

Mother had asked this stranger to our house? I guess she tried in her own way to make this day memorable, and in this she succeeded.

Keeping close to the floor, I peeked around the couch. The man loomed, and I knew just one wrong step from those enormous shoes could crush me flat. I took in his black suit, tie, and pressed white shirt, wondering how they made clothes to fit someone so big. He was monstrous—a good four inches above six feet, with a face as round as a dinner plate, a doughy double chin, and a shock of salt-and-pepper hair. As he beckoned me, his booming voice seemed capable of rattling the paint off the walls. There was no way on this planet I was going to come out and talk to this Goliath-like man.

Even though he claimed to be my father.

What was a father, exactly? I had never seen him before in my life. My mother and Aunt Marilyn told me my father was an important man, a senior apostle in the FLDS Church—fourth in line to the prophet—and I should respect him.

But what a father *really* was, I had no idea. What I did know was that this particular man's presence seemed to suck the very air from the room.

I lived with my mother, Sharon, and my sister, Vanessa, who was six months old, in Sugar House, a southeast neighborhood of Salt Lake City, Utah. On the other side of the house lived Aunt Marilyn and her eight children. The original home had been converted into a duplex with two full kitchens and basement access from one side to the other, so it was perfect for our two families.

I felt gratitude that Aunt Marilyn was on her side of the house and we were on ours. This man was overwhelming enough without adding the volatile Aunt Marilyn into the mix.

"I brought the boy a present," the stranger said, giving a package to my mother. Sneering down at me and without bothering to lower his voice, he added, "That boy has some serious issues. If you don't take care of him, he'll grow up to be a loner."

He spoke to her as if I didn't exist, not attempting to disguise how little I meant to him. I wished I could melt through the floor. He seemed disappointed, but I had no idea why. I held my tears, vowing that this man, who didn't like me yet claimed to be my father, would never make me cry.

When I glanced at my mother, my spirits sank a little lower. Though she tried not to show it, I could tell by her wounded look that she felt as devastated by his pronouncement as I did.

LATER, AFTER HE FINALLY LEFT, I CAME OUT OF MY HIDING PLACE. AT Mother's encouragement, I opened my present. The gift turned out to be a new Tonka truck, something of my very own and not a hand-me-down.

I should have been happy about it—no one had ever given me a present before—but I only felt relief that the awful man was gone.

As I played with my new toy, the words *serious issues* and *loner* kept ringing through my mind. I wasn't exactly sure what they meant, but from the way that man had said them, they seemed like something I should be deeply ashamed of.

Within what seemed like moments, the part of the day I dreaded most arrived—evening. When Mother was home and not sleeping, she, Vanessa, and I lived in peace on our side of the house, with little or no interaction with Aunt Marilyn and her children, especially the annoying know-it-all Warren. But now Mother was smoothing her nurse's uniform so the skirt skimmed just past her knees.

This birthday was just getting worse.

Mother worked mainly night shifts at the hospital, so generally we would see her for only about an hour each evening before bed, and sometimes on the weekend. Often, when we woke in the morning, she would have just gone to sleep, so I always tried to be quiet.

"Please, Mother, can't you stay home with us tonight?" I whined. "Just for today?"

As Mother pinned her cap onto her auburn bun—she never wore braids like the other aunts—she said, "I'm sorry, son, but I have to go to my job."

She didn't seem very sorry.

But why should today be different than any other day? Whenever it was time for Mother to leave for work, a happy bounce appeared in her step. She walked out of the house with no backward glance at my tears.

As if she were leaving her problems behind.

And then baby Vanessa and I were subjected to unpredictable moments with Aunt Marilyn.

On the evening of my birthday, I watched Mother through the window until I couldn't see her anymore. She was just over five feet and of medium build, so she disappeared from my sight all too quickly.

With her deep brown eyes, Mother garnered admiration for her beauty. In standard society, Mother probably would have been considered average in her looks. However, in the redheaded, freckle-faced majority of the FLDS, Mother's dark coloring made her seem exotic. When she joined the FLDS Church, she was considered quite a catch because of her attractive appearance and her ability to make good money with her degree as a registered nurse. Many of the aunts were heavyset, yet Mother had a trim, buxom figure. When she first joined the community, she even wore makeup.

But what most made Mother unique from the other wives was her rare distinction as a convert to the FLDS Church. This was extremely unusual—after the 1960s, it would basically be forbidden. Following in the footsteps of her mother, she left the Church of Jesus Christ of Latter-day Saints (LDS), commonly known as the Mormons, to join our church. Though the FLDS and LDS religions are often confused because of their name similarities and common origin, they are two very separate religions and are not affiliated in any way.

Mother had worked since the day she married Father. She was a valuable breadwinner for his family. With seven wives and somewhere in the neighborhood of forty-five children to support, Father desperately needed her income.

In 1963, when I turned two, Father had announced that our family would live under the same roof with Aunt Marilyn so she could babysit me. When my sister was born, Marilyn had to take care of her too. Though our two families lived so close, there was never any real connection between us and Aunt Marilyn. She and Mother were civil, even friendly to each other, but they rarely spent any time together unless they had to.

Mother enjoyed her nursing career, and plural marriage suited her just fine. She had all the advantages of a marriage, most notably children, without the drudgeries often endured by 1960s-era full-time wives and mothers.

But I hated that my mother was different.

None of my other aunts worked. None of my other aunts had to live with each other in the same house. Most of my aunts had a lot of children, but my mother had only two.

Our family was unusual, and I was painfully aware of how much we stood out.

I cringed against the wall as Aunt Marilyn growled at me. "The sinful things you do make you unworthy to be part of my family. If you don't straighten up and start behaving, you will be damned to hell."

Aunt Marilyn's yellow teeth flashed, her awful breath flooding out. I wanted to turn away, but she jabbed her finger too close to my eyes for me to move.

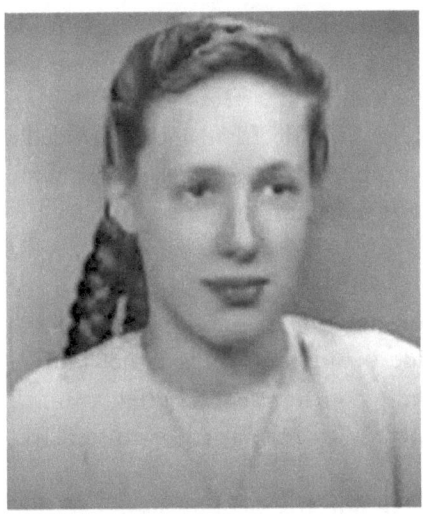

Warren's mother, Marilyn, around age sixteen when she married our father, Rulon T. Jeffs.

Mother hadn't been gone for more than an hour, and I was already in big trouble. I had made too much noise, and then Aunt Marilyn started showing signs that she was losing control. Her head tilted down, she glared at me with the same look I imagined the vengeful Jehovah of the Old Testament used—seemingly capable of annihilating you by a single glance.

Marilyn never corrected our wrongdoings in a loving manner; guilt and shame were her weapons of choice. She utterly terrified me. At six feet, she loomed as an incredibly tall woman with unusually long arms and fingers. She had the look of a farm girl, rough with not an ounce of femininity about her. Whenever she became angry—frequently with me—her skin would turn a deep beet red. She would back me into a corner by moving her body closer and closer, engulfing me in her scent of rubbing alcohol, until there was nowhere for me to go. She would shove her narrow, horse-like face right into mine.

Now, Marilyn's lips curled into a sour pucker and her disdainful eyes bulged wide. Waves of negative energy rolled off her and slammed into me, making me literally shake in my shoes. She whispered again, "You will be cast into hell."

I ran out from under her arm. Her voice chased after me. "Unlike you, my children and I are of the royal bloodline. You are getting in our way of fulfilling our destiny and reaching exaltation."

To escape my fear, I ran as fast as I could to my sanctuary, Sugar House Park. I had previously discovered this wonderful place during one of my many roams around the city. Neither Aunt Marilyn nor any of my half-siblings seemed to care that I wandered all alone as a preschooler; my only rule was I had to be home by dinner.

In the park, separated from my family's chaos and the uncaring attitude of Aunt Marilyn, I relaxed in the quiet. I watched the ducks in the pond and listened to the breeze rustle through the many trees.

Because of these moments of peaceful solitude, I had already learned a true appreciation for the beauty of nature. It was only in the park, alone in the precious quiet, that I felt genuine relief and happiness.

EVEN WHEN MY SISTER AND I WERE YOUNG, AUNT MARILYN WOULD leave us alone every night to sleep on our side of the duplex while she stayed with her children on their side. I can't remember either mother ever tucking us in; we just went to bed by ourselves, and I often assumed the role of caregiver for my baby sister. With zero structure to our lives, we just existed.

Marilyn treated Vanessa and me like outcasts, as if we were parasites she would just as soon smash with her broom. But being ignored by her was better than being forced to endure her disgust. Nothing we ever did was good enough to please her—we were not her children.

Marilyn's second child, Warren, was five years older than me. He received the most preferential treatment of all the children. Whereas no matter how hard I tried, I could do nothing right, whatever Warren did, he could do nothing wrong.

He was the miracle child.

Warren had been born six weeks premature. He was the only one of Father's children to be born that early and live. With Father's wives hiding in various parts of the country and so many of them giving birth, he didn't see every birth. However, Father had attended Warren's delivery in Sacramento, California, where Marilyn lived in 1956. To keep everyone hidden and safe from prosecution, all the children needed to be delivered at home. During Warren's difficult birth, Father said he felt the presence of past prophets watching over the child. Both Father and Aunt Marilyn considered Warren a wonder, meant for greatness. Father believed that God brought forth the infant Warren and saved him for a higher purpose. From his very first breath, Warren received the highest treatment.

To prove that her children were superior to us, often Aunt Marilyn would brag. She made sure we knew that her family line, the Steeds, came from royal blood. One of Marilyn's ancestors had received a patriarchal blessing from the original Mormon prophet, Joseph Smith. In this blessing, her ancestor was told that his seed would eventually rise to become rulers of the church. Aunt Marilyn believed this constituted a prophecy for her and her children.

Occasionally, someone from the Steed family would stand up in meetings and pull out the "revelation" and read it. At family gatherings, Aunt Marilyn would gush to anyone within earshot, "It was foretold that the prophet who will lead the church into the next millennium will come from our royal bloodline!" No matter what any of the Steed descendants did, it was never wrong because their lineage allowed all of them special rights. This gave the entire family an air of arrogance and pretention.

Aunt Marilyn didn't just assume this prophecy would be fulfilled; she was convinced of her role in creating destiny. She was determined to make it happen for her miracle child, Warren.

Chapter Four

Plyg Kid

Because of her work schedule, it was rare for Mother to fix any meal. One day when I was around five years old, she arrived home early and decided to make dinner for our little family of three. As a nurse who washed her hands so often, she suffered from dry skin. She was a huge fan of Jergens lotion. Bottles of it were all over the house.

On this particular night, Mother made frozen peas, one of my least favorite foods. I got the idea that if I squirted lotion on them, I would be saved from the awfulness of mushy peas.

I doused them.

"What are you doing?" Mother cried when she came back into the room.

"I accidentally dumped lotion on the peas when I was getting some for my hands," I said smugly.

"Eat them anyway, and clean your plate!" she ordered.

Choking down every bit of the goopy mess, I became physically ill. I realized that wasn't such a brilliant idea after all.

To this day, the smell of Jergens curdles my stomach.

Several days later, Mother stayed home for a rare overnight. Normally I felt comforted with her presence nearby, knowing Aunt Marilyn had no control over us.

In the middle of the night, I awoke from a terrible nightmare. Close to tears, I made my way to Mother's room to see if she would let me sleep with her.

I stopped short when I noticed there were *two* lumps in the bed, instead of one. It freaked me out to see a man sleeping next to Mother, so I crept closer. Maybe he was one of those bad Gentiles we were supposed to stay away from, here to hurt Mother. I looked around to see if there was some kind of weapon I could use to protect her, but I found nothing. I'd just have to be brave.

As I crept closer, I saw that it was the man who had given me the Tonka truck the year before. I dashed back to my bed and buried myself under the covers. I had no idea why he was lying in bed with Mother. I spent the rest of that night in an awful state.

This was the one and only time I saw my mother and father sleeping in the same bed.

FALL OF 1966 BROUGHT MY FIRST DAY OF KINDERGARTEN AT GARFIELD Elementary School in Salt Lake. I'd looked forward to school so I could learn and finally make some friends, but my excitement disappeared when our teacher asked each child to stand in front of the class, give their parents' names, and tell what their fathers did for a living. My heart sank to the floor. I knew my mother's name, but my father? I was still unsure exactly who he was, let alone what he did. All I had were hazy memories of a man with harsh words and a Tonka truck. He'd slept once with my mother and joined us once for dinner.

When it was my turn, I stood in front of the class, fumbling over my words. All the kids laughed at me. It was completely humiliating.

In my family, we were told not to stick out or draw attention to ourselves. But that was impossible even with just the way we dressed. Imagine going to public school every day in long pants and a long sleeve shirt—fully buttoned at the wrist and neck—with boots, even on late-summer days when it's common in northern Utah for the temperature to top one hundred. FLDS girls looked equally out of place with their braided hair and long dresses. Our clothes were well-worn, purchased at the local thrift shop, Deseret Industries. While all the other children wore either jeans, T-shirts, and tennis shoes or shorts, tank tops, and sandals, we polygamist children wore our prairie clothes.

So, on my first day of school, standing in my unusual, threadbare clothes with nothing to say about my father, I drew far more attention than I ever wanted.

I NEVER DID MAKE ANY FRIENDS AT SCHOOL. I WAS ROUTINELY OSTRAcized and constantly teased. I was called names like plyg kid, prairie boy, and weirdo.

But I didn't care, because I had a loyal friend waiting for me when I got home.

Mother had bought me a red-eared slider turtle. It came in its own little plastic aquarium, complete with a little island, and I named him Turtle. He was the only creature I could confide in. At home, I spent every waking hour with him.

I hand-fed him flies, grasshoppers, and anything I could catch. We had so much fun together. When I was with him, I didn't have to spend time with Aunt Marilyn's family.

But then one day, tragedy struck. Without any warning, Turtle died. I held the little guy in my hands, sobbing, willing him to move again.

Mother came home from work and asked, "What's the matter?"

I showed her his tiny body. "Can you make it come back to life for me?" I begged.

She just shook her head. "I'm a nurse, but I don't know about turtles."

I was heartbroken. I finally had a friend, but after only three short months, he was gone and we couldn't get him to come back. So I did the only thing I could: I held a funeral.

Carefully wrapping Turtle in a cloth, I placed him in a casket I made from a matchbox and lowered him into the hole I'd dug. For two weeks I visited the grave every day, mourning the only being I'd ever considered my ally.

Though I would never think of my half-siblings as pals, sometimes I did hang out with some of them. There was a creek—a gully, really—that ran through Sugar House. With my half-brothers Leroy, Warren, and Lyle, I liked to go down there and play. A steep hill led down to the water at the bottom. Since we were instructed to never get near the gully, we would slide down the hill and stop right before we entered the water. One day, momentum flung me into the creek.

Ten-year-old Warren began to laugh. "I'm going to tell Mother."

I begged him not to. I truly feared Aunt Marilyn and what she would do to me.

He said, "Okay, if you'll stick your head in the mud, I won't tell."

Sticking my face in muck held more appeal than facing the wrath of Aunt Marilyn. So I did it—I put my face in the mud.

Warren protested, "You didn't put it in far enough." He came over and shoved my whole head into the mud.

Leroy was a kind child who wore his heart on his sleeve. He was probably the most decent and down-to-earth of Aunt Marilyn's sons. He was older, and I hoped he'd stick up for me. But because of the fear that Warren caused in all the siblings, Leroy just stood there, staring at the ground.

No one dared to say anything against Warren or tell him no. He was a consummate tattler. All the kids felt uneasy about Warren's ability to turn the tables and call attention to others for wrongs he often was involved in himself. Rather than face the unpleasant consequences, we children would often just let him get away with whatever he wanted, not daring to tell on him in return. If we did so in a moment of stupidity, we faced the explosive Aunt Marilyn and her preaching of doom.

To save ourselves from her rage, we tried our best to stay away from Warren. We discovered that if Warren wasn't present to witness us doing something wrong, even something small, then he had nothing to manufacture into a larger story against us.

Warren was skilled. If deflecting people's attention onto someone else so he wouldn't get punished was an art form, then he was its master.

ONE THING I LOOKED FORWARD TO AS A YOUNG CHILD WAS SUNDAY classes. They were held at what we called the stone house, bunkhouse, or farm at the mouth of Little Cottonwood Canyon on the east side of the Salt Lake Valley. Aunt LaRue lived there, while the other six wives were spread around the valley.

The stone house was constructed of crudely cut granite blocks. It originally had been used as a bunkhouse for the silver miners who worked the Alta mine. On Sunday mornings at ten o'clock, all the mothers and their children would gather at the farm. The boys of priesthood age, twelve years old, would arrive early to push Aunt LaRue's furniture to the side and set up chairs so we could meet in her living room. This was the only time the family all came together. Except for Aunt Marilyn—she exempted herself and her children from Sunday classes and never received a reprimand.

When a child turned eight and received the ordinance of baptism, it was a big deal to be able to go to class. Prior to that time, the unbaptized children went to another room with a mother to watch over them.

After class, Sundays became even more enjoyable, something I looked forward to each week. One of the mothers would be in charge to prepare a large lunch. Once the lunch was finished, we had the afternoon to play with our siblings until we all had to return to our separate homes again.

In 1968, everyone began to buzz with excitement when Father announced he'd commissioned the building of a new house on the same property as the stone house. As we went to family classes, it was thrilling to see this large house grow in shape and form.

People from the Short Creek, Arizona, FLDS community were called Crickers, and we referred to the town as the Crick. People from Salt Lake were called Lakers. Crickers were called on missions to travel from Southern Utah to Salt Lake and build the big house, donating their labor. It was common at that time to go on what were called work missions. Father's sons frequently used to go down to Short Creek to fulfill work missions.

The Crickers would arrive in Salt Lake in groups of twenty to thirty men. Their missions could last a few weeks or up to a month. Drywallers, framers, and electricians began to complete sections of the house. No work was hired out. Allen Steed did the excavating. This was before large excavating machines were common, so he used a backhoe to dig an eight-foot-deep foundation.

This was the first time I got to know people from Short Creek. I'd been there only once, to meet my maternal grandmother. Father would go down to the Crick about every other weekend.

When my eighth birthday arrived in 1969, a date was set for my baptism. This was a big deal in the life of an FLDS child, but since I did not yet attend family classes, I had no idea why. All I knew was that when Mother discussed my upcoming baptism, she would beam at me with anticipation and pride.

That was enough for me to be excited as well.

On the day of my baptism, we traveled uptown to a building that had a six-foot-square baptismal font. I'd brought one of my clean, white shirts from home, along with a thrift-store pair of white pants Mother had purchased. After arriving at the building, I changed into my white clothing.

When I entered the baptismal font, there was my half-brother Hyrum. This confused me even more, causing me to take a step back. Although Father was in attendance, he and two of my brothers just acted as witnesses to my baptism. Why wasn't Father baptizing me? I knew he'd baptized some of my other siblings.

I moved forward in the water again, but with growing trepidation. Hyrum was twenty-three. Although I knew he was my half-brother, I didn't really know him personally. He was considered quite handsome, but he also had a violent temper and thought nothing of beating people up who crossed his path. Yet here he was, clothed in white like an angel. My instincts told me that entering a big pool of water with him was not the smartest idea. But not wanting to disappoint Mother, I did.

Hyrum took me by the wrist and uttered the baptismal prayer. With no other preamble, he plunged me deep into the water, a terrifying sensation. When I came up sputtering, I tried to smile at my mother. Luckily, the witnesses deemed that I had been fully immersed in the water, or he would have had to dunk me again. I had seen children be dunked several times simply because a bit of their toe popped out of the water.

SINCE I WAS NOW A BAPTIZED MEMBER OF THE CHURCH, THE TIME HAD come for me to attend my first family class. Although it was a huge honor, I felt frightened and thought everyone was staring at me as I sat on the front row. I was too scared to look at Father, who stood before me teaching. As a child, when I would get nervous, I had an unusual habit of looking at the ground and pretending I was flipping things from off my knees. In the first family class I ever attended, as my nervousness grew, I flicked away with my fingers. It apparently became distracting to Father.

He finally got fed up with me and stopped the meeting. "Wallace, what are you flipping?"

This only made it worse. I was so embarrassed that I started to cry and had to leave the room. For a while there, Father called me the Flipper.

AFTER THIS, I TOLD MY HALF-SISTER VALERIE, WHO WAS THREE MONTHS younger than me, all about the terrors of the family class that she would soon experience. Valerie had become my best friend. She was Aunt Norma's daughter. They lived across the valley, and we would sometimes get together to play, especially while the older people were in family class.

I guessed Valerie would probably be okay during family class. She was always so happy and cheerful. I wanted to be around her because she made me feel better just by being in the same room. Her laugh was contagious, and she giggled constantly. Throughout my childhood, she was the sibling I was closest to.

I would have given anything to spend every waking second with the vivacious Valerie.

Soon, I learned this dream would come true as the big house neared completion. In a matter of weeks, we would all move in together. I anticipated days of joy, romping and playing with my abundant siblings and spending every free moment with Valerie.

I never dreamed that this single event would turn into a nightmare, spinning our already fragile families into chaos.

Chapter Five

A Living Hell on Earth

In January 1969, the month before I turned eight, the big house was finally completed after a full year of construction. The event of Father combining all his wives and unmarried children together into this home became known as the Gathering.

Father informed his older boys and his seven wives of the date when the entire family would move into the big house. All my older half-brothers were charged with making the move happen. It became a massive undertaking.

My small family was one of the last to arrive. By the time our house was sold and we could pack up and move, it was late February. Most of the other wives and their children were already settled in.

The term *big house* turned out to be an understatement. It was a cavernous space of twenty-two thousand square feet. In the center of the house, a large meeting room doubled as our dining room. The rest was built around this one gigantic room, in the shape of an H. Our home had twenty-five bedrooms and fifteen bathrooms, connected with four-foot-wide hallways and equipped with an enormous commercial-grade kitchen.

Father built his own secluded wing off the dining room, private from the rest of the house, where he stayed when he was in town. We children were absolutely forbidden to enter his sanctuary, although sometimes Warren would sneak in. To me, this area of the house seemed something like Fort Knox.

Aunts Norma and Marilyn were given their own wing with their children, completely taking over one of the verticals that formed the H shape of the house. Aunt Elba never had any children, but she was put in a large room of her own. Once settled, these three aunts never moved, which was

Located at 3601 East Little Cottonwood Road in Sandy, Utah, my father's big house was razed in 2014.

highly unusual. About once a year, particularly if the children who shared a room started to bicker, they and their mothers would have to move to a new location in the house.

Because we were not allowed into Father's secluded space and some of the aunts had separate living areas, I never noticed his schedule for spending time with his wives. To most of us, he stayed private in his relations with the mothers. Occasionally he would take one of them when he traveled, but it seemed by random choice.

HERE, UNDER ONE ROOF, OUR LARGE FAMILY NOW PARTICIPATED IN A higher religious law. The mothers were living the Law of Sarah, the highest order a woman can achieve in the FLDS religion. As wives of Rulon Jeffs, they were to be shining examples to the other members of our church.

Under the Law of Sarah, mothers sacrifice by generously sharing their husband among them and allowing their children to be nurtured by all the women in the household. We children were instructed not to consider our biological mother as our actual mother—rather, every woman in the household was our mother. After the Gathering, Father commanded that we stop using the term *aunt* for his multiple wives and use *mother* instead. We were to call all the women by the name Mother. Even the women referred to each other that way. Father's wives included Mother Kay (given name Kathleen), Mother LaRue, Mother Ruth, Mother Norma, Mother Marilyn, Mother Sharon, and Mother Elba.

Mother Leona was Father's sister. She and her five children lived with us, and we considered her one of our mothers. She had been married to Rulon Allred, but when he left our church to start his own, she moved in with us. We were told that in the afterlife, even though they were siblings on Earth, she and Father would be sealed together as husband and wife.

This supposedly higher law that we were forced to live was actually a living hell on Earth, especially for the wives. The stress of combining eight women, who were used to raising their children in their own homes, and on average fifty children, ranging in age from infant to teenager, under one roof often proved too much for even the most docile mother. Chaos escalated as the number of children in the house constantly changed due to new babies and older half-siblings who would frequently come and go.

To run a house this size required a lot of work. Each day, chores would rotate among the women, each given a specific job for that day. It could be laundry, yard work, cooking, cleaning, or childcare. Each mother would have a contingent of children to help with the assigned tasks. Boys and girls worked side by side on the same chores until they turned eighteen or got a job outside the home.

Though we all knew how to work hard, none of us wanted to be assigned to Mother Kay. Of all the mothers, she was the worst. She was a slob, a true hoarder. She couldn't throw anything away, including used tissues and empty gum wrappers. Her stuff was piled four feet high everywhere in her room, with just a small pathway leading from the bed to the door. The stench that filled the hall when she opened her door was repulsive.

Besides being a mess, she was never happy—in fact, she was one of the grouchiest people I have ever met. And she did not get along with the children, at all. For some reason, she felt the only way to get us to do anything was to intimidate us. "If you don't pull every weed in this flower bed, I'm going to beat you within an inch of your life!" she would scream. Another favorite saying was, "If you don't sweep and mop that floor, I'm going to cut off your fingers at the third knuckle." To be honest, all of us thought she would follow through with her threats.

Whichever children she oversaw would be forced to go to bed at 6:00 so she wouldn't have to deal with us. We could not leave our rooms after that time, even in the middle of the summer when the sun wasn't going down until late evening. Since we were not tired, we ended up stuck in our rooms for hours until we were finally ready to sleep. This lasted for about one year before Father took her off any assignment that dealt with children.

Kitchen duty always seemed to result in some kind of chaos, as each mother had a different idea of what constituted a proper meal. Just imagine putting meals on the table for nearly seventy people, three times a day, and the feeding frenzy that ensued.

Father would call on someone to offer the prayer before the meal. Father would kneel first, and then the rest of us would all kneel, fold our arms, and bow our heads. If it was a child saying the prayer, it was usually short, offering abbreviated thanks and asking for a blessing on the food. But if a mother would pray, some of them would go on and on with long, teary prayers that tried our patience to the limit. Usually prayer would end with the words, "May we use our strength for building up your kingdom."

That was our cue.

The instant the amen was uttered, we children would jump up and push each other away from the coveted chairs at the end of each table, where there was more elbow room, or at the centers of the tables, where the food had been placed in serving bowls or on plates. There were always two loaves of bread on the table and lots of peanut butter and honey. We would dive in like a bunch of piglets in the barnyard.

The cost of feeding our family nearly broke us each month, so the mothers became extremely frugal in their meal preparation. Because of this, we had some interesting meals. We lived close to a vegetarian lifestyle since meat was so expensive.

For breakfast, we rarely had store-bought cold cereal. Instead, we grew up mainly eating a dish we referred to as *musheto*—mush, eggs, and toast. The mush was either cream of wheat, corn meal, or oatmeal, which was by far the worst! All sticky and clumpy, oatmeal would glop into our bowls with a big splat.

The mothers made a soup that we called kitchen sink stew because it looked like they took the kitchen sink and made a soup in it. They used the cheapest ingredients possible and added any leftovers they could throw in. On most days, it was just split-pea soup or chicken-wing soup that consisted mostly of water.

Eighty percent of our meals ended up being peanut butter and honey sandwiches, thanks to my half-brother Leroy. If an exceptionally horrible meal was prepared, he would eye the food on the table and then rudely stand and declare, "This is a peanut butter and honey meal!" We all tried to copy the near-artist precision with which he spread the peanut butter and honey on the bread. He would hold contests to see who could cover the bread most thoroughly or spread the peanut butter most evenly.

Without fail, every Sunday night for dinner we were served bread, milk, and cheese. As kids, we hated it. But in the end, it was food and it filled our bellies.

For each meal, the large meeting room doubled as the dining room for the family, with five long, custom-built dining tables set in a circle. Meals were a social event. It was the only time during the day when the family all gathered together.

LIKE MOST WOMEN IN THE FLDS CHURCH, FATHER'S WIVES SEEMED to have zero domestic skills; they lacked even the most basic idea of how to prepare food. They rarely used salt or any seasoning, and the food was always extremely bland, though Mother Kay did put mint in everything, giving it a strange flavor. Because the women married so young, they did not receive proper training, and most came from poor families, so there wasn't much to learn with. However, the common consensus was that food was meant to be nourishing, not fun or exciting, so it didn't matter how it tasted. Only those who had a lot of money and were in the top echelon of our community learned how to cook and could eat like kings.

But growing up, I really didn't mind that we had meat so infrequently, because when we did have it, the mothers always overcooked it, making it dry and tasteless.

I remember one time Father splurged and bought some beautiful steak for the entire family. This extravagance cost nearly a thousand dollars. Mother Kay was assigned the cooking for that day. She wanted this to be a special meal, so she marinated the steak in wine before cooking it. If that was all she had done, it probably would have been somewhat edible, but no, she also cooked it in the wine. It tasted repulsive.

Father took one bite and then stared, fuming, at his plate. "You ruined it!" he finally exploded.

This was the first time I'd ever seen my father show anger in public, as he carefully guarded his emotions around groups of people. If Father was angry, it was as if God was angry, so he really worked hard to keep his emotions in check.

The mothers also appeared clueless about basic hygiene principles in the kitchen. One night at dinner, my half-brother Blaine got a strange look on his face as he ate a piece of bread. After fishing around in his mouth with his fingers, he pulled out a Band-Aid, still curled in a circle, as if it had recently left a finger.

"That's disgusting!" he said.

My mother, Sharon, glanced over, saw the Band-Aid, and looked at her finger. "Oh, so that's where that went."

IN 1970, ONE YEAR AFTER MOVING INTO THE BIG HOUSE, OUR FAMILY went on our annual fishing trip to Moon Lake in the Uintah Mountains. We children always looked forward to this trip. I was especially excited as a nine-year-old boy, because not only was I out of school, but I was surrounded by nature. It was so peaceful and quiet, unlike the chaos in my home. I could finally go off on my own and explore.

When I stepped out of the car, I breathed deep the cool, crisp mountain air. It was filled with the scent of pine, aspen, and fir trees, mixed with sweet, fresh water and clean, rich soil. I wished I could stay there forever.

We quickly set up camp, then grabbed our fishing gear and set off.

Though Warren was five years older than me, he and I were both feeling adventurous, so we walked around to the other side of the lake, away from the rest of the family. I felt honored and happy that my older brother, the chosen one, would spend time with me, since he rarely showed any interest in me at all. Finding the perfect spot, we had fun casting our lines out as far as we could. Some of the casts were pretty amazing.

I should have known my joy would be short-lived.

It wasn't long before a man trolling in a boat happened to catch our lines.

Warren yelled, "Hey, you're crossing our lines!"

The man stared at us, then began to turn his boat around. "You can go to hell!"

"Quit trolling so close to shore. This is our spot!" Warren shouted back.

"I'll troll wherever I want. I'm gonna come and kick your ass!"

As soon as the boat pointed in our direction, Warren dropped his pole and ran, leaving me alone to deal with the furious man.

The angry boater kept yelling. "I'm gonna beat the shit out of you!"

I couldn't leave the fishing poles, and I didn't have time to reel them in before he came to shore. So there I was, a scrawny young boy, shaking in my shoes and terrified of having to face this physically imposing man. Because I was so young and was frozen in place, he knew I wasn't going to run away. He took pity on me and left me alone.

He yelled out one more time to Warren, who was still running, before he climbed back into his boat and left. When I could move again, I gathered the poles and rushed back to camp. Warren was already there.

I had seen this kind of cowardly behavior often with Warren and some of his other brothers and sisters. It was not the first time he'd left me standing alone when he was the culprit who started the problem. Unfortunately, it wouldn't be the last time either. That day I learned the danger of following Warren blindly or believing everything he said. This was one of the first incidents that proved to me his lack of character and integrity. But I held my feeling inside, not wanting to cause any more trouble than was already happening at home. It wasn't as if anyone would listen to me anyway.

THAT WAS THE LAST YEAR MOTHER MARILYN WOULD GO TO MOON Lake. After that time, she declared the outings too "worldly" for her and her chosen children. Like a martyr, she would sigh and say, "We'll stay and protect the house. We'll make the sacrifice."

Secretly, I was pleased that Warren wouldn't be there to make trouble again.

ON OUR PROPERTY, WE USED A LARGE IRRIGATION POND TO KEEP OUR seven acres of land watered. My oldest brother, Hyrum, was in charge of keeping the reservoir filled up and the property watered. Wanting to put ducks and geese in the pond, he asked Father if that would be okay. With Father's blessing, he moved ahead with his plans.

I was an animal lover, and I spent a lot of time up at the pond. Most days I felt like I connected with the ducks better than with the people of the house.

When a duck hatched a bunch of eggs, one duckling turned out to be a sickly runt. Knowing how much I loved animals, Hyrum put me in charge of making sure the underdeveloped duck would survive. Hyrum told me to separate it from the others. So, I began to hand-feed the duck. I let it sleep in my room in a box. After about a month of almost constant care, it eventually grew and became a healthy duck.

When I tried to introduce this duck back into the flock, it was picked on. Instead of letting it fend for itself, I slowly began to reintegrate the duck into the flock.

Having so many ducks and geese resulted in a lot of poop in the reservoir. One day Father looked around, disgust written all over his face. "No more geese and ducks. Slaughter them! We're going to eat them."

Hyrum knew I was attached to my hatchling. He told me to find the duck a home, or it would have to be slaughtered. But in our isolated existence, I didn't know anyone who lived around us. I had no contact with the Gentile world. I was too afraid to just go up to a random farmer and ask if he could take my duck.

As slaughter time approached, I began to panic. I wanted to take my duck back home, but I knew Father would never permit that. For the first time ever, I began to pray for an answer. I felt constantly agitated—I didn't want the duck to die.

One night, we were sitting down to dinner. I stared at my father. He was such a Godlike figure to me. I thought, *If I don't slaughter the duck, Father will be mad at me. He doesn't like ducks.*

I felt impressed that I should slaughter the duck. Hyrum had built a special structure for the task. I cut the duck's head off, cleaned the carcass, and then prepared it. I asked one of the mothers to specially cook it, and then I presented it to Father with a timid, "Here, I want you to eat this."

And he did.

It was the hardest thing I had ever done in my life. But it felt good to do what my father wanted me to do. I sensed I had learned the importance of personal sacrifice to please Father. It was a defining moment for me, and I felt so close to him, as if this had drawn me to him. I believed I had finally done something worthy of his praise and honor, that he might respect me. I decided that Father was tremendously important to me. Making him happy and bending to his will were my priorities.

IN 1972, WHEN I WAS ELEVEN, ANOTHER CHANGE IN OUR FAMILY occurred: my father married his eighth wife, Mother Gloria. Soon, they started having children, which added more chaos to the already overcrowded big house.

As kids, we learned to adapt to this lifestyle pretty well. We made friends with each other and teased one another as siblings always do. For instance, we had an industrial-sized dishwasher in our huge kitchen. We loved this dishwasher. Without it, we would have had to wash all those dishes by hand. The best thing about this appliance was that, if the door was opened while it was running, water would spray everywhere. So, as fun-loving siblings, periodically we would maneuver an unsuspecting person to stand next to the running dishwasher and open the door, drenching the unfortunate victim.

Leroy continued his teasing. If a dish was prepared that we didn't like, he'd say, pointing to the food, "When I get married, I'm going to invite you over, and we're going to have this!"

Leroy was also the split-pea soup expert. Because our food was so bad, split-pea soup was actually a favorite. If a mother happened to ask what we wanted for dinner, we would say, "Steak!" knowing there was no way we could afford it. The alternative, what we really wanted, would be split-pea soup. Leroy taught us to add things to the soup to make it taste better. He would stand and declare for all to hear, "I love you so much, dear brother, that when I get married, I'm going to invite you over and make you the best split-pea soup ever."

However, among the wives, things were not nearly so amicable. Adding another wife and more children upset the tenuous balance that had just started to form. There were constant jealousies and arguments. Each mother would try to protect her own children from the other mothers. If a mother thought her children were being treated unfairly, or if someone was picking on her kids, all hell would break loose. Often, the mothers would focus on food, complaining to Father, "My child isn't getting enough to eat."

Mother Elba was childless. During mealtimes, she took it upon herself to look after all children ages five and under. She made sure they were fed first. She especially loved a couple of Mother Gloria's sons, Isaiah and Peter, and watched over them always. One night, Mother Elba tried feeding the boys before one of Mother Ruth's older children could dish up his own food. Mother Ruth grabbed Mother Elba by the wrist and dragged her from the room, screaming, "You think you're doing good, but you're ruining those boys!"

These fights between the mothers often turned physical, resulting in kicking, slapping, and ripping out each other's hair. The arguments usually started in the kitchen but soon moved to Father's office for him to settle the dispute. Father would generally speak to the disputing wives quietly and use scriptural doctrine to diffuse the situation. Then he would send the women, shamed and humbled, on their way.

However, Mother Norma was the rebel of the wives. She was an alcoholic, and she always got her own way with Father. She would go into his room and yell and scream, domineering his time. At age twelve, Mother Norma had been married to the former prophet, John Y. Barlow. After her husband died when she was sixteen, Mother Norma was given to Father "for time" but remained eternally sealed to Barlow. Quite often we could hear her yell at Father, "You will never be as good as John Y. Barlow! You should be honored to take care of me." She would say this even though her children were Father's.

Father's room was right off the dining room. One day, as normal, Norma was in there screaming. Suddenly, there was a loud clatter and then an eerie quiet descended over the whole house. After a few seconds, Norma tore out of the office and ran to her room. We found out later that day that Norma had stabbed Father in the thigh, clear through to the bone. When asked about it, all Father would say was, "She took my own damn letter opener and stuck me in the leg with it."

The women didn't limit the fighting to each other. If a mother thought you were picking on her child, even if it was just sibling teasing, you got in trouble. Or, if a child was hurt while playing and that child's mother thought you were responsible, you were punished.

Mother LaRue had a son, Spencer, who'd contracted polio, so he had a short leg. We never mocked him, but sometimes a little teasing occurred. Spencer was pretty cool with it, even joking around with us, but his mother did not think it was funny in any way, shape, or form. She would holler at us if she thought we even looked at him wrong. She would come unglued, shouting, "He has endured more than you ever could!"

Mother Marilyn sheltered her children and shielded them from the consequences of wrongdoing. This was particularly true of Warren. If you witnessed one of Warren's transgressions, she would deflect his actions onto another child and put the fear of God into you to forget about the incident. If she thought you mistreated him in any way, she either had

Father take care of it or she would do the honors herself, even if the child was very young.

At any hint of someone mistreating Warren, she would growl, "You leave him alone! If you don't, you'll have to deal with me."

No one wanted that to happen.

Father rarely yelled at us. His main form of punishment was to use scripture to shame us into behaving. But Mother Marilyn didn't even need to speak her spiteful words; the projection of her body and the disdain in her eyes spoke volumes. Mother Marilyn had violent mood swings. She was completely unpredictable. One minute she would be relatively nice, and within a second she would turn into a raving witch. She terrified us.

Even though we now all lived together, we still had our Sunday-morning family classes. Father's married sons, along with their wives and children, would join us, but the married daughters would go with their husbands to the husbands' family classes. We would meet in the large meeting room with Father on a raised stage, dressed in a suit and tie. The young children would sit in front next to their mothers, while the older children and adults sat in back. Mother Norma played the organ, so she sat next to the organ. Mother Elba, because of her age, had a nice, soft chair to sit in.

The classes followed a strict structure, beginning promptly at 10:30 with a prayer. Father would call on one elder and one priest to bless and administer the sacrament. The priest would bless the bread, the elder would bless the water, and both would pass the bread and water to the whole family. Fulfilling this assignment was considered extremely sacred and a great honor. If you were guilty of any sin, you could not participate in performing this holy ordinance until you repented and made restitution.

After the sacrament, a family member or members assigned by Father would offer a song or reading. This was a round-robin rotation, as he tried to involve everyone. I did not enjoy it, and I wasn't the only one. Often, a child would stand up, start to cry, and need to sit back down.

One reason why we were all afraid to offer a thought in family class was because if you messed up or said something silly, others would intensely ridicule you afterward during lunch. With Mother Marilyn always crowing about being of the chosen seed, one of the most common taunts was, "You're a *frozen* seed. You had to be artificially inseminated."

After the "song and dance," as I liked to call it, unbaptized family members would go downstairs and be tended by one mother while baptized members would remain upstairs in the main room for class. We would all move up to the front, and Father would begin teaching.

Father was a gifted orator. He would talk for an hour using his wonderful vocabulary. He knew the scriptures well and could find references with no preparation beforehand.

Initially, Father conducted the family classes, but eventually Warren was given this job.

Even though it was a big deal when I became old enough to go to class, my fear did not dissipate with time. I found the lessons either boring or frightening, and I hated them. In every class, Father talked about the destruction of the evil world and how it would happen any day now. It was terrifying to think about being destroyed. Was I righteous enough to escape the desolation? If not, what would it feel like? I would sit there in my chair thinking, *I'm never going to survive the next year. I'll never get my driver's license. I'll never get married.*

I was so grateful when the classes ended at noon and we could play together as siblings after lunch. I hung around Valerie a lot. I always loved Sunday afternoons.

Family Sunday classes were considered important to our salvation, and attendance was mandatory. Everyone was required to be there, unless they were ill. They would be considered an apostate if they missed more than two meetings. However, once again, Father gave Mother Marilyn more freedom, and she was the exception to the rule. Making excuses that she had to answer the phone for Father, she would spend Sunday mornings by herself in her room. She was never censured for this behavior.

We were taught not to make any distinctions among the wives; all were equal. In reality, Father allowed a class system to exist within our family. Even though Mother Marilyn was not the first wife, she became the matriarch with that aura of power and self-righteousness about her. What set Mother Marilyn apart from other women was her long, thick, blond hair that fell to her knees. This was the sign of an extraordinary woman, one more worthy than those who could not grow their hair long. Women in the FLDS are forbidden to cut their hair. Marilyn's hair was in stark contrast to my own mother's short, thin hair.

In the future, we were told, women would use their hair in a special ordinance to wash the feet of their husbands. This is one reason why Marilyn was one of Father's most beloved wives and received special treatment.

Upon moving to the big house, Marilyn forced herself into the role of Father's secretary. This allowed her to be with Father all day every day, so she knew everything he did and everyone he met with. Because of her work, she said she was much too busy to spend breakfast and dinner time with the family; instead, she would gather her children into her bedroom every night to talk to them, telling them to stay close to Father because he was a great man and would be prophet one day.

As one large family, we were supposed to participate in family functions together; however, Mother Marilyn refused to join in. She did not get reprimanded in any way for this behavior. A true narcissist, she demanded to be treated better and that her children receive special treatment as well. She would claim she was doing right, following the Law of Sarah, but when she put herself above the other women because of her superior bloodline and long hair, and when she demanded special treatment for her children, she became a hypocrite, living in exact opposition to what we were taught.

We all knew Father had a different attachment to Mother Marilyn. Although he didn't do anything openly, it was just understood that she and her children were special to Father, much more than the rest of us. Mother Marilyn had control over the family. She wanted to exalt her own children; rules had nothing to do with them. The lesson I learned as a young child was that the business of attaining favor by God was a competitive one. None of us were as good as her children, especially Warren.

Mother LaRue also tried to ingratiate her children with Father to get special treatment, but she was not as successful. She did not possess the manipulative, passive-aggressive cunningness of Marilyn, nor was she descended from the Steed line. Mother LaRue emphasized that her son was the oldest son, but she seemed to have no other ammunition to place her children close to Father like Marilyn did. LaRue was always trying to push her boys by telling them, "Go to Father and help him."

For example, Father wanted a large fence put around the big house to keep us separated from the Gentiles. LaRue pushed and pushed to have her son Ward placed in charge of this important project. Unfortunately, once Ward was established as the fence project manager, he was drafted into the military. Marilyn immediately campaigned to get Warren, then about seventeen, put in charge of the project. And once again, Mother Marilyn won, and Mother LaRue lost.

Mother Marilyn was a brilliantly calculating woman. She knew that our father would someday be the prophet, and that the next prophet after him would most likely be one of his sons. She always instructed her children to stay close to Father, to obey and respect him.

Mother Marilyn also had a win with poor Leroy. He was the one chosen to take over Father's CPA business. Leroy despised being an accountant and wanted to be a farmer. At first, Leroy seemed to be Marilyn's chosen son, in line for the position of prophet. Eventually, however, Leroy fell out of favor because Warren had more charisma. But Marilyn saw the tactical advantage of having a son in control of not only Father's business but the church finances as well. If positioned correctly, Leroy could also possibly become a trustee of the United Effort Plan.

The United Effort Plan, or UEP, was a holding trust put together by Father and the other apostles in 1942. They believed that plural marriage and the United Order could not be safe unless there was a legal document that the government and courts could not tear apart. The UEP held all church property and was managed by the FLDS Church trustees. The UEP allowed faithful members to live on church property and improve it through the trust. They were considered tenants at will. When they built a home, the home and property remained in the trust.

Through her manipulation, Marilyn assured that her sons were in key positions, Leroy financial and Warren spiritual.

Mother Marilyn made it her mission above all else to ensure that her son Warren, no matter what sins he committed, would be the next prophet of God after Father.

Chapter Six

"I Will Not Tolerate Rebellion"

PERUVIAN PARK ELEMENTARY SCHOOL.

Valerie and I looked at each other and then at the building that loomed before us. Now that we had moved into the big house, this was the school we would attend. We wondered if we'd be treated any better than in our previous schools, but our hopes weren't set too high. At least we had each other and were in the same class together.

I was three months older than Valerie. We were told to say we were twins because of our age.

"You and Valerie live in the same house?" I was asked many times by the other students.

"Yes."

"You have the same last name?"

"Yes."

"How can you be twins but have two different birthdays?"

"Um..."

"And why do you wear those funny clothes?"

"Um..."

Having never been coached by my family on how to respond to these questions, I didn't know what to do, so I just kept quiet. This didn't go over very well with the other students. Soon we were being made fun of again.

Ridicule from my classmates wasn't the only thing I had to deal with. One kid was our next-door neighbor. He apparently wasn't too pleased to have a polygamist compound right next to his house. He became determined to beat me up every day at recess. He was a pathetic fighter. Even though I was small, growing up in a large family like mine had made me scrappy. I would beat the crap out of him every single time.

However, one day after school, he and two of his larger, older friends attacked me. This time, I didn't fare so well—they were able to batter me pretty bad. He thought he was really cool for pummeling me. A few days later, even though I still sported a few bruises from our last encounter, he thought he'd have another go at me. The problem for him was that I'd decided I'd had enough. I clobbered him. With my fist clenched tight, I punched him hard, imagining my hand slamming all the way through to the back of his head. His face was just something that got in the way. He never tried to fight me again.

I realized that kids are kids, no matter where one lived. If you were different in any way, you were picked on and made fun of. This was my life. So, to protect ourselves from the other students, my siblings and I learned to keep to ourselves, hoping unrealistically that the teasing would stop.

SIXTH GRADE WAS A TURNING POINT FOR ME. FOR THE FIRST TIME IN my life, I became friends with a Gentile. On the first day of school, my jaw dropped when a buxom young woman with flowing blond hair showed up in class. My heart pounded in my chest, and I had a hard time breathing. She announced that her name was Miss Susan Lamont and she would be our teacher that year.

Miss Lamont walked to the chalkboard and stood there, trembling. She looked around the room, seemingly in a panic, and caught my eye. I felt a real connection with her at that moment.

Then, without saying a word, she ran to her desk, put her head down, and began to cry.

All the kids stared at each other, unsure what to do. Because of our brief eye contact just seconds earlier, I felt like I should be the one to see if everything was all right. Tentatively, I approached her. "Are you okay?"

She sniffled. "I'm so sorry. This is my first day. I've never done this before."

"Well, we aren't going to hurt you." I tried to sound kind, in hopes that somehow my voice would calm her fears.

She smiled. "Thank you. That makes me feel better."

My chest swelled with pride, being the one who made her smile like that.

But though she tried diligently to do her job, she cried off and on all day.

I've always hated to see women cry, so even though she broke out in tears multiple times every day, I would still try to comfort her. Sometimes I brought her apples, just to be graced by that beautiful smile. She knew that I came from a polygamist family and that we were weird, but she never talked about it, nor did I feel that she judged me.

Miss Lamont was a playful person, so as soon as she'd start on one of her crying jags, I'd call out, "Let's go have recess!" She would then take the class outside and play football with us. Of course, I loved tackling her; it gave me a reason to touch her.

One day during football, she came running right at me and I tackled her good, knocking her backward and toppling over with her. I face-planted right into her ample bosom.

She just laughed. "What are you doing there?"

It was embarrassing, but it also felt pretty good. She was so soft.

As the year progressed, our friendship grew stronger. I loved to hike the mountains around my house, and I'd found an old turquoise mine. I asked her several times if she'd like to see it. One day she surprised me and said, "I've got some time off this afternoon. Let's go check it out." I was so excited that she wanted to spend time with me and share in my discovery.

Miss Lamont met me across the street from my house, right at the base of the mountain, since she certainly couldn't come up to my front door. We talked and talked as we trekked up the mountain. I felt like I actually had a friend outside the family.

It turned out that she didn't care about the mine, because she all but ignored it. When we sat down to rest, she said, "Tell me about your family."

I was self-conscious, but eventually I opened up. I told her how much I hated being weird and how hard it was when everyone teased me.

She looked at me not with pity but with sympathy, without a trace of judgment. She said, "We're all raised in different ways. Who knows what will happen in the future?"

It was a warm feeling, this unusual sense of acceptance. My love for her deepened.

These feelings for Miss Lamont caused a swirl of confusion within me. My father had given the young men in our family many lessons, quite a few of them instructing us about our behavior toward girls. We were told we should never talk to or think about girls. Touching a girl was forbidden, and we certainly could not have a crush or a girlfriend. He would caution, "Think of girls like snakes, because they will bite you." And, "A man has no right to take a girl's hand, unless she offers it to take her across the street."

In other words, we were to wait patiently and chastely until the prophet placed us in a marriage.

We were also told that if we had to speak with a girl, the only place we could look was chin level. Yet here I was staring into the big, beautiful blue eyes of Miss Lamont. When I clasped my hands together, I was surprised to find them all sweaty.

I knew Father would be terribly angry and disappointed with me if he knew I'd not followed his counsel and I'd allowed myself to fall in love with my teacher, a Gentile.

THERE WAS ANOTHER SLIGHT PROBLEM: MISS LAMONT HAD A FIANCÉ. My evenings were filled with paralyzing bouts of jealousy. To make matters worse, one day he came to class. I hated him. All I could think about was how much I wanted to beat him up.

One day after school, she had another one of her crying fits. She confided in me that she'd been in a fight with her boyfriend.

She said, "I don't know about the wedding. What should I do?"

I thought, *This is my opening!*

I said, "Have you kissed him?"

"Yes."

"Oh, that's terrible. Do you really love him?"

"Yes," she sniffed, "but I don't know about marrying him."

I blurted, "You can't marry him. You need to marry me!"

She cried even harder and ran out of the school, sobbing.

THE NEXT DAY, SHE CAME UP TO ME AND SAID, "I WANT TO APOLOGIZE about yesterday. My behavior was not appropriate. I shouldn't have put that on you."

After that, my jealousy disappeared because I focused more on the fact that she liked me and could open up to me. This made me feel important, a unique feeling that I'd never experienced before. I also learned another lesson that would help me for the rest of my life: for no apparent reason, women changed their minds a lot!

She got married one week later.

When she returned to school after her honeymoon, I asked her, "Have you had sex with him?"

Her face blossomed red, and that was all the answer I needed. I'd learned enough about sex from listening to kids in school to know what her blushing meant.

AFTER I FINISHED SIXTH GRADE, FATHER HAD HAD ENOUGH WITH HIS children going to public school. He started an exclusive FLDS-only school called the Alta Academy, held in the east basement wing of the big house. Father had a banner made and hung it on the wall for all to see: *Nothing Is More Important than My Getting and Keeping the Spirit of God.*

Within a few years, the school would expand and Father would build another building. Eventually, the big house would become the school and Father would build another house to live in. From the beginning, Father claimed that the current prophet, Leroy S. Johnson, had appointed Warren Jeffs, just seventeen and barely graduated from high school, as principal. Unfortunately for the students, Warren continued as principal the entire time Alta Academy was open.

That first year, our school had thirty students, most of them my siblings, from first to seventh grades. The second year they added an eighth grade. Though we were no longer in public school, my family still received strange looks, even from other FLDS students. It wasn't because of how we acted or dressed—being FLDS themselves, the others were the same as us—but because of the food we ate at lunch. All students went upstairs and used the large gathering room to eat. We could use the kitchen to prepare our food, but the mothers usually had lunch already made for us, so we just grabbed our food and sat down to eat. Our homemade bread was not typical. We called it either "brick bread" because it was so heavy or "kitchen sink bread" because leftovers were added to it. Peas, carrots, beans, hard meat chunks, and even spaghetti found their way into our bread. To mask the flavor, we would slather on peanut butter and honey. The few students who didn't come from our family would eye our lunches suspiciously, cringing at the strange odors coming from our sandwiches.

WARREN RAN THE ACADEMY WITH THE IRON HAND OF A DICTATOR, obsessed with rules and order. His hero was Adolf Hitler. He obsessively studied Hitler's life and his leadership of the German people, and he implemented what he learned. Warren even went so far as to secretly study the German language. Once he became fluent, he relished the chance to show off and speak it as often as possible.

Warren's attitude was that if a student didn't meet his precise standards, then he needed to break the student any way he could. He would do anything to get us on our knees in front of him, even to the point of tripping us to make us fall. He was delighted when we bowed to his authority and supremacy. Once we were humiliated enough to beg for forgiveness, he would break out into a smug grin, knowing he had succeeded.

In general, punishment was a joy to Warren, and he personalized it to the individual child. With his "I will not tolerate rebellion" mantra in mind, Warren knew and studied each student to figure out the worst thing for that child to go through. Then, as he implemented his punishment of choice, he would do his best to make us feel small, stupid, and emotionally debilitated. Through the duration of our punishment, though we cried tears of shame and embarrassment, he would laugh.

The punishments could be public spanking or sitting in the corner of the classroom. A few children were afraid of the dark, so Warren forced them to sit in a windowless bathroom with the light turned off. Many times Warren could be seen dragging students through the school by the hair or ears. If you were shy, you would be forced to speak or pray in front of the class. He would even note which food a child disliked and require him or her to consume it while he watched. It was not uncommon to see a student being beaten with a yardstick. During these punishments, Warren would say things like: "I will break you." "You will conform, or there will be hell to pay." "You will obey, or else." And the one he spoke to me most frequently, "I will not tolerate rebellion." Quite often he told me that I was his greatest trial.

One instance of Warren's cruelty sticks out in my mind. There was a terribly shy boy one year younger than me in our school. One day, Warren called him up to pray in front of the group before we began our noon meal. The boy started mumbling a prayer but, because of paralyzing shyness, he began to sob as he spoke. He grabbed two tissues, one pink and the other blue, and stuffed them behind his glasses to soak up his tears. It was as if he thought that since he couldn't see us, we couldn't see him.

Our principal berated the still-crying sixth-grade boy. "You're a big baby." Warren made him sit there for the whole lunch hour with those tissues stuffed in his eyes while he openly laughed at him.

Public humiliation was common, and no student was immune. Whenever a punishment happened in public, we all felt awful for the unfortunate child, knowing that any one of us could be singled out next.

Warren's behavior trickled down to most of the teachers as well. He knew it made me uncomfortable to be singled out, so that was how he instructed the teachers to handle me. For example, the staff at Alta Academy decided to begin a music class. I wanted to play the guitar, but instead they made us sing hymns, which I did not enjoy. Because of my disinterested attitude, and to make an example of me, the music teacher, Sheryl, the wife of one of my half-brothers, made me sing a solo in front of the entire class. This happened not just once but every single day. I hated it!

One time, I refused to sing the solo. I was called into Warren's office. "Do as you're told, or you'll have hell to pay!"

What could I do? Nothing. For my entire seventh-grade year, I was made to get up and sing a daily solo.

Finally, I got the chance to play the guitar. One week after we began our instruments, Warren instructed that each of us needed to play a solo. Once again, I had to go first. Well, I played my solo, which was only five seconds long. Of course, it was awful. Warren grabbed me by my neck, stuck his finger in my spine, and pushed me into his office.

He said, "That was terrible. You don't have your heart in it."

"Duh," I answered.

He didn't appreciate my response. But on that day, he didn't get the upper hand because I refused to let him know how much the experience bothered me.

One punishment we actually sought out was running up a steep hill behind our school. It was at the base of the mountain, perfect for hiking. A group of us would get in trouble just so we could run up the hill.

"Please, Uncle Warren, don't make me run the hill!" We would cry and plead with him, hoping that if we slipped up and laughed out loud, it would sound like a hiccup.

"You will obey, or else! Now get going!"

Joyfully, yet trying not to smile, we would charge up the hill.

Warren never knew we were playing him. We would secretly time each other's ascent, competing for the fastest time. Those moments running up that hill were a small win for us, a time we could manipulate Warren right back.

I really began to hate school. Almost from the day it opened, I'd been called Black Sheep. I was okay with my new title as an insubordinate. I remembered how the Gentile families in the public schools had acted and how happy they'd seemed. For the first time, I began to secretly question the lifestyle I'd been raised in. My family life was not something that brought any semblance of joy to anyone, as far as I could tell. So, little by little, at barely twelve years old, I allowed my rebellious nature to trickle out.

Simple things such as wearing clothes that Warren didn't approve of and passing notes to my girlfriend, Gail, would frequently land me in trouble. I knew I wasn't supposed to have a girlfriend, but Gail was so beautiful and kind that I couldn't help it. I had a really hard time looking only at her chin.

One day in seventh grade, in trouble yet again, I sat in Warren's office. He stared at me through his owlish glasses, shook his head, and said, "You are my greatest trial." Sighing, he continued, "You leave me no other choice than to kick you out of school."

I loved being out of school! I went hiking and spent time in the mountains by myself. However, when Warren saw how much I was enjoying myself, he decided it was time to drag me back.

I continued to rebel against the authority of Warren and my teachers. Warren labeled me the bad student. I became the catalyst for his dictatorial behavior. Lecturing us that he would tolerate no rebellion, Warren would inform the other pupils that because of me, he was forced to make harsh rules that others must obey, such as the dress code.

I wanted to wear stylish clothing, not the boring things that the rest of the community wore. The dress code was actually fairly simple: we could wear anything as long as it went to our wrists and ankles. For our shoes, we could wear either boots or Sunday shoes. I stretched the rules as much as possible. I had a favorite shirt that I found at the thrift store we always shopped at. I loved it! It was bright yellow, with a huge collar and cuffs. It fit tight. I felt like a movie star.

After people got used to seeing me in my awesome shirt, I pushed the limit again. I rolled up the cuffs on my sleeves, just one roll. No one had ever gotten away with that before. I knew I was the best-looking kid in the school!

Warren couldn't have been more furious. But my victory was shorted-lived. Soon, Warren came up with a dress code that he claimed Father and Uncle Roy had approved and given him permission to enforce. Now we had to have button sleeves on our shirts and the cuffs had to be buttoned, preventing us from rolling up the sleeves. Also, at least the second button at the neck had to be done up.

More changes were slowly added, each one a little stricter. We were still allowed to wear jeans, but they couldn't have any holes, and we had to wear belts. By the middle of my seventh-grade year, we had to prove we were wearing our belts by tucking in our shirts.

Then hair was added to the code, so of course I started to grow mine out. Our hair could not touch our ears or collars. To hide my longer hair, I would tuck it behind my ears and under my collar. Once Warren was onto me, he started inspecting all the boys' hair by running his finger along our collars, pulling out the hair from underneath. There went my hair.

Then it was announced that all tight-fitting and bright-colored clothing was no longer allowed. Warren had to be able to pull one inch of fabric off the thigh and chest areas. There went my favorite yellow shirt.

Girls were not exempt from the new dress code. A lot of the girls were quite buxom, especially my friend Sally, and they could not wear tight-fitting clothing either. Warren had to be able to pull one inch of fabric from their chest and waist areas. If bra lines were visible across the girls' backs through their clothing, that was unacceptable. Dresses had to cover up to the collarbone and down to the wrist and mid-calf or ankle. Heels could not be higher than one inch, and shoes could not expose feet in any way. Years later, even the one-inch heels were revoked.

Warren's office was in back of the school with a large window overlooking the playground. He would stand at the window observing the children at play, watching for any infractions of his rules. If Warren felt that any of the children violated the dress code, he called them into his office to inspect their clothing. My half-sister Valerie and one of my good friends, who I will not name to protect her privacy, both told me that when they were called into his office, Warren would grope them while attempting to pull the fabric away from their waist and breasts.

WARREN'S POSITION AS PRINCIPAL FED HIS FIRE FOR SEEKING POWER. I began to notice his predilection as a pedophile, though it didn't really become a conscious thought until later, when I was about eighteen years old. At a younger age, I was innocent; I never thought it was possible for sex between an adult and a child. The thought never even entered my mind.

Yet I knew something wasn't quite right.

Warren seemed infatuated with young girls. He was touchy with them. This went against Father's teachings of not touching girls. Warren constantly hugged them and put his arms around them. He rationalized this behavior by stating that the age of twelve was a blessed age for girls because the virgin mother, Mary, was twelve years old when she conceived Christ.

Warren seemed obsessed with how to exercise control over girls. According to some media reports over the years, he was also interested in boys. This may or may not be true, but I never witnessed any evidence of it. I noticed only his attraction to young girls.

THOUGH I DETESTED SCHOOL, I MUST ADMIT IT WASN'T ALWAYS BAD. Warren did one thing that made me very happy: he recognized that I had a strong affinity for math. He helped me by creating a special curriculum so I could get through algebra, calculus, and part of trigonometry all within a year's time. Then, when the lessons slowed down because Warren didn't have time to learn the math himself, I was bored once again. This resulted in my getting into more trouble.

By age twelve and a half, I felt like I could not stand school any longer. Father had a business that Ward, one of my half-brothers, ran for him. They made plated-leaf jewelry and display boxes.

"Father, please let me work for Ward," I begged.

"No. You are too young to be out of school," he answered.

"Please. I promise I'll work hard."

He looked at me for a few moments without saying a word. Finally, he spoke. "You can work on one condition: you must remain in school."

My heart sank, but then I saw the opportunity before me. If I had to stay in school, that meant I would have to work in the evenings. I wouldn't have to spend all that time with my family!

I smiled and agreed. Though I still had to stay in school, I loved my new freedom and my ability to work hard.

School lost even more appeal when I learned something that crushed me. Though I frequently got into trouble for passing notes to her, I still had a major crush on Gail, who also attended Alta Academy. I thought she was beautiful, smart, and completely wonderful. She had long, deep-black hair, a slender figure, and brown eyes. She had been adopted into the FLDS.

Blaine, my older brother, started doing yardwork at her house because her adopted father was crippled. Boy, was I jealous that he might get a chance to see Gail more than I could.

Everyone knew that Gail and I were considered boyfriend and girlfriend. That is, until I heard that my older brothers Blaine and Lyle had both seduced her and were having sex with her. Finding out this news devastated me. I couldn't believe my older brothers would do that with a girl I truly cared about. I never wanted to go back to that school again, but I had made a promise to Father.

I continued attending school full-time and working part-time until halfway through the eighth grade, when I reached my limit with school. It was then that I permanently dropped out and began working full-time in the jewelry store. I continued my employment there for five years.

Being free from school didn't alleviate problems at home, so I worked as many hours as I could. But my busy schedule did not preclude me from the dreaded "produce runs" we boys were forced to participate in.

The Strattons were an older couple who converted to the church. They lived in Salt Lake City in an ancient farmhouse that had been built in the early 1900s. It was located on Redwood Road at about 7800 South. The Strattons acted destitute even though they lived off inheritances and pensions. Since they didn't have to work, they took it upon themselves to become FLDS benefactors and gather food for the community. They accomplished this mission by traveling around to various grocery stores to pick up leftover items that were going to be thrown away because they were too old or rotten to sell.

At that time, Father was the bishop of Salt Lake City, and he would send his sons once a week on what he called a "produce run." The Strattons had a little shop at the back of their farm where they bagged up all this food for us. As we would get out of the truck, we could hear swarms of buzzing insects. It was a steady hum that sent chills up and down our spines. And the smell was awful, reaching us long before we made it to the shop.

As we entered, we saw literally thousands of flies buzzing all over barrels of half-rotted chicken wings and produce. A single electric fly zapper sat on a corner rafter, constantly zinging and sizzling the vermin. The building also housed colonies of mice and rats. Cats, dogs, chickens, and goats roamed the grounds. There was shit everywhere. It was a health-code nightmare. I'm surprised the neighbors didn't turn in these loathsome people to the authorities.

We would run and hide when we heard it was time for a produce run. Not only was the food sickening and the flies horrible, but the Strattons had no sense of personal hygiene. Mae was a skinny beanpole compared to her husband, who sported one of the biggest guts I've ever seen. Their hair looked like it had never seen a showerhead, and their body odor suggested they'd never owned a bar of soap or stick of deodorant. I doubt they ever bathed. When they would come to church, their smell reached us before they entered the building. Once they stepped inside, their stench would overpower the entire room.

Mae had a thing for young boys, and she would come on to us, trying to flirt. She'd pull us aside and say things like, "We oughta meet up sometime." Although her advances were repulsive, with the condition of her husband, I guess I could understand.

After we'd loaded up the stinking mess in the truck, we would have produce-throwing parties on the way back to the big house, about a half-hour drive. We would throw the rotting food at passing vehicles, people we didn't like, random mailboxes, and parked cars. By the time we got home, the produce would be about halfway gone.

I had a friend named Stan. He owned an old pickup truck that was useful for covert throwing activities. One night, we loaded up the bed of his truck and went to a grocery-store parking lot. While Stan was driving, I stood up in back and pelted cars and any other stationary or moving items we passed. Stan took a hard turn, and I flew out of the truck, getting pretty banged up. When I got home, one of the mothers asked what had happened. I couldn't let her know we were wasting our food, so I gave the standard, "Oh, I just fell down the stairs."

After we'd done this for several years, the mothers started to get wise about our produce-throwing parties. Mae would call them and ask whether specific items had arrived. We were busted. It's a miracle we didn't get arrested. Each time we traveled to the Stratton home, we could still see the previous week's trail of rotten produce along the roadside.

Because this was food no one else wanted, the most common items for us to receive from the Strattons' benevolence were chicken wings, squash, lettuce, rotten tomatoes, and lots of Brussels sprouts. Perhaps this is why the mothers always overcooked the food—they were trying to make sure all the germs were killed and it was as harmless as possible. I can still see those chicken wings floating on top of a greasy layer in the soup. By the time the squash would be served, it had the consistency and appeal of baby food. The mothers did everything they could to make the Brussels sprouts into something we would eat, but we all hated the bitter flavor.

Eventually, the Strattons apostatized and we lost this ability to get free food. None of us missed this. It was a miracle someone didn't die from eating that rot.

MORE AND MORE, I JUST WANTED TO GET AWAY FROM THE CHAOS OF my household and spend time alone in the mountains. My mother became concerned. She would take me into her room and sit me down to have a talking-to. However, she was a weak woman and hated conflict, so as she started to talk, she would immediately begin to cry. She would just sit there and sob, "I'm so sorry. I'm a bad mother. I'm so sorry." I never knew what to say when she did that, so I usually just sat there and stared at the walls and floor until she told me I could leave.

One of the mothers, Mother Ruth, had all girls. She had given birth to one stillborn son, and she did not like the boys of the family. On one occasion, she walked up to me and started yelling and screaming for no reason. Honestly, I hadn't done anything this time. She said I was bringing damnation to the family with my rebellious behavior. The mothers were still struggling with accepting the other children as their own, and she accused me of being the cause of all the fighting. It didn't help matters that my own mother felt that since I was her only son, she didn't have to share me with the other women in the house.

Some of the wives overheard Mother Ruth's tirade and told Father. It wasn't long before he called me into his office. *Great*, I thought, *another interrogation*. I never liked going into his office. It was a cold, unwelcoming atmosphere with his desk situated in the center of the room, surrounded by bookshelves.

When I entered the office, there was Father, looking as he always did, dressed in his suit and sitting behind the desk. As usual, his full, dark hair was neatly combed straight back, exposing his forehead.

Without smiling or getting up, he said to me, "I want you to know that I don't agree with what Mother Ruth said. She's not right. She has no reason or cause to say that to you. You need to get over it."

Though he was stern and matter-of-fact like always, his reaction to what Mother Ruth had done surprised me. He was actually on my side. It was one of the few times I felt somewhat close to my father.

When Mother heard what Mother Ruth had done, I witnessed something I'd never seen before: my mother angry.

"What the hell happened?" she asked, fuming. When I told her, she said, "That is totally wrong. That is not who you are."

Another surprise.

This would prove to be a unique experience, the one and only time in my life that both my mother and father ever defended me.

Chapter Seven

Tomorrow Is the End of the Earth

An irrigation creek ran through our property. Playing in the water proved a huge temptation for all us kids. The younger children would squeal as they watched the silvery bodies of fish dart here and there in the little stream. The chilly mountain water refreshed us on blistering summer days. But our parents feared that a small child could fall in and get swept away. Once the water left our property, it flowed swiftly under the road and traveled beneath 9400 South, the street our house was on. We were all banned from the creek, which, of course, made it all the more appealing!

One day, Warren, Blaine, and Gary were chasing fish in the creek. One of the mothers saw them and went to tell Father.

"What the hell do you think you're doing?" Father shouted as he stormed out of the house.

The boys whipped around, terrified that they were caught.

"Each of you, get a strong stick. I'll teach you to stay out of the water." Father's loud voice carried across our property, drawing our attention.

A few of my brothers and I positioned ourselves around the corner of the house to see what would happen. This would be a rare opportunity to see Warren take a beating. Finally he would get the punishment he deserved! My heart raced with excitement.

Father used whipping only when he felt his usual lecture wouldn't be enough to teach us a lesson. Gary and Blaine went in search of a stick that would meet Father's approval, but Warren got a wimpy one, all rubbery.

Visibly shaking, the boys offered their sticks like a reluctant gift to Father. He spanked Blaine and Gary with a heavy hand, but when he got to Warren, he became emotional. Warren looked at Father with big puppy-dog eyes and said, "I'm so sorry. I want to do your will."

Father barely tapped him once with the stick and then said to the other boys, "This is how you repent. Warren is sorry, and therefore I can't do to him what I did to the others."

It was as if Father wanted to prove to us that Warren was extra-holy and didn't deserve punishment. As I got older, I realized that Warren just had to go overboard when he said he was sorry, and the mothers and Father always fell for it.

"Don't ever go anywhere alone" was another family rule we had to live by. I normally followed this guideline, but it wasn't always possible. Valerie and I were best friends, and we spent a lot of time together. Whenever we could get away, we went hiking because I loved the peace and quiet of the mountains. If Valerie wasn't available, I would go by myself. But whenever I did this, I was almost always caught because Warren would be on the lookout with the binoculars. Invariably, I'd return to see him standing there, waiting for me on the property line. "I saw you. I'm going to tell Father."

He was so annoying! It seemed that Warren constantly looked over my shoulder, even when I did something as innocent as trying to escape the fighting and yelling at home and be by myself.

The mothers still struggled to live the Law of Sarah. There were constant arguments and trips to Father's office to place blame on each other.

Father began trying to force the mothers to live in harmony. But mandating certain aspects of life only made matters worse. In about 1975, when I was fourteen, Marilyn made a rare appearance in family class. Father addressed his attention to her and said, while pointing to my mother, "Sharon has no young children. I am going to give Esther to Sharon to raise."

Noah and Esther were Mother Marilyn's four-year-old twins. Would Father really split up a set of twins and give one to another woman? Everyone looked around in shocked disbelief. Did he really mean it?

He did.

Mother was now charged to take on Esther and raise her as her own child. Because all the mothers already did the mundane activities surrounding our physical needs, such as food preparation and laundry, Mother's role was more spiritual. She would be Esther's guide and teacher, and her new "daughter" was to report directly to her. This did not affect our day-to-day living arrangements, because, since our family was so small, we were always sprinkled among the children of the other mothers anyway. It's not like my mother had her own wing of the house like Mother Marilyn.

In the long run, this lesson in the Law of Sarah never really worked. Esther was old enough to know Marilyn was her real mother. However, it did send fear shockwaves through all the mothers. Who would be next to lose her child? And at what age? Would Father start taking away their infants next?

FEAR—A CONSTANT AND UNRELENTING PART OF AN FLDS MEMBER'S life. "Tomorrow is the end of the world" is a theme the people believe, reinforced by continual messages of destruction. It becomes the norm to live in terror because the end is coming any day now. If you are found lacking, you will not be saved. You will suffer annihilation alongside the wicked.

Because this was all that was ever taught, both in church meetings and family class, I bought into these world-ending scenarios with my entire soul. I began to despair that I would ever attain a driver's license, marriage, and a family of my own. So, at age fifteen and a half, I became depressed.

Knowing I had to do something to overcome these horrible emotions, I gathered up my courage, went to Father, and asked him to allow me to get my driver's license.

"You are not worthy to have your license," was his stern reply. "If I gave you that privilege, you would only do bad things with it."

Anxious that I would miss out on major events if my life was suddenly cut short, I kept at him. Over and over, I hounded him for my license. After many days of my cajoling, he finally gave in. We loaded ourselves into his old green Cadillac to start the five-hour drive down to Arizona, where, at the time, one did not have to take driver's education. I would only need to take the test.

I felt intimidated alone with Father in the car. I had to keep wiping my sweaty palms on my pants. Even though I was almost sixteen, this was the first time I'd ever been one-on-one with him. We did not say more than five words to each other the entire time. I usually enjoy silence, but the tension in the car made it the longest five hours of my life.

I'd never studied a driver's manual, but I'd learned the laws while driving with my family, so I felt confident I would pass the written test. The only time I'd actually been behind the wheel was when I'd snuck out and stolen my father's new truck.

When I was thirteen, my friend Sally, from Alta Academy, had a crush on me. We were both in eighth grade. Since we weren't supposed to talk to others of the opposite sex, she started passing me notes. So, of course, I would pass notes back to her. She was so pretty and quite buxom. She was also a hopeless romantic.

In one of her notes she wrote, "I really want you to be my boyfriend."

Since I no longer considered Gail my girlfriend, I wrote back, "Okay."

Then she quickly wrote another note. "Since we can't talk in school, pick me up tonight so we can talk."

She told me she would sneak out of her house and meet me at a certain corner in Salt Lake near where she lived. The last part of the note had me grinning: she called me her knight in shining armor.

At that moment, I didn't think anything about the fact that I lived in Sandy and she was in Salt Lake, twenty miles away. I only knew that I wanted to meet her and impress her. My father's new truck was a beautiful bright-red, four-wheel-drive Chevrolet Cheyenne. I knew if I picked her up in that, she would be in awe.

So, at 3:00 a.m., I snuck into the yard where all the vehicles were parked and "borrowed" my father's new truck. Since our property was fenced with a locked gate, there was never any fear of someone stealing our cars, so the keys were kept in the ignitions. My hands shook as I attempted to grasp the key. But I was a clever kid, and I figured out how to start and drive the truck. Once I'd closed the gate behind me, I was off to meet my new girlfriend. Electric nerves and excitement shot through me, making it hard to focus on the road.

I found the corner where she waited for me, and we drove the short distance to Liberty Park, a huge area of trees and grass near downtown Salt Lake.

From the moment she climbed into the truck, she seemed calm, but I still jangled with nervous tension. We talked for a while before she slipped from the passenger seat and scooted closer to me. Then she put her arm around me.

"I really want you to kiss me." Her voice was soft in my ear.

How could I refuse? This was my first kiss, and it was amazing. I never knew a girl's lips could be so soft.

We continued talking and kissing until I noticed it was 5:00 a.m.

"I really need to take you home. We have school in just a few hours. If I'm not home for 6:00 breakfast, I'll be in so much trouble."

She agreed and quickly scooted over to her side. I sped to the same corner and dropped her off, then I hurried to cover the twenty miles home before the sun rose.

No one ever knew I was gone.

For the next couple of weeks, Sally continued writing me notes calling me her knight in shining armor because I was going to sneak her out of her family—like me, she didn't want to live the FLDS lifestyle.

Then, in one note, she said, "We need to talk again. Tonight. Pick me up at the same place and same time."

So once again I snuck out, stole my father's truck, and drove to Salt Lake. This time while we were parked at Liberty Park, there was only a little talking and lot of making out.

It was shortly after this that I dropped out of school, so we never had another rendezvous, though we did talk a couple of times after that.

Since I'd taught myself to drive my father's truck, I felt confident I'd also pass the driving test.

Imagine my joy when I did! On the way home, Father let me drive while he slept. I was speeding, and I got pulled over in Nephi, Utah, a small town about eighty miles south of Salt Lake. I tried to ease the car to the shoulder in silence, but when I pulled over, Father woke up.

"What the hell's going on?" Father's voice bounced around the interior of the car.

I started shaking from head to foot. My elation at receiving my license was torn apart by my father's rage. The cop only gave me a warning because it was my first day driving, but Father refused to speak to me for the rest of the trip home. The tension in the car was so thick, I could hardly breathe.

On that uncomfortable drive home, I decided once again that this FLDS life was not for me. As I pulled up to the house and Father slammed the car door, the all-too-familiar sense of dread settled over me. I saw no reason for me to stay in my family. Why should I? Behind our closed doors, there was nothing but fighting between the mothers and a cold, disinterested father who didn't have time for his family. Yet I knew I was too young to go out on my own. I was stuck. I stood beside the car and gazed up into the mountains, wishing for release from my unloving situation.

My only consolation was that I still worked at the jewelry company, and now I also worked at a cabinet shop. I relished the freedom this gave me. I could work whenever I wanted, which became more and more frequent as the tension between the mothers increased. Law of Sarah or not, yelling, screaming, slapping, and kicking were becoming the norm. I would volunteer to work overtime for free, just to stay away from home.

I TRIED REALLY HARD TO GET ALONG WITH MY MANY SIBLINGS AND STAY under the radar of the mothers, but it seemed impossible.

One day, Mother Norma became angry because I teased one of her twins. It was just normal brotherly teasing. Later, as I sat watching TV, someone came from behind, grabbed me by my hair, and began violently shaking. It was Mother Norma. I was so angry—I have rarely been that mad—that I rose with my fists clenched and almost hit her. But I do not believe in hitting women, so I ran out before I could do something I'd regret.

"I'm done with this!" I shouted. Bolting out of the house, I ran to an old Chevy station wagon of Father's in the yard. I got in the car with virtually no money and little idea what to do. All I knew was that I was done with my family and wanted to go to California to see the ocean. The car was full of gas, so I took off. I stopped to buy a map.

As a sixteen-year-old, I had no thought about what I'd do once I reached the coast. I'd never seen California before, but it sounded beautiful. I felt positive my life would be better in a completely new setting.

About a hundred and forty miles later, at the Utah/Nevada border town of Wendover, I ran out of gas. A cop pulled over to ask what was going on. When I explained, the cop said he was sorry, but since I was a minor, he had no other recourse than to take me home. My heart sank.

When I arrived home, the family stayed quiet and avoided me. I was being shunned. I just went to my room and lay on my bed. Surprisingly, Mother Norma came in.

"I'm sorry," she apologized. Then she turned and left my room. I've never heard words spoken with so little emotion. They left me feeling empty.

Immediately after Mother Norma left, I went outside to find Father so I could talk to him and receive counsel. He was in the yard telling people what work needed to be done. I took a deep breath and walked up behind him.

Because Father was so important in the church, he seemed almost like a God to all of us. We couldn't just go up and talk to him. Even though I was now sixteen, I had no idea how to approach my own father. Like I'd done in the past, I just shadowed him as he moved around, hoping he would turn and ask what I wanted. I made enough noise that it was impossible for him not to realize I followed behind. But he never acknowledged me. After a while, I realized he too was shunning me.

During the next week, the entire family continued to ignore me. I was allowed to eat meals with them, but they refused to engage with me in any way. A stray glance was their only acknowledgement. After this week of silence, they slowly started talking to me again. Things eventually returned to normal.

I DESPISED EVERYTHING ABOUT PLURAL MARRIAGE. I DID NOT WANT TO live that way. To me, plural marriage was a living hell with constant bickering and fighting between the mothers. I fantasized about having one wife and only four or five kids, so I could form a close relationship with each child, something I did not have with my parents. I wanted my children to enjoy the security of a dedicated father and mother. I would dream about going on bike rides together as a happy family.

By age sixteen, I wanted to get married. In my limited experience, I assumed this was the only possible way to improve my life. Since marriages were arranged and I could not choose my own wife, I went to Father and asked him to choose one for me.

He replied, "You are too damn young."

I said, "Then I'll leave."

Positioned behind his desk in a severe suit, Father turned his stern gaze fully upon me. "If you leave, you will be cast off. You will be considered an apostate." In excruciating detail, he explained that I would never have contact again with my family.

Even with everything I'd gone through, I never thought my family would completely reject me. I believed I had the agency to choose the way I wanted to live. I thought that if I wanted to leave, I would be able to. If I changed my mind, I would always be welcomed back.

Now that view was changed.

How could I have been so wrong? I was trapped. I had nowhere else to go. The idea of losing my family made me feel something like paralysis. Along with the members of the church, my family were the only people I knew.

I would have to postpone my plan of getting married.

Many people wonder why members of the FLDS Church stay in such challenging conditions. What they don't understand is that the FLDS members have little notion of anything outside the community. Their cloistered life is all they know. They don't understand laws, cultural aspects, or even how to make a living in the Gentile world. So, for FLDS people to leave the church and go out into that frightening world constitutes physical, financial, spiritual, and emotional abandonment.

Leaving the safety and familiarity of the community was a terrifying thought. I would need to ease into it.

A FEW MONTHS BEFORE MY SEVENTEENTH BIRTHDAY, IN THE LATE FALL of 1977, I was moved into the big bedroom on the third floor with Warren, Dale, and Lyle, who were all older than me. The bedroom was in the center of the house, above the big meeting room. Four or five boys always shared this room.

Our beds lined the wall, and Warren took the prime spot under the window. I had lived there about a month when Warren started thinking he was the boss of the room. His constant nagging drove me crazy. "Pick up your clothes, Wallace." "Make your bed right now!"

As the youngest boy, I felt embarrassed to get undressed in front of my older brothers. I didn't want them to tease me because of my scarecrow-thin body, so I'd often sleep in my clothes. Being a teenager, I didn't care too much about my appearance. Since I no longer had a girlfriend, who was I trying to impress? Sometimes I wore the same clothes two days in a row without showering. We showered at night, but it never occurred to me that I could take my pajamas into the bathroom and change into them after I was clean.

Whenever Warren saw me sleep in my clothes, he tattled on me. This prompted Father to make step-by-step rules about how we needed to shower each day. We were to turn the water on and wet ourselves. Next, we had to turn the water off while we thoroughly soaped our bodies and hair. Only then could we turn the water back on to rinse.

Warren always watched for wrongdoing and ingratiated himself with Father by telling, which made him seem holier than us. Quite often, Warren would stand outside the bathroom with an ear to the door. When I showered, I loved standing under the running water. One day, I was called into Father's office.

"Warren told me you are not showering properly," Father said. "You are taking food out of the mouths of your family by using too much water and electricity."

First I wasn't showering enough, then I was showering too much. I couldn't win.

AT THIS TIME, THE CHURCH WAS FOLLOWING SOME OLD RULES ESTABlished by the Musser family. No matter how warm it was, we were never to roll up our sleeves or go without a hat. We were to do everything we could to keep from getting a tan. Having a tan was considered a sin, showing that you wanted to be a black person and live under the biblical curse of Ham. The Mussers would wear gloves, huge hats, and sleeves down to their wrists.

Since we had to follow this rule, we were often hot and miserable while working out in the unforgiving sun. Some of the boys were charged to tear down our old wood fence and build a six-foot concrete wall to surround our property and keep out Gentile eyes. To be called to the crew indicated that we were special and capable of protecting our family. The mothers all campaigned to have their sons included in this honored work detail. However, the labor proved backbreaking in the stifling heat. It was made even worse by our foreman, Warren. When we complained we were roasting because we couldn't roll up our sleeves, Father would not relent.

Father also said we couldn't cuss about our intolerable circumstances, but Warren continued saying *damn, hell,* and *shit.* Lyle, Dale, and I didn't know what to do with all this swearing. We finally confronted Warren and said we were going to tell Father he was swearing too much.

He said, "Well, I'll tell Father you're lazy."

This was a complete lie. We were working our butts off. But we knew that if Warren told this lie to Father, he would believe the golden child and we would get in trouble. So, we kept quiet.

We were hand-digging the footings for the fence. Since we were at the base of the mountains, the ground was terribly rocky. I used shovels to pry rocks out of the hard ground. One day, I broke three shovels.

"Damn you!" Warren shouted. "Those shovels are expensive. I don't have the budget to keep replacing them."

"I'm sorry," I said. "But I can't get these rocks out any other way."

"If you break another shovel, I'll tell Father you have moral problems and can't work on the project anymore."

It was another lie, but I feared he would actually do it. Then I'd face more serious problems than not being able to work on the coveted fence project.

In my family, I learned there are two kinds of fear. One is mental, and the other is physical. My oldest brother, Hyrum, was large and aggressive, mean even. This helped him do well on the football team in high school. He also had a terrible temper, and people feared him. If you crossed him, he would beat the shit out of you. When he fought with someone, he would literally pick them up and throw them on the ground.

But with Warren, the fear was all mental. His kind of trouble could get us cast out or damned to hell, which was more frightening than any physical harm. It was a great way to exert control over us. Warren was a master at cataloging things in his brain. He kept an inventory of anything we'd ever done wrong in our lives, so he could use it against us. This manipulation affected not only our hearts but also our minds.

IN ADDITION TO LIVING IN CONSTANT FEAR OF BEING DAMNED OR getting beat up, we had to stay aware of church doctrine. The church leaders would dictate rules and guidelines, like what food we could eat and what clothes we could wear.

The Word of Wisdom was a revelation given to the original Latter-day Saint prophet, Joseph Smith, concerning what members should and should not do to keep healthy and strong. For example, followers are warned to stay away from alcohol. However, since the Word of Wisdom was considered only a suggestion and not a commandment, few people in our church followed its counsel.

My father, some of the mothers, and most of my siblings loved to drink. Father didn't keep his alcohol to himself—he was more than happy to share with others. In fact, it was Father who offered me my first beer, when I was fourteen.

One day, shortly after my first drink, I followed Father around the house while he checked on people. He had been drinking heavily and was fairly intoxicated. Father was a big man, standing six-foot-four and weighing about two hundred and eighty pounds. When Father was drunk, he acted jovial but didn't realize his own strength. I must have been following too closely behind him. He turned around and punched me on the shoulder, knocking me down. Then he just laughed, not concerned that I was injured.

On Fridays, we had family home evening. This was when Father would teach his family regarding a variety of church topics in the sanctity of our own home. The goal was to make us well-versed on all aspects of our religion. Sometimes the younger children participated in activities so they could learn as well.

After class, Father would break out the vodka and ask the kids, "Want a screwdriver?"

This was how he controlled Mother Norma, by keeping her drunk. It's no surprise that Norma struggled with alcoholism.

My half-brother Blaine is six years older than me. At twenty-one, he was a real rebel, and I looked up to him. I knew he went out drinking, and I wanted to know what it was like to get drunk.

At this time in Salt Lake City, teenagers loved to "drag State." State Street is a main thoroughfare in downtown Salt Lake that leads to the State Capitol Building. In all seasons except winter, the city's youth would drive their cars and motorcycles up and down the street, flirting with each other. It was where the Salt Lake Valley's cool teenagers spent their Friday or Saturday nights.

Blaine would drag State in his Pontiac Grand Prix and get drunk. I thought he was the coolest guy ever.

One night during a produce run, Blaine asked, "Hey, Wallace, you want to get drunk with me tonight?"

The biggest smile spread across my face, and I could only nod my head. I loved fast cars, and I was excited to get drunk and meet girls.

After driving up and down State for a while, Blaine stopped at the liquor store. Being a big spender, he bought a couple fifths of Annie Green Springs peach wine. It put him out $2.69 a bottle.

We stopped at Dee's, a local fast food restaurant. Blaine ordered a large cup of ice and poured in the wine. He handed it to me, and I took my first sip. It was nasty. I don't think I've ever tasted anything so vile.

Blaine said, "Come on, drink it fast."

I didn't want to disappoint Blaine, so I drank the first fifth in five minutes. When he offered the other fifth, I drank it too.

I was checking out the scenery from the backseat when everything started to swirl. This wasn't anything like I thought it would be. I didn't feel so good.

"I've got to go home." I could barely speak.

Blaine said, "Don't you dare throw up in my car. I'll kill you."

That was one of the longest drives of my life. The car felt like a merry-go-round and roller coaster combined. I was so sick, I wished I could just die. Once we were home, I stumbled to my room. I thought if I could lie down, I would be okay. But when I did, the room started to spin topsy-turvy, making my nausea worse. I barfed all over.

Warren's bed was right next to mine. He woke up, sniffing. "What the hell is that?" he yelled. "It stinks like shit in here." When his eyes focused on me, they narrowed to slits. "What have you been doing? You went and got drunk! I'm going to tell Father, and you're going to get in so much trouble!"

Because it was Warren, I knew he would tattle on me. But since I felt like death warmed over, I didn't really care at the moment.

Blaine got into serious trouble with Father, and he was mad at me. The whole family bagged on me for getting drunk and stinking up the house.

Mother helped me clean it up, but she was angry and scared. "What have you done?" she asked. "I taught you better than that. You know what alcohol does to a person. You have to stay away from it."

I think Mother was particularly concerned because of Father's heavy drinking. She hated alcohol. I was super-annoyed with her, and I wondered what her problem was. It bothered me that Father, who was a leader in the church, and anyone else could drink, but not me. Blaine and Lyle drank all the time, but I was the one who got into trouble.

I replied, "Well, Father drinks vodka, and that's okay."

She didn't like that answer. I knew I'd disappointed her. But I didn't ever want to feel that sick again, so I never did any heavy drinking after that. I'd learned my lesson.

Even as a child, I wanted to improve my station in life. This drive carried through to my teenage years and kept me going, but it irritated Warren. If he thought anyone was getting ahead in any way, he would try to cut us down by bringing up a wrongdoing from our past. So, from the moment I vomited after drinking, he would say to me, "Well, you stunk up the whole house."

I'VE ALWAYS LIKED TO WORK. FATHER LET ME GET A JOB AT POLYSEAL, a hydraulic seal manufacturer in the rubber products industry. I started out as a laborer and later advanced to shop foreman. PolySeal employed both polygamous and Gentile workers.

This was the first time I'd lived and worked in a Gentile world, and it was an eye-opening experience. Talk about culture shock! A few wild people talked about drugs and sex. This was my first exposure to Gentile girls, of which this company had plenty. I was intrigued by their ability to be soft, quiet, and cool all at the same time.

I started to experience a flutter of feelings for a coworker, Stacy. Like my mother, Stacy was considered a convert to the FLDS Church. However, her mother had joined the church when Stacy was three, so she didn't know anything different. Stacy scared me a bit, as I'd been taught to fear Gentiles, and she had a worldlier upbringing than me because of her mother's Gentile influence. Stacy was small, about five-foot-two with a medium build, light blond hair, blue eyes, and a shy personality. She was pretty cute.

But what brought us together was not so much feeling physically attracted as sharing concerns with each other. Neither of us wanted placement marriages. We both sensed a solution to our problems in each other, though neither of us had the foresight to really think through how things would look long-term between us and with children. We both just wanted out, but we didn't want to lose our families. In my inexperience, all these complicated emotions seemed like young love.

I asked my father if I could marry Stacy. I was still only seventeen. Once again, he said I was too young and to forget about it. My half-brother

Blaine also had a crush on her, and I worried he'd ask Father to arrange for their marriage. Luckily, his crush was short-lived.

Even though I was an older teenager, I still had to abide by a 9:00 p.m. curfew. I bought a red 1978 Chevy Camaro with my earnings. I thought I was pretty cool. I liked to cruise around and do a little drinking. I relished the sense of reckless abandonment this car gave me.

One night, my friends picked me up and we went to the movies. When they dropped me off at ten o'clock, one hour after curfew, Father was at the gate waiting for me.

"Where the hell have you been?" he screamed.

This really upset me because my half-brother Lyle broke curfew all the time, yet he never got in trouble. Just like Warren, Lyle always got away with things, no matter what he did. It seemed that someone always covered for them. I, however, lived under constant scrutiny. It was as if Lyle and Warren were always right and I was always wrong.

This curfew incident was a last straw for me. I was tired of the injustice and inequality in my life.

I insisted to Father that if he did not marry me off, I would leave.

In my ignorant mind, marriage was the only way to get out of my house and away from oppressive rules and bickering mothers. Naively, I truly believed that once I married, my problems would evaporate. I trusted that as soon as I had a family of my own, I would be free to set my own rules and create loving relationships with my wife and children.

At this tender age, I had no idea how foolish these ideas would prove to be.

Chapter Eight

Brotherly Love

Though Valerie and I had been inseparable throughout our childhood and teenage years, almost as soon as we moved into the big house, Lyle started to act in a proprietary way toward her. It was almost as if he thought he owned Valerie. He was a year and a half older than us.

Valerie had developed a gorgeous hourglass figure. She was breathtaking. She had flowing auburn hair and the deepest blue eyes that seemed like they glowed, making a person want to fall into their depths. Her eyes were undoubtedly her most striking feature. To match her beautiful appearance, Valerie was always happy and bubbly. She never had anything bad to say about anyone.

Because of Valerie's attractive looks and fun personality, Lyle acted like she was his prize that he could wear on his arm. Lyle had a gangly and athletic build, but he certainly would not be considered handsome. He had a goofy mouth and a stuck eye. When you talked to him, you never knew which eye to focus on or where he was looking.

Even though Valerie and Lyle were half-siblings, I started to see them secretly hold hands and kiss while keeping out of sight of the mothers. I found myself shivering in disgust whenever I saw it. I tried ignoring it, but it was hard avoiding them, so I learned to shift my focus to other things.

I grew to love engines and cars. By age sixteen, I'd become the mechanical talent in our family. One day, I was working on a car in the barn and Valerie came in. It was great spending time with her again. We started talking about the different parts of the engine.

Out of the blue, Valerie said, "If you teach me about engines, I'll teach you about sex."

I felt my heart drop. A sick feeling grew in the pit of my stomach. "What do you know about sex?"

She shrugged her shoulders. "I'm having it with Lyle."

What? My mind went blank. My brain was not processing what she said. I was still naïve about sex—it was never spoken of in church or among family members. All I knew was what I'd overheard the Gentile boys saying in sixth grade. The idea of incest never entered my imagination.

Years earlier, Father had gathered all his sons together one Sunday afternoon in his office. Sternly, he said, "I've heard about some of my boys playing with their sisters . . . touching their private parts. If I ever hear of any of you touching your sisters, I'll beat you within an inch of your life."

His formidable glare told us he meant what he said.

When I finally realized what Valerie was attempting to tell me—she was having sex!—I felt the blood drain from my face. I became light-headed. Lyle was our brother! Valerie was my closest sibling and confidante, and I loved her. I wanted her to be safe and happy. But I knew if she was doing this, she would have neither safety nor happiness. Why was she doing this? We were only sixteen years old!

I tried speaking, but my voice shook. "How long has this been going on?"

"Oh, for about two years," she answered.

I couldn't believe it. I didn't know what to say, so she just left. My mind could not stay focused on the engine—I couldn't get the two of them out of my head.

Valerie's situation concerned me enough that I actually went to Father to tell him what was going on. He said, "I know all about it. I have it handled."

But nothing changed.

ALTHOUGH VALERIE SEEMED LIKE A WILLING PARTICIPANT, AT LEAST with the hugging and kissing part, after another couple of months she confided in me that she was tired of Lyle's behavior. "All he wants is sex."

This didn't surprise me.

Lyle never loved Valerie; he never loved anyone. He was a conqueror, and he told everyone he could that he was having sex with both Valerie and

Gail, the girl I once considered my girlfriend. Eventually, Valerie broke up with him and stopped seeing him.

However, weeks later, she came to me nearly in tears. "Warren is forcing me to have sex with him now."

"Are you boyfriend and girlfriend?" I was almost afraid to ask her; surely she couldn't be that stupid.

"No!" she shouted. "I don't have any choice."

I didn't know what to say to her. I knew only too well the threats and lies Warren gave when he wanted to get his way. What was worse, Father believed everything he said. This behavior continued for years, though Valerie wanted it to stop.

WHEN WARREN WAS ABOUT TWENTY-TWO, JUST BEFORE HIS FIRST MARriage, I was seventeen and still sharing that same room with him.

I never really had a strong bond with my mother, so I was surprised one day when I was lying on my bed and she came running into my room sobbing.

I jumped up. "Mother, what's wrong?"

But she couldn't answer me. She appeared to be in the depth of sadness, her body racked with gut-wrenching sobs. It disturbed me to see her so upset.

"Mother, please tell me what's wrong."

She was unable to speak through her tears.

"What did I do?" My hands turned to ice, and I could not tear my eyes from her. I assumed I'd done something wrong and would be kicked out of the church. I continued to beg her to tell me what was wrong, positive I'd committed a grievous sin.

She still could not speak. Finally, I just stopped talking and let her cry.

After what seemed like an eternity, she blurted out, "Something terrible has happened."

"Please, you've got to tell me. What did I do?" I was so indoctrinated in the church of guilt and shame that this was all I could think of. I must have unknowingly committed a horrible sin.

Mother took a deep breath and grabbed my hands. "I have something to tell you. I have to get this off my chest. But before I do, you have to promise me you'll never tell another soul." After a great sigh, she said, "This is eating at me, and I can no longer keep quiet."

"I promise." Now my mouth was dry. My tongue felt like it was stuck to the roof of my mouth.

Mother choked out, "Warren did something terrible to Vanessa."

Instantly, the blood froze in my veins. What did he do now? Vanessa was my only full sibling, three years younger than me and only fourteen at that time. I'd always tried to keep her protected and be the best brother I could.

"How did Warren hurt her?" I could barely get the words out.

My mother in her mid-forties.

She whispered, "They were found without their clothes on and touching each other." Mother sobbed. "Warren forced Vanessa to massage him."

"What kind of massage?"

"Full body."

At this point, I wasn't sure what the big deal was. A massage didn't seem horrible. But if they didn't have their clothes on, that was something else entirely.

Finally, Mother admitted, "It became sexual."

Cold enveloped me. I hoped and prayed that he wasn't forcing himself on Vanessa like he was with Valerie. "Did he rape her? Did he penetrate her?" It was strange how raspy my voice sounded to my own ears.

Mother shook her head. "Warren tricked Vanessa into rubbing his shoulders and then forced her to massage his genitals."

At least it wasn't all the way. I felt relieved they were caught before it could go any further.

"How is Vanessa? How does she feel?"

"She feels dirty." Mother started to cry again. "What am I to do? I can't face her." Mother never could handle any kind of conflict and would do anything to avoid it. "Promise me again that you'll tell no one."

"I promise." All I could think of was that Warren had to be punished. This behavior must be stopped. Surely Father would punish him now.

As if Mother could read my mind, she said, "Don't worry about it. Warren will be dealt with."

"How? Have you told Father?"

As FLDS children, we were taught to never go to a mother with an issue. If we had a problem, or if we knew of a problem, we were to go directly to Father. After you reported the issue, you dropped it, trusting the person in authority to handle the concern. Your hands were then washed clean of it.

Mother nodded. "Yes, Father knows what happened, and he's going to handle it. But you must help Vanessa because she's a victim and she feels so dirty and bad. Can you go to her? You don't need to do anything else."

Because of my strong training on the proper way to take care of problems, after Mother left I went to Father anyway. I felt I must follow the chain of command for reporting a problem, just as I'd done a year earlier with Lyle and Valerie. It was my duty to my sister.

Father was less than helpful. He told me, "I'm aware of it. I want you to drop it right now. Don't talk about it or mention it to anyone. I am handling it."

"But what about Vanessa?"

"I am taking care of Vanessa. Do nothing further."

Then he dismissed me.

I went to Vanessa and talked to her about the incident. In tears, she confirmed that it had happened. My heart broke for my little sister. I wanted to punch in Warren's face.

Though I didn't discuss it any further, I wondered what kind of punishment Warren would receive. This was a terrible sin. I kept remembering Father threatening to beat us if we ever touched our sisters in a sexual way. So how would he handle things with Warren? What would be his punishment? Though I anxiously watched, I didn't see anything happen to him, which frustrated me more than anything.

Later, I learned that Mother Marilyn went to Warren and told him that Father knew about the incident, that Warren had been forgiven, and that he was to forget about it and never mention it again. She didn't want him to think about it or get stressed because he was the righteous and holy one. Why was I not surprised?

Warren didn't know that I knew what had happened, although I think he suspected. As instructed, I forgot—or at least didn't talk about—the incident and didn't mention it to anyone. I had no idea that twenty years later, I'd be forced to break my silence, and it would turn my whole community against me.

Chapter Nine

Father-Prophet

FLDS MEMBERS DO NOT APPROACH COURTSHIP IN A TYPICAL MANNER. It's not boy meets girl, they fall in love, and he proposes. Dating isn't even a concept that exists or is permitted in the FLDS culture. Instead of the classic romanticized notion of Prince Charming riding up on his white horse to rescue the maiden, an FLDS teenage girl dreams that she will someday be the favorite wife of her husband. The only proper way to get married is if the prophet approves it and, with direction from God, assigns you a spouse of his choosing. This is called placement marriage. Every Sunday meeting, we were read scriptures about placement marriage. The importance of this saving principle was drilled into us.

I was more than ready to get out of my chaotic home life. But it wasn't as if I could leave my community and go off on my own. I had no contacts or resources that could help me in the Gentile world. As members of the church, we had access to computers, television, and newspapers, but we were told not to believe anything we heard, read, or saw because everything reported by the media was a complete lie. I didn't know any different kind of life outside of polygamy, and I was raised to believe and blindly trust everything I'd been taught since birth. With my limited world knowledge, the only way I felt I could improve my situation was to marry someone so I could escape my house.

After weeks of begging, I was determined to get my way. I approached Father once again. "Father, please, Stacy and I want to get married."

"I've told you before you're too damn young. There's no way in hell you're ready."

"But Father, others have been married as young as sixteen. I've been working full-time for three years. I'm able and willing to take care of a family. Please ask permission for us to get married."

Continuing to rebel and cajole, I eventually forced his hand. Father went to the prophet to receive approval for Stacy and me to wed. Uncle Roy agreed, but he said we could not get married through the priesthood. It would need to be a civil marriage, and then I'd have to prove my worthiness for a full year before I could get back into the priesthood's good graces.

Both Stacy and I desperately wanted to improve our situations. Neither of us wanted the shunning that would come if we turned our backs on the placement marriage principle, but we were also afraid of who the prophet would place us with. After much humble contemplation, we decided to move ahead with marrying each other. But first we needed to overcome one more obstacle.

Years before we met, Stacy's ex-stepfather, then divorced from her mother, claimed he'd received a revelation that Stacy belonged to him. When Stacy and I became friends, he reacted with jealousy and tried to persuade his ex-stepdaughter to *want* to marry him. He then attempted to force her to have sex with him so they'd *have* to get married. Luckily, the priesthood council did not agree with him, which allowed us to marry. We were both thrilled and intimidated to be able to move forward. We became man and wife on March 17, 1978. By this choice, however, we also became FLDS apostates. I was seventeen, Stacy eighteen.

Now we faced the enormity and the reality of our decision.

INITIALLY, WE LIVED AT MY FATHER'S PLACE. HOWEVER, BECAUSE OF the teachings ingrained into our minds about the principle of placement marriage, we felt wicked living there in our apostasy. My family ostracized us and treated us as outcasts. By the end of the first month, our shame had become unbearably intense and stressful. We were so uncomfortable that we moved to an apartment in Midvale, Utah. Although I still had relationships with the people in my community—I could visit once a month—things were cold with Mother, Father, and many of my siblings and friends, who disapproved of my actions.

Stacy and I continued to work at PolySeal and were happy overall. Neither of us wanted to repeat the family life we were raised in, and we both dreamed of creating close relationships with our children, so we started our family with that united goal in mind. To be outside the religious community that had been our life really trashed our self-esteem, but Stacy and I had each other, and we worked together to enjoy a peaceful marriage.

Within a year, our daughter, Danielle, was born. Father came to me and said he wanted me back. He said Stacy and I could have a priesthood-ordained marriage. By being sealed through the priesthood, we would be brought back into the FLDS fold. We were being offered a spiritual marriage, assuring our salvation in the last days.

During the months I'd been away from my family, and after desiring to get away from them for so long, it surprised me how much I missed them. I longed for acceptance from my parents, siblings, cousins, and friends. As I'd been trained from birth that the world is a wicked place, that first year of marriage had been a struggle both on a spiritual level and an emotional level.

Although I was not interested in going back to the religion, I desired to be with the people I loved again. We gratefully returned to the fold.

ONE OF THE COMMANDMENTS IN THE FLDS CHURCH WAS THAT WE were to have one child each year, or as many children as we could, as quickly as possible. At age eighteen, I became a father for the second time. My son, Seth, born in January of 1980, was six weeks premature, weighing in at a measly one pound, four ounces. His first days on the Earth were a real struggle as he fought to live. He was one of the Salt Lake Valley's first children to be admitted to a hospital neonatal unit. How grateful we were for their skill as they attended to our tiny infant son.

During that uncertain time, Father came a couple of times to the hospital. On one of his visits, he gave my son a priesthood blessing. I felt honored that he was there with me, especially after our uncertain and often volatile relationship. I'd always maintained what felt like an unworthy and guarded connection with him. Father was still an apostle in the FLDS Church and had a high standing with the people. We were taught by our mothers that Father would be a mighty leader and that he was a great and holy man of God. It was wonderful to have a father who was held in such regard, but it also made him incredibly unapproachable to his children. Because of this, I felt that he was too good for me, and I did not possess the worthiness to be in his presence. Now, finally, while in the hospital, we learned to appreciate each other a little bit better. For the first time in my life, I felt a true connection with him, much more so than when he'd defended me against Mother Ruth's attack years earlier.

Thankfully, Seth grew stronger and was finally released from the hospital two months later. I cannot express my joy at finally being able to bring him home.

With one health scare behind us, another soon followed. Father suffered a heart attack in about 1984. As an accountant and church leader, Father just sat at his desk and talked to people all day. He'd always had problems with varicose veins, wearing compression socks and keeping his feet elevated. He loved food and ate like a horse. Steaks, pies, and cakes were some of his favorites. He loved to go to lunch with the brethren—other leaders of the church—and eat whatever he wanted. He drank a fifth of vodka every day for forty years. Whenever we'd go into his office, he would ask, "Want a screwdriver?"

After Father's heart attack, the doctor told him to lose eighty pounds and stop drinking alcohol, or he would die within a year. He went on a radical high-fiber diet and quit drinking vodka, moving to wine as his beverage of choice. Father had a tremor disorder; it wasn't Parkinson's disease, but his hands shook. It was an inherited condition. He said wine calmed his nerves and steadied his hands when he needed to give blessings. Mother was so happy when he gave up vodka because she hated his drinking and had nagged him for years to stop.

From that point forward, he would brag to men who had a potbelly, "I lost eighty pounds, and you can too!"

The year 1984 also brought in a new aspect of our FLDS dress code. Uncle Roy banished all whiskers or facial hair on men. Suddenly, if you dared to wear facial hair, you were cast out. The prophet claimed Christ had no facial hair during his lifetime. Despite all the art that portrayed a bearded Christ, Uncle Roy made it seem like he'd recently seen Christ in person with a cleanly shaved face, so the many sculptures and paintings were all wrong.

Uncle Roy also started making changes in how marriages were arranged.

There had been a time in the FLDS when girls presented themselves for marriage, and the prophet would ask them if they had anyone special in mind. The prophet would then take their suggestion and pray for revelation. Sometimes the girl got the man of her dreams, and sometimes the prophet was inspired to go in a different direction.

However, during this time, Uncle Roy started drilling into people that they shouldn't ask for a certain person anymore. Placement meant letting the prophet decide through revelation who you should marry. It was the "pure way to get married." Whenever a marriage was announced, it was common for the gossiping to begin: "Did she ask for him?" If it was a pure placement, the couple was held in high regard; if not, they were treated like scum.

There began to be a class system in the FLDS. If you were a faithful and favored woman, you could ask for a certain person and maintain your reputation. But if you were rebellious in any way and offered suggestions for your marriage partner, you were automatically considered an apostate.

Of course, the fact that Stacy and I had asked for each other made us linger in our guilt as shameful outsiders.

I CONTINUED TO WORK HARD TO PROVIDE FOR STACY'S AND MY GROWing family. In 1982, I'd begun working at a company called HydraPak. Grant Lund was one of the owners; he was an excellent businessman and mentor, and I learned much from him. One of the main lines of business was manufacturing O-rings.

In 1986, the space shuttle *Challenger* exploded seventy-three seconds after lift-off, killing the entire crew of seven, including Christa McAuliffe, who was chosen from eleven thousand applicants to be the first schoolteacher in space. NASA blamed the disaster on faulty O-rings. Not believing that his company could survive such harsh media coverage, Grant decided to put his business up for sale. My brother Brian, a coworker named James, and I got together and started talking. The three of us thought this was still a sound company with a lot of potential. We made an offer to buy HydraPak and pulled together every dime we could for a down payment.

We were now business owners.

We worked hard during those first couple of years, and we were successful in our endeavors. We negotiated multimillion-dollar contracts with NASA and Morton Thiokol. By the age of twenty-five, I was a millionaire.

Little did I know how radically this money would change my life.

On November 25, 1986, Leroy S. Johnson, the FLDS prophet, passed away. He was ninety-six years old and died of natural causes. Our prophet had been afflicted with painful shingles for four or five years and suffered greatly, even to the point of missing years of church and being confined to a wheelchair.

At one point when Uncle Roy had been so ill with shingles, Father and Truman, Uncle Roy's bodyguard, gave Uncle Roy a blessing. It was read throughout all the church. The blessing said that Uncle Roy would be saved and renewed as a new man and that he would be the last prophet. We believed this as revelation from God and never doubted it.

Because of the revelation, everyone felt shocked when they heard about the prophet's death, most especially Father. Heading down to Short Creek, we drove up to the mortuary just as Uncle Roy's body arrived. I went inside with Father. They placed our prophet on the slab, and I just kept looking at him.

We'd been told that, on many occasions, Uncle Roy's spirit had left his body and then come back. Witnesses said he'd appeared dead before his spirit returned, and it had been shocking to see the lifeless body of the prophet. I stared intently for any twitch or movement, watching for when his spirit would return to his body. I knew he would get up. Frozen in place, I thought, *This isn't right. He's going to wake up. I know he will. This is just a test.*

My confusion was compounded because we'd been told time and time again that Uncle Roy would never die. He would be the prophet to lead us to Zion.

But now, he did not move and obviously never would again. This was real.

With troubled minds and hearts, we returned to Salt Lake. I immediately went to Father's office and asked, "How do you feel, Father?"

He answered, "This is an awesome responsibility."

It was not the answer I expected. Instead, I thought he would say, "I'm confident he'll wake up any minute now." But no, it seemed that Father knew he had to move immediately into his ordained role. The FLDS believed that if a prophet was not present on the Earth, there was no priesthood and the Earth would fall apart. The men who'd been in line before Father had all either died or been excommunicated.

So, my father, Rulon Jeffs, became the new FLDS leader.

FATHER WAS RESPECTED BUT NOT HIGHLY REGARDED. THE INFLUENTIAL Barlow family had many sons who were liked and well-known. They believed one of them should be the next prophet because they lived in Short Creek, which was church headquarters and where Uncle Roy had lived. Father was from Salt Lake and was popular there, but not in Short Creek.

It was almost as if a competition arose between the Crickers and the Lakers. Only about three hundred members lived in Salt Lake at the time, and the three thousand who lived in the Crick began to grumble, "Great, now we have a *Laker* prophet."

The Barlow boys wanted Father to move immediately to Short Creek, but Father hated the Crick and stayed in Salt Lake as much as possible. At first, he would go down to the Crick every other weekend, but gradually he ended up spending half his time in the Crick.

Overall, it was a difficult transition for everyone. Uncle Roy had been universally loved. He was a kind and serene man. When he spoke, he was not a pulpit pounder. He rarely raised his voice and was considered a father figure. And, of course, we all fervently believed he would be the prophet to lead us into the millennium.

WHEN THIS CHANGE FIRST OCCURRED, FATHER BECAME WITHDRAWN, as if he didn't quite know what to do with his new position, but that didn't last long. He soon grew more confident, took control, and led the church with strength. Mother Marilyn stayed close to Father, seldom leaving his side. It was as if she wanted everyone to know how close they were and that her sons were his greatest supporters and heirs. This was her time to shine, and she displayed pride when she let everyone know she was the prophet's wife.

Whether because of fear or uncertainty, Father performed no marriages for two or three years as he learned his new role. When it was time for him to start giving women in marriage again, many women in their mid-twenties were available for him to marry off. However, after he'd performed many sealings, a shortage soon arose of women to give to the men who were interested in plural wives. This was a real dilemma for Father, as there was nowhere he could go to get more women for these men.

Father's predicament over the shortage of brides, however, did not keep him from noticing my newfound wealth. Suddenly, on the days Father was in town, he began inviting me to the daily luncheons he held with all the influential church leaders. I went from being a black sheep to one of the chosen few, simply because I was a successful businessman who paid a large amount of tithing.

It wasn't long before Father informed me that, as the new prophet, he needed me to pay him a salary for his position, which I did. I also paid for fancy lunches and even rented Father a Learjet so he could fly from Salt Lake to the Crick at his convenience.

It was quite a heady time, going from complete nobody to an influential member of our faith. But not everyone was so enthused. One day, after I'd just bought a new Mazda 929, Grant Lund, an elder in the church and highly regarded because he had a college education, got up in a meeting and publicly said, "There are men in this very room who go out and buy boats and cars while the rest of us are starving."

I attributed this comment to sour grapes, since we'd bought the business from Grant and were now flourishing. Whatever his motivation, this public shaming only served to fuel my fire, and I went right out and bought a bigger boat.

Around this time, I was called Uncle in a church meeting for my first time. Initially, I didn't realize who the speaker was talking about, and I looked around the congregation, trying to see who "Uncle Wallace" was. It wasn't until I saw Stacy's beaming face that I understood who he meant. It was me! I was in total shock. To be called Uncle was an honor. Only those who were held in high esteem were given this prestigious title.

My new wealth had bought me status in the community.

Chapter Ten

Blood Atonement

FATHER GREW MORE POWERFUL AND AUTHORITATIVE IN HIS ROLE AS prophet. In about 1988 or 1989, he stood up in a meeting and said we could no longer wear red ties or red anything.

In Isaiah 63:2–3, Christ states: "Wherefore art thou red in thine apparel, and thy garments like him that treadeth in the winefat? I have trodden the winepress alone; and of the people there was none with me: for I will tread them in mine anger, and trample them in my fury; and their blood shall be sprinkled upon my garments, and I will stain all my raiment."

Father interpreted this scripture to mean that at the second coming, Christ's robe would be red. So, if an individual wore or possessed anything with red in it, they openly mocked Christ. The FLDS people were eventually banned from possessing anything red, even something as small as a pencil or a child's toy.

DURING THIS SAME TIME, GRANT LUND INTRODUCED THE COVENANT of wearing long underwear. As a religious group, we were already highly modest. We always swam fully clothed. It was forbidden to expose your body below the neck, above the wrist, or above the ankle. We could roll up our sleeves only if we were doing work that required it.

However, Grant had converted from the traditional LDS religion. He'd been through their temple and worn the LDS undergarment—in fact, he said he'd received his "second anointing." He wanted to introduce the covenant of long underwear to the FLDS people. He modified the LDS garment style to match the clothing we were already wearing and be exclusive to our church. The purpose of FLDS long underwear was to keep the people pure and hold off sexual impurities. It was a reminder of the covenants we'd made. Before we got naked, we would see our long underwear and stop whatever improper action we were about to participate in.

After Grant's announcement, Father got up and said, "What you have heard is the truth. I require you to wear long underwear from wrist to ankle."

We could not figure this out. Grant Lund really had no status in the church. Why did he get to make this highly inconvenient rule?

It was not uncommon to hear members say things like, "My father was a good man. He never lied. If he said it, it was the truth." Members often used this same reasoning when we were told to believe something that seemed strange, including Grant's new "doctrine."

We could take off our long underwear only in the bathtub. Children out of diapers and over age two needed to wear the long underwear or be cast out. The mothers had to immediately start sewing long underwear for everyone.

ALL THESE CHANGES WERE CONFUSING, BUT NOTHING FROM THIS uncertain time compared to pivotal events that would change everything the FLDS had ever known or believed in.

Uncle Roy had been a bit lax about correcting people who committed adultery. He followed the scriptural injunction that if adultery was committed but the person confessed, repented, and forsook the sin with all his or her heart, this individual would be forgiven and welcomed back into the church with no further action.

Within a few years of Father becoming prophet, however, he began what he called the cleansing. He stood up in priesthood meeting and said, "I am overloaded with the immorality of this church. I am calling for confessions of sexual sin. I'm going to clean the entire church."

Everyone shifted in their seats and stared with downcast eyes. What did this mean?

Father began speaking and acting more in line with a principle that had been followed by John Taylor, an early LDS prophet. This doctrine said if a man or woman committed adultery and it was their first offense, they could repent and the sin would be forgiven. However, if it happened a second time, they would be cast out.

Our prophet demanded that adulterers come to him and confess, but this idea terrified the people. Father began to actually cast out a few men, something that had never been done before. Soon he got even stricter. Some early church prophets believed that if a man or woman had been sealed in celestial marriage, they could not be baptized back into the church if they committed adultery, because no person can inherit the celestial kingdom who does not keep the celestial law.

Father started quoting another talk by John Taylor. While John Taylor was prophet, a woman committed adultery while her husband was away, and the husband wanted her forgiven by the church and back in his life. But she was penalized for her sin and never allowed back into church fellowship. John Taylor said, "We cannot have such people in the Church." The reason for his harshness, he said, was because "she had entered into covenants which were sacred. She had violated those covenants. The Book of Covenants says that such people shall be destroyed. I could not change it. I did not make that law." He believed that if the church allowed her to stay a member, they too would be partakers in an unforgivable crime. No matter how much the woman and her husband begged, she was not granted back her membership in the church.

This doctrine, although not new, was new to us. It rocked our foundation, going against everything we thought and believed.

Quoting scripture that said they "shall be destroyed," Father began informing FLDS members that if a man committed adultery, he would be unable to exalt his wives in the next life. If he properly went through the repentance process and received forgiveness, this man would be allowed to go to the celestial kingdom, but not to the highest degree within this kingdom. His punishment would be not having wives in heaven—in other words, he would lose his family forever. In the afterlife, he would become a eunuch servant to men who had remained worthy.

Since such a man could not exalt his wives, his family should be taken from him in this life, just as King David's wives were removed by the Lord after he committed adultery. If the sinner was truly a great man, he would voluntarily give up his family so they could reach exaltation with another man. If a man obediently confessed to immoral acts, as the prophet demanded, he could be part of the congregation but would watch his family from afar, thriving in the presence of a worthier man.

This new punishment happened to a man who, after confessing to adultery years earlier, had been forgiven by Uncle Roy. Father retroactively took his family away from him. Many wondered how a new prophet had the right to punish a man for a sin that the old prophet, under the direction of

God, had forgiven. Father responded that this man could be a single man in the church as well as a single angel in heaven, but he could not attain the highest glory of the celestial kingdom.

Father made sure we knew that both men and women would be held accountable for sexual sin. No one was immune. It wasn't a surprise that people were terrified to come forth and openly and willingly confess sexual wrongdoing.

But then the sin of adultery became even more serious—deadly serious.

Father began reading the sermons of early prophets regarding blood atonement, which some considered necessary to cleanse the sins of adultery and murder. Blood had to be spilled to pay for these grievous sins. The sinner had to shed their own blood in this lifetime to be exalted in the next—Christ's blood was not enough.

Father liked reading a certain quote by Brigham Young: "I do know that there are sins committed, of such a nature that if the people did understand the doctrine of salvation, they would tremble because of their situation. And furthermore, I know that there are transgressors, who, if they knew themselves, and the only condition upon which they can obtain forgiveness, would beg of their brethren to shed their blood, that the smoke thereof might ascend to God as an offering to appease the wrath that is kindled against them, and that the law might have its course. I will say further; I have had men come to me and offer their lives to atone for their sins."

Father even began preaching that fornication, or unmarried individuals engaging in sex, was a dire transgression, likened unto adultery. To add to the confusion, he never clarified whether, if someone actually went through blood atonement, it would qualify them to have their family in heaven.

Although these thunderous sermons seemed almost theoretical, we witnessed people losing their families for past offenses. Would we soon be expected to die for sexual sins?

Chapter Eleven

Marriage Middleman

Placement marriage continued to become more integral to our community, but I'd never been interested in having another spouse. I'd always dreamed of having a close relationship with one wife and our children, and I felt I'd succeeded in this goal. Aside from this, I'd always considered myself unworthy for plural marriage, and I still felt this was the case. Those with the birthright were deserving of the blessing of plural marriage, but I never felt I was one of the chosen to be asked to live this higher law.

However, soon after our financial horizons broadened, Brian and James, my co-owners at HydraPak, were both given a second wife. Then, a few years later in October 1991, I received a call from Father. With no preamble, he said, "I am going to give you another lady."

I was stunned. The shock only increased as he continued, "I've got a wife for you and one for Merrill Steed."

I wondered why he would even mention Merrill Steed, who had nothing to do with me. But then Father surprised me even further. "I am going to give Merrill and you Adrian's daughters. You will have Jessica, and Sarah will go to Merrill."

My astonishment could not have been greater. Jessica was the daughter of the influential Adrian Morgan, Father's bodyguard and a highly regarded member of the church. At the time, Jessica was eighteen years old and I was twenty-nine. Blessed with a mane of brunette hair, Jessica loved horses and the outdoors. She also tended to be a little on the wild side. I suspected they were giving her to me because they thought she was beginning to go in the wrong direction. I found out later that she initially refused the marriage, but her father talked her into going through with it.

My confusion came from the fact that Jessica was my half-sister's daughter and my half-niece. The thought of marrying a blood relative completely shocked me. This had to be a mistake. I felt certain that Father must be in error, that Jessica was for Merrill and Sarah was for me. Sarah was the daughter of a different mother than Jessica and therefore was not a blood relative to me.

As my silence continued, Father asked, "Are you okay?"

I couldn't answer. He repeated his question.

I finally found my voice and replied, "Whatever you say." I would not dare question the prophet, even if he was my father.

He instructed me to call Jessica's father, Adrian, to make the arrangements. Because we were old golfing buddies, I had no problem with the idea of asking Adrian if things had been mixed up.

When I contacted Adrian and asked if my father had mistakenly told me the wrong daughter, he said no, the prophet had named the right woman. The marriage would take place the following week.

I spent the next seven days in a swirl of confusion. How was this going to work? I kept thinking Father had made a mistake, but I did not dare utter any doubts for fear that Stacy and our children would be taken away from me. I kept it all to myself.

I never asked for this second marriage. The thought of a second wife had never crossed my mind. However, this was a priesthood placement, a revelation from God to the prophet. To reject it would be unheard of, basically walking away from one of the greatest blessings an FLDS person could enjoy. It would be a sin to refuse, and if I did so, the real threat loomed that I would lose everything. There's an FLDS saying: "A blessing offered but rejected becomes a cursing."

In general, a second wife is given to a man as a test. If you cannot manage two wives, then clearly you cannot manage multiple wives, and therefore you are unworthy of salvation. In the FLDS religion, it is believed that to survive the destructions and be exalted, a man must be spiritually sealed to at least seven wives. In addition to never committing adultery, you need seven wives to reach the highest level of the celestial kingdom. Without seven wives, you would become a slave eunuch to men who had seven or more wives. Any wives you had would be taken from you and given to someone else.

In my secret thoughts, I felt I'd rather go to hell than live without my wife or wives. But the concept of seven wives really bothered me. It seemed like salvation wasn't about the sealing between a man and a woman—it was a numbers game. You were deemed worthy to become a god only after you had seven wives.

Though I don't know that it's written anywhere, we were told that the original Mormon prophet, Joseph Smith, saw a vision of 144,000 men who had become gods. To prove they were part of a quality family, they had the name of the earthly father to whom they were sealed upon death written on their heads. In the world's entire history from Adam onward, these 144,000 men were the only men qualified to go to the highest level of the celestial kingdom. All the rest would be eunuchs.

It was believed that women would never be cast into hell against their will. Only men could be damned and called a Son of Perdition, and only if they'd held the priesthood. However, if a woman was unworthy of exaltation, she could not be sealed to a worthy man. She would be given the opportunity to choose between going to hell or becoming a heavenly slave to a man or woman who was worthy to reach the highest degree of glory.

I kept thinking about billions of women married to only 144,000 men in heaven. It boggled my mind.

By assigning me a second wife, it appeared that Father felt I was ready to progress on the path toward exaltation. However, I believe this was also a personal test. Father wanted to ascertain my loyalty by seeing if I'd agree to marry my half-niece.

Although women supposedly had somewhat of a choice in the placement marriage principle, men were never given an option. If you were offered a wife, you either accepted this assignment or were kicked out and damned.

In reality, women weren't really offered a choice either. They either acquiesced to the situation, or they were forced to leave. *Accept it or go* was the prevailing thought.

Obedient to the Law of Sarah, the current wife or wives had to accept a new wife, just as Sarah gave Hagar, her handmaiden, to Abraham so he could father children. Often, we were instructed from Genesis 16:3: "And Sarai Abram's wife took Hagar her maid the Egyptian, after Abram had dwelt ten years in the land of Canaan, and gave her to her husband Abram to be his wife." The emphasis was always placed on the word *gave*.

In that spirit, no marriages were done in secret within the FLDS. In the latter part of October 1991, a grim-faced Stacy, belly swollen with our ninth child, placed my hand in Jessica's and then took Jessica's other hand in her own. Forming a sturdy line, we presented ourselves to the prophet for our placement marriage.

After the ceremony, when they instructed me to kiss my new bride, Jessica turned so I kissed only her cheek, showing everyone she was not happy. I found this awkward and humiliating in front of seventy witnesses.

I BEGAN THIS SPIRITUAL MARRIAGE WITH A STRONG SENSE OF UNEASE, not understanding how this could possibly work. But I pushed forward with the deep-seated FLDS mentality: I could do anything for one year. Because all our teachings were focused on the end of the world, we always believed we had only one year left before the destruction hit.

Anything can be endured for a year.

Because it was a pure placement marriage and I took upon myself a rebellious girl, I was elevated another notch and held in even higher esteem than before.

THE FIRST THREE MONTHS WITH JESSICA WERE HARD WHILE WE ALL tried to learn to get along. Starting a sexual relationship with another woman didn't bother me from a moral standpoint. After all, I was raised with this as the norm. To be fully involved in the religion, you had to procreate or risk losing your salvation. Sex was almost a chore—if you weren't trying to impregnate your wife, she could report you to the prophet. After you had relations with a wife, you needed to wait a month to see if she conceived before you had relations with her again. If successful, no further sex could occur until after the baby was born.

What gave me pause was jealousy among the wives, which could become debilitating. In polygamy, sex was a delicate precept, a law you must conform with even though you knew it would rip your house apart. This resulted in secret meetings and quick liaisons, with little or no preamble and often without removing clothes. The act rarely involved love or affection—it was a job you must do to be exalted.

In addition, Stacy's pregnancy created constant hormone changes, making it much more difficult for her to deal with the placement than she'd expected. However, things settled down, and Jessica and I quickly began a family of our own. Stacy and I already had eight children. Including the one she was expecting, we would go on to have five more. Jessica and I would have seven children together. So, I have twenty incredible children. Words cannot describe how much I love my family.

Jessica and Stacy could not have been more opposite, not only in looks but also in personality. Stacy was a wonderful homemaker, while Jessica was a tomboy who loved being outdoors and getting her clothes dirty. Jessica was good with children and had a strong sense of fun, always making up creative things for them to do. Each of their strengths complemented the other's, and my children had the blessing of a well-rounded upbringing in a home full of love.

I bought a rambling house in Draper, Utah, an affluent southern suburb in the Salt Lake Valley. It was a beautiful spread with pastoral fields, a swimming pool, and three acres of land, including a barn. My home became a gathering place for the people of the church, and we would host large parties, picnics, and dances quite often.

As a highly regarded member of the priesthood, I enjoyed perks such as special dinners and golfing trips with senior church leaders. I was included in many hush-hush meetings with them and the FLDS attorneys. Father would invite me to join him on his Learjet to Short Creek on weekends. He also invited me on camping trips and vacations to Lake Powell. During these trips, we would talk with other leaders and attorneys concerning church business.

For the first time in my life, I was in the know.

IN 1996, FATHER HAD A SEVERE HEART ATTACK AND REQUIRED SURGERY to insert a stent. No doubt his health had deteriorated due to poor lifestyle habits and the stress of running the church.

Despite his health challenges, Father instigated many new restrictions on church members during the mid-to-late 1990s. For example, he never liked parties or social events because he felt they distracted us from preparing for the future. In 1996, all socials were suddenly banned because they were considered frivolous and wicked. I could no longer hold any function for the church at my beautiful home.

Additional restrictions involved tightening up the dress code. For the girls and women, Father did away with pigtails, ponytails, and braids. Women could have a single French braid down the back of their heads, but no braids like the "reins of a horse" or any hairstyle that included two plaits of hair.

Father called curls around the face "boy catchers," and he also banned these. Women had to pull their hair back, leaving a huge wave in front with their ears exposed. No boy catchers or hair straggling from a bun or French braid were allowed.

Women could trim their hair to get rid of straggly ends, but cutting their hair was considered taboo, and they would be cast out if they did it. This was when the ordinance of women using their hair to wash their husband's feet began to be discussed.

One-inch heels had been permitted before, but now only flat shoes were allowed. Girls had to cover their feet—no exposed toes, ever.

Not only the women had to make adjustments. Father got up in priesthood meeting one day and said we could no longer wear gray suits to priesthood. He'd already demanded that we button our shirts all the way up, so I'd taken to wearing a suit and tie continually because I thought it looked stupid to button a collar without a tie. But now we had to wear black suits with a white shirt—no colored shirts.

On one of his visits, Winston Blackmore, the bishop of Canada, noticed the men taking off their suit coats due to the heat. He almost shouted, "How dare you men take off your suit coat unless the prophet has already done so!"

After that, during meetings we all mirrored what the prophet did. We sat the way he sat. If he crossed his legs, we did. If he crossed his feet, we did. Father wore his hair combed back from his large forehead in a wave. So, we were supposed to do our hair that way too. Even if we were boiling, we could not take off our suit coat unless Father did so first.

I'd felt doubts as a youth and into early adulthood about the FLDS religion. Because of my new station in life, if any disbelief ever reappeared, I pushed it away, ignoring it. I did not want to jeopardize my high standing in the church in any way. If I voiced any concern or a single thread of unbelief, I would be cast out and lose my family, home, and wealth. I would be doomed to be destroyed with the wicked people of the world.

The shortage of marriageable women began to be a real problem for Father.

The people were instructed, with even more force, that it was wicked for a girl to request a certain man to marry. Doing so showed she did not trust the leader of the church and his gift of prophecy. Rather, Father had a revelation that, when a girl was ready to marry, she was to go to him as prophet and say these exact words: "I place myself in your hands to be placed with a good man."

To solve the problem of too many young men wanting to marry, as well as to reserve more girls for the older men, Father began kicking boys out of the FLDS religion. He and Warren started using the Alta Academy as a filter to expel young boys if they showed any sign of rebellion, no matter how slight. Father had Warren command that if a boy showed even a hair's breadth of rebellion, he would never get a wife.

Women were now a tool used to control the men.

I often thought to myself that if I had been in school at this time, I would have been the first boy kicked out of the church for rebellion. I breathed a mental sigh of relief that I was older now and no longer subject to Warren's dictatorship in school.

If a young boy obeyed every rule with exactness and was given a wife, she usually didn't appear as pretty or intelligent as other girls. The beautiful and smart girls became plural wives to Father, Warren, or men who were wealthy and loyal to Father. In other words, if you were an attractive or clever FLDS girl, you were most likely destined for a relationship with a man two or three times your age. The injustice was obvious, but no one dared confront the church leaders for fear they'd be kicked out themselves.

Everyone could see the church faced a critical dilemma. As a closed society that no longer welcomed new members, the FLDS did not have enough women for the prophecy of every man needing seven wives to come true. Many people grumbled, "How is this going to work?"

Father had no answer, even when asked by his special priesthood luncheon buddies.

A new doctrine came forward in the male-only priesthood meetings. Father introduced the Law of Chastity in Marriage. This law was not contained anywhere in the scriptures. It seemed like something Father made up to solve the bride shortage.

He stated that, in order to have more than two wives, a man must be sexually pure and realize that sexual purity made up the celestial law. Therefore, no one was to engage in sex unless it was for procreation. Father stated that procreation could bring comfort to a husband and wife, but sex could never be recreational. Oral sex was strictly forbidden. Sex during pregnancy also became a huge taboo.

Father liked to quote us the teaching of Heber C. Kimball, an early LDS apostle, that men were not to "weary their wives." For example, touching a woman sexually who was beyond childbearing years equated to "wearying the tree." An infertile young woman could not be touched sexually, as that would be the sin of "wearying the fruit."

These new rules were difficult, if not impossible, for everyone to follow.

IN THE LATE 1990S, EVEN AS FATHER AGED INTO HIS EIGHTIES, HE KEPT taking younger and younger wives. Every one of the younger girls he married was thin. It seemed like thinness was the first thing he looked for. He did not like women with big breasts. He called bras "over-the-shoulder boulder holders," and he said breasts that were bigger than boulders were too big.

After class, Father would go around looking at women's bodices. Stating that large-breasted women looked strange, he really pushed that women needed to be lean. Before long, he began getting after men to lose their potbellies as well.

Years earlier, I'd started noticing that Warren seemed to enjoy the underdeveloped or flat look in a girl. I ignored—or pushed aside—these clues that Warren was leaning toward becoming a pedophile. I told myself he was just following Father's example. But it didn't stop with Warren. Others began adopting this way of thinking.

Stacy was not flat-chested in any way. People began to scorn her for her body type, leaving her feeling threatened and vulnerable. I comforted her any way I could, telling her I loved how she looked and didn't care what others thought. It wasn't hard for me to say this because it was the truth.

Father also liked a thin face on a woman. The higher a woman's hair rose above her forehead, the thinner her face appeared. The wave hairstyle had started with Father's wives and then spread to all the people. The wave got higher and higher over time, until it looked almost ridiculous. My

Destroying Their God 105

My father, the prophet Rulon T. Jeffs, with some of his wives, circa 1990 when he was about eighty-one. My mother is seated on the first row, fifth from the left.

understanding of the hairdo was simply that Warren and Father preferred a woman with a narrow face.

With our prophet preaching the doctrine of sexual purity, we believed he was not touching or behaving toward his wives in any sexual manner. To do so would have been hypocritical. I found out later that this belief was false. The doctrine was put forward to hide the reality of what many high-ranking men in the religion were actually doing.

WHEN AN FLDS MAN GIVES HIS DAUGHTER INTO A PLURAL MARRIAGE, he never really retreats. It's up to the new husband to keep the father-in-law happy. If his son-in-law falls out of his good graces, a polygamist father thinks nothing of taking his daughter and her children away from the husband. This action is supported by the prophet.

The prophet becomes more important to an FLDS wife than her own husband. Women are chosen and placed with their eternal companion by the prophet. He is the controlling entity within every FLDS marriage. If you are not a good and faithful priesthood man, if you do not teach your children exactly how you're told, or if you don't make your wife happy in every way, she can go to the prophet and ask to be released from the marriage. This means she'll be given to another worthy priesthood holder. Your children from this wife will be given to him as well.

I was terrified that I could lose my family at the drop of a hat. The prophet was the middleman in my relationships. He meddled with the free flow of love between my two wives and me.

Many people think an FLDS man takes multiple wives so he can participate in group sex and other deviant rituals. This is the farthest thing from the truth. It is difficult for others to understand the stress of being forced into a plural marriage in order to be saved and redeemed. If you do one thing wrong, you are cut off forever and lose everything. It's just one more aspect of how the FLDS live in complete and utter fear.

Plural marriage is not really a true relationship between you and your spouse when the prophet is right there. With him always in the back of your mind, ready to tear your family apart, no genuine bond is formed between husband and wife. I would say ninety percent of FLDS men marry multiple wives out of fear for their livelihoods and families, not for any perverse sexual reasons.

Chapter Twelve

Lifted Up

Though things were going well for me with my family and business, things were not so positive for my beloved half-sister and friend Valerie.

When she was about sixteen years old, Valerie hooked up with a real loser who, at age eighteen, earned his living at an auto-body shop, but he was also a drug dealer. His family had converted to fundamentalism in the 1970s, and the boys were all obsessed with sex—it was all they seemed to live for and talk about. Valerie had started a relationship with this young man, and he constantly bragged about them having sex. Valerie was seventeen when Father finally found out and made them get married. I think she went along with the marriage just to get out of the house and away from her abusive mother, Mother Norma, who was a terrible alcoholic.

They had a few children together, but they also did a lot of drugs. Over time, Valerie became a coke whore, completely addicted. Eventually she left him and their dysfunctional marriage, which allowed his parents to take custody of her children.

About eight years after leaving him, Valerie moved in with me, trying to clean up her life. I was happy to help her, but it nearly broke my heart when she couldn't give up her lifestyle. After only one week, she abandoned any hope of changing and moved out.

Five years later, she ran into the arms of another abusive partner, this time a Hispanic man. She was with him for three months. One night, they got drunk and high together, and he took her outside, banged her face on the pavement, and then refused to let her back in the house. The hospital called us and said she was about to die.

But Valerie was a survivor. She eventually recovered. She called Father and said, "I want to clean up. Can you help me?"

With no warmth or concern for his daughter, he answered, "No, but Wallace can."

Father instructed me that I should help my half-sister. Of course, I said yes.

I picked her up from the hospital and moved her into my house again.

We sat down together. I stared into the sunken eyes and almost-ruined face of this once-beautiful sister I loved so much. I wanted nothing more than to help her clean up. This time, I knew we would need ground rules.

"To stay here, you have to stay away from your partying friends," I said. "Absolutely no going out at night. I'll cover all your expenses, but I need to take your phone. Agreed?"

She nodded, handed over her phone, and said, "I want to clean up."

"Fine. You need to go one month with no phone and no contact with your friends. If you can do this, then you'll need to get a job. You've got one chance. Do you think you can do this?"

I struggled with being so hard on her, but I knew I had to be strict to get her to where she could function on her own. Otherwise, she would just revert to her destructive ways.

"Yes. I'll do whatever you say."

Though she agreed, it almost seemed as if Valerie had given up. I hoped she would follow through and straighten up. More than anything, I wanted Valerie back in my life. Even though she was an absolute mess, I felt pleased to have her with me. I gave her a room in my basement.

Jessica, however, was not so sure about having this woman in our home. Valerie appeared physically destroyed, and her terrible smell permeated the entire house. The kids were confused why such a wild Gentile woman lived with us.

VALERIE DID REALLY WELL FOR ABOUT ONE WEEK. THEN SHE DISAPpeared, and I couldn't find her anywhere. I called all her friends, but no one knew where she was. The next morning, some people dropped her off. Valerie smelled rank. She immediately began puking everywhere. She was so stoned that she would pass out and wake up screaming and hallucinating.

When she finally came down from her high, I asked her, "What happened?"

She began to cry. "Let's work this out," she begged.

When I didn't say a word, her body deflated. She confessed, "My friend invited me for a drink."

"Is that all?"

She sniffed. "Yeah, that's all." But she refused to make eye contact, and her lie was obvious. I let her sit there until she continued. "Well, then my friend had a buddy come over, and we smoked a joint." Now that the real story had begun, it tumbled out of her. "Then we went to this other guy's house, and he had coke. I couldn't say no." She admitted that she'd had sex with five guys.

With tremendous sadness, I asked her to leave. She cried and sobbed. It was heart-wrenching, but I couldn't go back on my word. She knew she had only one chance to prove herself. If I backed down now, what would that teach her, or my children? Besides, I had to think of my own family. I was feeling pressure from my children and my wives—they did not want her there. Her behavior really scared them. I was torn between my love for my sister and my love for my family. It was one of the hardest decisions I've ever had to make.

I called Father and asked him what I should do. He was our mutual father and the prophet, so I knew he'd be inspired to guide me. For my entire life, I'd been taught to follow the prophet's counsel without question, and this time would be no exception.

My father, the prophet, instructed me, "Take her to the homeless shelter."

My heart died a little when he spoke those words.

This was a typical FLDS reaction to sinners: if you were not part of us, you were not one of us, and you had to go away. No compassion was given to those who had made mistakes. We feared them, as if their lifestyle would somehow rub off onto us and damn all the faithful to hell.

It was such a cold reaction to a formerly cherished daughter and sister. Didn't Father and Mother Norma feel any love for their child? Was I the only one who still cared for her? It was heartbreaking. Though I knew I had to follow the prophet's guidance, I also had to try to do everything I could for Valerie. When I called the hospital, they said they had records of her being an overdose patient several times. The hospital administration refused to admit her because she had no insurance, but they said they'd give her some medication if I brought her in.

I drove Valerie to the hospital and got her some basic care. Then, weighed down with guilt and anguish, I drove her to the homeless shelter.

After I escorted her inside, Valerie broke down, begging, "Please don't leave me here!"

In tears, I said, "This is the best thing for you until you can get off the drugs."

My soul felt broken as I drove away. Even though I knew this action was necessary to help her clean up and become healthy again, it felt as if I'd just abandoned my best friend.

That anguished parting would be the last time I ever saw Valerie.

Five years later, in the mid-1990s, Valerie overdosed. Her family had given up on her; her friends had deserted her. She died alone, without reaching her fortieth birthday. The medical examiner found a lethal combination of five different drugs in her body.

Utah state representatives called Father to ask him for final instructions, but he would not claim his daughter's body. Mother Norma wanted nothing to do with the situation either. As Valerie had become a ward of the state, she was cremated.

Valerie was never a bad person; she never hurt anyone. I do not blame Valerie for the unfortunate decisions she made in her life. I'm convinced her mental trauma led to her tragic life and eventual death. Beginning at age fourteen, she was forced to have sex with her older brothers Lyle and Warren. Her parents knew what was going on and could have stopped it, but they did not.

In 1996, Warren's circumstances began to transition. Mother Marilyn persisted in pushing Warren toward Father, and she still covered up any sin or wrongdoing he'd committed, even though he'd recently celebrated his fortieth birthday. Warren soared under Father's wing; he was the chosen one, the carrier of the word of God. Their relationship evolved from father and son to something more like partners. They seemed to think they would go forward together and lead the people into the new millennium.

Warren was now Father's spokesman. His message centered on preparation. If we were not qualified when the end came, we would die. Father encouraged his revered son to get up each week in church and say he'd been directed by the prophet to reveal key principles to the people.

The year 2000 loomed ahead, which the FLDS prophesied would begin the seventh millennium, ushering in one thousand years of peace as foretold in the bible. Warren rationalized that because the FLDS Church used the Mayan calendar, which could be off four years either way, everyone needed to be watchful because the end of the world could come in 1996, 2000, or 2004.

Warren preached that when the judgment came, the FLDS people who were righteous would be "lifted up" as the Earth burned in a fiery inferno. The original revelation that introduced lifting up was given by the prophet Leroy Johnson, or Uncle Roy. However, years later, when Father became prophet, he received additional inspiration that the only way to endure the Earth's destruction was to be lifted up—in other words, only worthy priesthood people would survive when the planet was torn asunder. The chosen people would literally be picked up and taken above the Earth. After watching the destruction, these survivors would be brought back down to live in paradise.

Warren referred often to the Old Testament and the story of the prophet Enoch, a forefather to Noah. He and his holy people, who dwelt in the city of Enoch, were removed by God from the Earth and never tasted physical death. Because of their righteousness, they were lifted up, including the land the city was on. This miraculous event left behind what was later called the Gulf of Mexico.

According to Warren, when the modern-day destruction came and the righteous FLDS were lifted up, we would join with the city of Enoch because both groups retained God's true priesthood. After the desolations were over, all these righteous people would return to Earth together, where the Lord's beloved saints would repopulate the Earth along with the lost ten tribes of Israel, who would also return.

Because this group of individuals would be perfect, Father and Warren had to keep teaching and correcting us with vigor, so we could become a sinless people.

INITIALLY, THIS LIFTING-UP MESSAGE STARTED ONLY IN PRIESTHOOD meeting, the group for adult males. But by 1996, it expanded out to the young-men meeting for those aged twelve to eighteen.

Father and Warren felt the people needed constant warnings and more protection from worldly influences. Prior to this, the media was not restricted, but we were told to believe nothing we saw or read because it was all lies and controlled by Satan. Now, Warren strictly forbade us to access any type of news publication, website, or television.

I STILL HAD SIGNIFICANT DOUBTS ABOUT THE CHURCH. WHEN 1996 went by with no prophesied destruction, I told myself that if nothing happened by the year 2000, I would leave. I was pretty done, but fear of leaving the community still lingered—the FLDS mentality of doom had been instilled in me from birth. It was frightening to consider walking away from the safety of the church. What if these teachings were actually true? What if I left the church and the next day the destruction hit? Besides, if I mustered up enough courage to face my fears and leave, I would lose my family.

I wasn't alone in my thinking. I started to hear the people of the church quietly murmur about why the supposed destructions never came to pass.

Despite my inner turmoil, I taught my family in the FLDS way, as instructed. I sent my kids to the Alta Academy, where Warren still acted as principal. He was now kicking out children who did not conform to the increasingly stringent dress code. He issued publications and recorded tapes of concepts that we should teach in our homes. I digested this information and taught it to my children. If not, I would be cast out and my family would be given to someone else.

My children were well-behaved and beloved by their teachers. Their only "complaint" was that my children did their schoolwork too fast. I was often told that teachers begged to have my sons and daughters in their classes because they were respectful and well-educated about FLDS subjects. We raised our model children this way because I feared what would happen if we did not teach them correctly. Though I regret it now, I lived the religion to the full extent, trying to believe it was of God.

WARREN'S DIRE SERMONS CONTINUED. BY 1998, THE LIFTING-UP IDEA moved from the male-only priesthood meetings into the main general meetings, to be heard by women and children alike. Because of Warren's position at Alta Academy, this message was also taught consistently at school. Within a short time, it became basically all he talked about. But not all the people believed, and it seemed to me that this intimidated Warren and the other leaders.

In his monotone voice, Warren would pronounce his fire-and-brimstone prophecies, then backtrack by saying, "I'm here to do the will of my father. I only do what Father tells me to do."

He became so intense that, in one meeting, he made us raise our right arms to the square and swear that we believed in being lifted up. He told us if we did not believe in this principle, we would have to leave the church, resulting in separation from our families. We took these oaths because of worry, peer pressure, and guilt trips. If we stated we didn't believe, we would be cast out.

As if sensing he needed new fodder, Warren began to meticulously define the judgment and destruction the Earth would go through. A massive fire would begin in the Arab countries and spread, eventually torching the entire Earth. He intimated that it would be a nuclear fire that would burn everything and everyone.

The FLDS people had to make their choice. Surprisingly, quite a few left the church. We were told they'd always had the "seeds of apostasy" in them.

ONE DAY, AS FATHER FLEW IN THE PRIVATE JET FROM SALT LAKE TO Short Creek—about a thirty-minute flight—he felt one side of his face go numb. He said he could feel an actual blood clot in his neck. He prayed mightily to the Lord to remove it. By the time they had landed, it was gone. He took a week off but downplayed the severity of this event.

A LITTLE WHILE LATER IN 1998, WE WERE ALL SITTING AT THE DINNER table in the big house in Salt Lake, as we did every evening. Father was subdued, which drew everyone's attention. Several minutes passed without him speaking, which was not like him. At one point, he sat for about four minutes with his hands just lying on the table. Father was normally an aggressive eater—if there was food in front of him, he ate it. Everyone stared at him, clearing their throats and glancing at each other for direction. Suddenly, he turned his head and collapsed, slamming down on the table.

Mother, being a nurse, jumped up and grabbed him. She cried, "He's having a heart attack!" She had others help her gently lay him on the floor. An ambulance came to take him to the hospital. He had suffered a mild stroke.

Later that year, Father had a severe stroke. He lost much of his memory, not recognizing many of his children and wives. Warren knew that Father was weak, but he could not take over the church as long as the prophet lived. The FLDS people believed that the prophet received revelation for the church even if he was not fully functioning physically or mentally.

To skirt the issue, Warren would stand up before the people and say, "I am close to my father. We are as one. I am only doing the will of my father, the prophet. All revelation comes from him. I am only the messenger."

These sermons occurred in every meeting I went to. Warren was just a humble servant doing what Father required of him. Because I knew Father's state of health, however, it felt to me like Warren was moving to assume leadership.

A YEAR PASSED, AND FATHER'S HEALTH IMPROVED. THE YEAR 2000 loomed large in Warren's sermons. As somewhat of a computer geek, he knew about the Y2K programming bug. He believed that as soon as the clock struck midnight on December 31, 1999, computers would go haywire and power would shut down. The Gentiles would panic.

On New Year's Eve, Father was well enough to have all the Lakers gather at his home. He had a generator with enough fuel to last for a year. He had three storage rooms filled with food, as well as two grain bins on the property. He was certain that the Gentiles would form mobs and commit mass suicides and murders.

However, Y2K passed with no fanfare. Warren explained that God was giving the FLDS people four more years to prepare ourselves, as we weren't yet worthy to be lifted up.

After our Sunday meetings, I would look into the faces of my children. It made me feel horrible to see their undisguised anxiety. But I remained trapped. None of us could go against the word of Warren or the prophet.

Warren seemed to glow with his power. It was as if he'd realized, "I have complete control over them. They will do anything I say!"

IN 2000, FATHER FINALLY SUCCUMBED TO THE PRESSURES OF THE Crickers and moved down to Short Creek permanently. The people built him a huge, castle-like home, as well as one for Warren. Mother Marilyn and all her boys—the "chosen seed"—moved down to be close to Father. It was only the "frozen seed" that stayed in Salt Lake.

After the move, Father had another major stroke. I was not there, but Mother told me about it. She downplayed the severity at Warren's insistence—he demanded that Father's health issues stay hush-hush.

Father remained hospitalized for many days. Everyone thought he would die. They performed some kind of surgery, but no one would be specific about which procedure. The doctors and Mother were certain he could not survive. He had a blood clot in his brain. People who knew the situation prayed that it would pass. When the clot dislodged on its own, it was considered a miracle.

Some of Father's young wives visited. When they entered his room, he would say, "Who the hell are you? What the hell are you doing here?" They left brokenhearted.

The Barlow brothers came and told Mother, who acted as Father's caregiver, that they needed to speak privately with Uncle Rulon. Mother allowed them a few minutes.

In the 1840s, a man named Israel Barlow was Joseph Smith's bodyguard in Nauvoo, Illinois. Israel and Joseph became close. Joseph gave his bodyguard a blessing that he would be great and mighty in the church. His seed would rule over the people.

Israel Barlow was a grandfather of the Barlow boys. They believed the blessing was a prophecy that applied to them—in other words, they would be leaders in the church. This created conflict between the Barlows and the Steeds, who believed they were the chosen seed to carry the church into the millennium. Both families believed they were superior. They were always right, and they couldn't fail. It was as if they'd been given a special pass to do whatever they wanted—they had a unique right to sin without consequence. In the FLDS Church, this attitude was true not only of the Barlows and the Steeds but also of the Johnsons and the Jessops.

John Y. Barlow was the prophet before Uncle Roy, and he was the Barlow boys' father. When he died, he was in his fifties. Most of his sons were teenagers then, too young to become apostles or other leaders. As Uncle John's oldest son, Louis was about twenty-five when his father died. He'd been ordained to the high-ranking position of seventy, the highest calling of any Barlow children. Because of his high standing, everyone assumed Louis would be ordained as the next prophet after my father died.

Anticipating this, Warren began circulating a story about Louis. Father corrected many men during his tenure as prophet. However, he did not normally cast men out. If they sinned, he would call them in. If they confessed, he would forgive them and then re-baptize them. Warren told people that Louis had been corrected by Uncle Rulon, but he'd never been re-baptized. Of course, if this was the case, it would be impossible for Louis to be the next prophet. Father, in his diminished state, was in no position to speak on the matter.

In Father's hospital room, the Barlow boys demanded that Father ordain one of them as apostle, so he could carry on the church if Father died. Even though Louis was the logical choice, they pushed Truman forward for the ordination. Father did not like Louis, and they felt Truman had a better chance with the prophet.

This action scared Warren. He feared the Barlow boys would worm their way in with Father. But he had little to worry about, as Father refused. He'd already said he would never ordain another apostle because he was the last prophet and would lead the FLDS people to Zion. Even in Father's weakened condition, the Barlow boys could not force the issue.

Later, Father said, "Those Barlow men are trying to gain power over the marriages." This authority was considered the ultimate power.

Warren tried to keep the Barlow brothers away from Father at all times. He acted as if he was offended and intimidated by their bold actions. This insecurity would lead Warren to do something unprecedented that would change countless lives, including my own.

Chapter Thirteen

Exodus to Short Creek

THE NEXT TIME I SAW MY FATHER, IT WAS CLEAR HE WAS NO LONGER the same person. He had a hard time walking. Mother warned me he'd lost his memory—he was not mentally there.

In January 2002, I visited Father at his home. He was sitting down to dinner with his family. As per custom, I went up to shake his hand. He looked at me with an utter lack of recognition. One of the mothers said, "Father, it's your son, Wallace."

He jerked as if startled. "Oh, yes."

It was sad seeing this once-great man deteriorate. But his declining health didn't prevent him from leading the church. He was still our prophet. We believed that God, regardless of my father's health, continued to direct the church's affairs through revelation to his mouthpiece on Earth.

IN THE YEAR 2002, SALT LAKE CITY HOSTED THE WINTER OLYMPICS. Father believed the Olympics epitomized wickedness and evil, akin to the Roman gladiator games. He prophesied that the Earth's destruction would happen during the Olympics. Something had to be done so the righteous FLDS people who lived in Salt Lake would survive.

The games were due to start on February 15, 2002. On January 1, Father announced that all Lakers needed to move to Short Creek, Arizona. At the time, roughly five hundred FLDS members lived in Salt Lake. Father said we must leave the valley before the Olympics started. This gave us only forty-five days.

Many FLDS owned homes and businesses and still owed money on them. They worried about the ethics of walking away from their financial commitments. Many Salt Lake residents had been good to them.

Father answered their concerns by saying it didn't matter. Their homes, their businesses, their cars, and their debt—none of it mattered. Everyone on the Earth would soon be destroyed. God's chosen people would never have to pay back their debts.

Following the prophet's counsel, members began turning over their homes to the bank or simply abandoning them. They left cars in the driveway, and they stopped making payments on their credit cards. They had faith that Salt Lake—and everything else—would be destroyed.

AT THIS TIME, I OWNED FIVE LONG-HAUL SEMI-TRUCKS. THREE OF MY sons and I had our CDL licenses. Father called me into his office and said we needed to dedicate ourselves entirely to moving the people with our trucks. I estimated it would take three hundred truckloads to move all the Lakers to Short Creek. I asked Father how I would pay for it. He told me to use my credit card because I'd never have to pay it back.

So that's what I did.

It took about five hours to drive the 315 miles between Salt Lake and Short Creek. A few others with trucks helped, but my sons and I did most of the work. In the forty-five days we spent moving a hundred and fifty families, I received one five-thousand-dollar donation.

About half of Father's wives were still living in Salt Lake. When we moved them, the job included lugging all the food storage and other supplies Father had amassed. With the end of the world coming any day, these preparedness items seemed almost as important to him as the people.

On the night of the Olympic opening ceremonies, I personally moved the last family.

During this exodus to Short Creek, I lost my home. I was forced to close my business. I used all my savings to fulfill my duties as assigned by my prophet. As we unloaded the last load, my sons and I felt totally exhausted and burned out. And now I faced extreme debt.

SHORT CREEK IS ACTUALLY THE TWIN CITIES OF HILDALE, UTAH, AND Colorado City, Arizona. The locals call this area the Crick. Despite the stunning red-rock Vermillion Cliffs and the nearby narrows of Water Canyon, Short Creek proved anything but spectacular to the stragglers from Salt Lake.

The town was not prepared to accommodate this influx of people. No homes were available, so families had to double up while new accommodations were built. My family went from living in a luxury home in Draper, Utah, with a sprawling yard to cramming into the basement of another person's home.

With the wells running dry, tap water turned orange like the sand and smelled like gasoline. Most everyone in the community, including my family, became ill with constant coughing and colds that would not go away. The children of Short Creek came down with an epidemic of RSV.

Financially, the move had destroyed the people's credit. We overworked ourselves to construct decent housing. Naturally, people began to grumble. This incensed Warren to no end. He would stare at us in his self-righteous way and say, "God has saved you from destruction, and all you can do is complain. How ungrateful can you be?" He made us feel like clumps of dirt.

Knowing Warren as I did, I could tell he sensed he was losing control of the people. We were becoming more skeptical about all the failed pronouncements. He responded by belittling us and using fear to control us. No one officially said they were leaving, but many people murmured that the situation was not right.

When no destruction hit Salt Lake City, we were told it was because we weren't yet worthy for the Second Coming. After we settled into Short Creek, Father forbade his cherished Warren from ever visiting Salt Lake City again because the city would soon be destroyed, along with the entire Wasatch mountain range.

As for the rest of us, we were commanded never to stay overnight in Salt Lake. If we had business there and needed to spend the night, we must find a hotel thirty-five miles west in Tooele or eighty-five miles south in Nephi. FLDS people still follow this rule today.

AT THIS TIME, WARREN HAD AROUND TWENTY WIVES, MOST OF THEM young. However, they were not producing many children. We were told that these pure and holy women were given to men who also remained holy and pure. The rest of us weren't worthy of this type of woman because we were not sexually pure and could not control our urges.

Birth control was taboo among the FLDS. Whether male or female, if you used birth control, you were guilty of adultery because you were having sex for fun, not procreation. You were failing to live the Law of Chastity in Marriage.

One day, I was talking to the town water master, who oversaw the sewer and water lines. He said that every Friday and Saturday night, the filter would clog up with condoms. A lot of the men worked outside the Crick, and they'd return on weekends for Sunday meetings. By Sunday, the filter began to work again as the men left town. I did not tell Father about this.

FATHER COINED A PHRASE: "KEEP SWEET, NO MATTER WHAT. IT'S A matter of life and death."

He preached that if you did not keep sweet, you would be physically and spiritually killed and sent to eternal damnation. Warren parroted the statement as a way of keeping control.

Failing to keep sweet was considered as grievous as adultery and murder. These heinous sins resigned an individual, and often their family, to destruction in the last day, while the worthy would be lifted up and saved. If you didn't keep sweet, you were evil, guilty of sin, and not worthy of the Spirit of God.

To prove they kept the Spirit of God with them, the FLDS people began to smile.

False smiles.

When you had an appointment with Father, he would check to see if you were smiling. If you were not, he would not allow you in his office. He refused to permit a negative spirit in his presence. So, everyone kept a big, phony grin on their face, especially when they went to see Father.

In his workspace, Father had a large recliner and ottoman. His feet were size twelve and extremely wide—they looked like snowshoes. On the bottom of Father's shoes, Warren inscribed a reminder: *Keep sweet.* When you first walked into Father's office, you saw his feet elevated and his shoes reminded you what attitude to have.

Father began expelling men from the church if they lost their temper or allowed their voice to rise in volume. That was not keeping sweet, so they could not be numbered among the people of God.

On the surface, this controlling doctrine worked. The people began to bless each other when they met. Many conversations went like this, with big smiles:

"Hello! So nice to see you. What can I do for you?"

"Oh, you're doing it already with your smiling. You're keeping sweet!"

People continued to get kicked out of the community for not smiling. They lived in fear of getting caught at the one instant they'd failed to paste a pleasant expression on their face. When they caught someone not keeping sweet, they began reporting each other to Warren. This is how people began to move into higher church positions, by proving their loyalty while selling out others. To be in Warren's favor, family members tattled on family members and best friends turned on each other.

Under this pressure, fissures started to show. My children began sneaking out at night, which they'd never done when we lived in Salt Lake. I worried their behavior was caused by a mix of peer pressure, the stress associated with the move, and Warren's constant message that we were not grateful and did not recognize the sacrifices made on our behalf. This combination created a difficult environment for my children's emotional health.

A lot of women started asking Mother to give them vitamin-B shots. We called these the keep-sweet shots. Over time, though it was hush-hush, women began turning to antidepressants like Zoloft and Prozac, due to our society's unrealistic expectations.

THOUGH FATHER CONTINUED TO DECLINE IN HEALTH, HIS PROPHECIES did not slow down. He came up with a new revelation for our dress code: all clothing had to be pastel. Father said he'd received a prophecy that during the millennium, the FLDS people would wear only rainbow colors. In a vision, he'd seen the ancient people of Enoch dressed this way, and we needed to dress likewise so they'd recognize us after we survived the destructions.

Thus, this time became known as the rainbow years.

This clothing revelation was trivial—a mere inconvenience—compared to Father's next revelation, which was downright bizarre. Father announced, through Warren, that during the millennium, the thousand years of peace after the Earth's destruction, Father would be renewed in the land of Zion. He saw himself running as a young man along streets paved with gold. God promised Father that he would live three hundred and fifty years into the thousand-year millennium.

At this time, Father had over seventy wives, most of them young. Many men had been asking why the young wives went to the elderly prophet, when they were women who could bear children. This new "revelation" addressed that problem. Because Father was extremely weak, he could not have sex right now. These young virgins were given to him so they could be kept sexually pure. During the millennium, when Father was renewed with a younger body, these wives would bear his children. God said Father would sire thousands of children. His posterity would cover the Earth like Abraham's seed.

However, many felt confused by Father's pronouncement that he would live three hundred and fifty years into the millennium. People could not imagine how this would happen. Concern and doubt churned in the community. Could it be true?

The FLDS are told that, if they don't understand a certain concept, they should put it in a bottle and put the bottle on the shelf. The Lord would reveal it to them later. "Put it on the shelf" was commonly heard advice. It meant don't worry about it—you'll find out eventually. As an elder in the church, I was told that if someone asked me a question I couldn't answer, I was to counsel them to put it on the shelf.

A lot of people put this concept of Father living three hundred and fifty years into the millennium on the shelf.

WHEN UNCLE ROY DIED IN 1986, FATHER HAD EIGHT WIVES. HE didn't take any additional wives for some time after that, until the early nineties. From 1996 until 2002, he acquired something like sixty wives.

Newell Steed had a beautiful daughter named Ora. After Uncle Roy died, everyone wanted her. Ora's father believed she was special, and he convinced her to ask my father to be her husband. She was the first of his many new wives to do so. Though this was forbidden, Father courted her and took her to dinner. When Father formally asked her if she would be interested in him, she agreed. They soon entered a spiritual marriage.

Following Newell Steed's example, men who wanted to get in Father's good graces began giving the prophet their daughters in marriage. Arthur Barlow gave two or three daughters. Frank Jessop and Lawrence Barlow each gave four daughters. Merril Jessop gave four or five daughters. After giving several daughters, Joseph Steed was put in a high position in Warren's organization.

Warren masterminded this scheme. These girls were among the Crick's most beautiful, all trim and fair of face. Men would go to Warren and say,

"I have a daughter, and I've had a revelation that she belongs to your father. Will you get me an appointment to see the prophet?" After receiving their appointment, they would go to Father and say, "Uncle Rulon, I had a revelation my daughter belongs to you and wants to marry you."

Another of Warren's orchestrations concerned two of Lawrence Steed's daughters. They were not so pretty, but they were of the Steed line. Father beckoned them to his office, asked for them at the same time, then married them both.

Men were not supposed to receive revelations about marriage, but it was okay in this case because the prophet and other key leaders were getting all the young, beautiful women. Numerous young men were growing up without wives. Many men reached age twenty-five without a wife, but Father had no shortage of them. These single FLDS boys and men could not court women, so they had no recourse.

Many would say these fathers married their daughters off to Warren and Father solely because they loved their daughters. Most of the people believed only Father and Warren were worthy to be saved during the destructions. They would be the only ones to be physically lifted up. If your daughter was married to one of these chosen men, perhaps she would be saved too.

In addition, with the common FLDS thought process that we would live for only one more year, it really didn't matter to these fathers that their daughters were married to an old prophet and couldn't have children. In one year, we would have survived the destructions and would be redeemed in Zion. So what did today mean?

But I think men like the Barlows and the Jessops knew this was all a scam. They went along with it for fear and also to gain status. They received money and young wives themselves for selling their daughters to a stroke-addled prophet.

Chapter Fourteen

Eliminating an Obstacle

THERE WAS A BRANCH OF THE FLDS IN BRITISH COLUMBIA, CANADA, and the bishop was a man named Winston Blackmore. The people revered him because he had a likable personality and behaved as a genuinely good person. He could win people over as a trusted leader, and he had a strong influence over the entire church. When he traveled down to Short Creek, everyone turned to him because he never preached destruction. Instead, he chose to speak of hope.

Father gave Winston authority to receive placement marriage revelation for Canada. Although he ultimately had to approve each pairing with Father, this gave him considerable power. Winston was a smooth talker. He made women swoon by playing his guitar and serenading them in romantic settings. He had about twenty-two wives. He participated in trading daughters back and forth, which is one of the few negatives I have to say about him.

When Winston became bishop, he assumed control of his father's logging business, Blackmore Brothers Company. The church provided free labor, which allowed Winston to amass a great deal of money. While many of the Blackmore company laborers lived in plywood-walled hovels, Winston had a spacious home situated on a gorgeous lot. Because of his charming personality and excellent lifestyle, quite a few women asked for him as a husband, in opposition to what we were taught.

Along with his other wonderful qualities, Winston was also smart—he knew what was going on with Warren controlling Father. By 2002, Father was basically crazy, with his mind gone and his speech nothing more than mumbling. This left Warren to lead the people, and it was obvious he felt intimidated by Winston's hold over the church, both in the United States and Canada. Winston understood it would be foolish to openly rebel against my brother. But he could work against Warren's despairing message with his own positive attitude. While Warren spoke negatively and preached destruction, Winston put forth uplifting ideas, such as all of us working together and living in harmony.

I CONSIDERED WINSTON A FRIEND. WE TALKED FREQUENTLY WHEN HE came to Short Creek. Once, Winston told me of an incident in Canada that proved pivotal in what happened to him later.

Down in Utah, a young woman, Deborah, married my half-brother, Dale. Only eighteen, she was somewhat rebellious and held a high opinion of herself. Because Dale was a little slow and not romantic in any way, she felt she'd married beneath her status and deserved someone better. Basically, Deborah hated Dale.

She wanted out of the marriage, but she didn't know how to go about it. I'm not sure if Deborah talked to her father about her dissatisfaction, but she decided to take matters into her own hands. To get out of her marriage, she committed adultery with some kid and then confessed to Warren, who immediately called her father.

Warren told Deborah's father that she had to get out of town. He and my half-brother Leroy were to take her to Canada. By this time, the preaching of blood atonement had increased. Warren told Deborah's father that blood atonement would pay the price for her adultery. Out of fear for his daughter's eternal salvation, her father committed to prepare his daughter to request this rite. If she did, Winston would make arrangements for her ultimate repentance.

Warren had concluded that proper blood atonement must be performed by a blood relative in a prescribed manner. A grave was dug. The sinner stood at one end of the hole. The chosen relative walked up behind with a knife and slit the sinner's throat. The family member held the body up while it bled out. When enough blood was shed, the person was pushed into the grave. There was no funeral or casket—they were just dumped in like a pile of worthless rags.

When Winston found out Warren might compel this woman to ask to be murdered, he was appalled. Winston argued that Deborah had falsely confessed adultery to get out of her loveless marriage, making her innocent of any sin. He called a friend in the Royal Canadian Mounted Police and asked for protection. His defense of Deborah was possibly motivated, at least in part, because he wanted her for his own wife.

Luckily, Deborah never requested the ritual. She soon married someone else. However, because Warren's dictates were not blindly obeyed, consequences followed.

First, Deborah's father fell victim. Warren claimed he was a master deceiver and guilty of sin. He kicked him out of the church.

One day, out of the blue, Warren stood up in meeting and said Father had received a revelation that Winston Blackmore was sowing seeds of apostasy and fighting against Father's teachings by no longer preaching prophet-approved doctrine. Because of his rebellion, Winston had received a warning from the prophet, and he'd accepted the correction.

Reacting to the shocked faces in the congregation, Warren asked, "Do you believe Rulon Jeffs is the prophet of God? Do you believe Rulon Jeffs will lead us to God? I want you to swear to it!"

We all had to immediately raise our arms to the square, affirming Warren's words.

Eventually, Warren talked Father into officially stripping Winston Blackmore of his bishop position. He informed us from the pulpit that Winston had been demoted because he was no longer complying with the prophet's warning. This took away all his authority and standing in the church, making him a lowly elder with no more power to marry.

The sad thing was that everyone bought into it, even me. To this day, I feel guilty for going along with this edict and not questioning these actions. We were used to obediently following whatever Warren said, and this was just another change that we blindly accepted.

But Winston Blackmore did not accept the demotion. Winston countered that Warren was usurping power and exercising control over Father, who was still the prophet. Winston continued to lead the people in Canada, but he eventually drifted away from the FLDS, leaving no one in authority to contest Warren.

This was the first of many actions against notable members by Warren. Though Father had kicked men out of the church before, it was usually for offenses like beating their wives and children. Never before had such extreme action been taken against a man who was higher up and had influence in the church.

Warren further stepped up his game by using informants. He started playing one against the other—if you told on someone else, it raised your standing in the community. He made the people perfectly aware that if they did not believe and support him, they were apostate.

Warren was not going to lose. With Winston out of the picture, he'd just eliminated a major obstacle in his climb toward his ultimate goal of becoming the FLDS prophet.

Chapter Fifteen

He's Just in the Other Room

FATHER'S PHYSICAL AND MENTAL CONDITION CONTINUED TO DOWN-grade. Although he attended our meetings, he was unable to walk, yet he refused to be confined to a wheelchair. When it was time for a meeting to begin, Warren and either Adrian or Leroy would hold the prophet by the arms and carry him in. Father would move his legs, but he was not walking.

Everyone tried to make Father appear as if he were still vital. However, when he took his place in the middle of the stand, with Warren always on his right-hand side acting as his guardian, Father didn't seem very strong to me. Hooked up to his oxygen tank, he would spend the meeting gazing down at the floor with a confused expression. He rarely looked at the congregation.

While in meeting, Father always wore a lapel microphone on his suit jacket. When it was Father's turn to speak, he would often begin rambling nonsensically. Warren would lean over and whisper things to him, covering the microphone with his hand. Then Warren would sit back and look at the audience as if nothing had just happened. Father would mumble whatever Warren had whispered in his ear. Then he would say, "Warren is my right-hand man. He always does my will. He speaks for me."

When Warren spoke, he would often say, "I only do Father's will" or "I am here to do my father's will." Ironically, before the prior prophet, Uncle Roy, had died, my father had said similar things. "I am only here to do Uncle Roy's will," he would say. "Uncle Roy will be the final prophet on Earth."

Warren frequently reminded the people about the revelation stating that Father would live three hundred and fifty years into the millennium.

He also made sure we recalled that Father had received this revelation, not Warren. Father would be renewed when the destructions came. Father would repopulate the Earth with all his young, virginal wives. Zion would be on the Earth, with the prophet as its father. The faithful members would be lucky if they survived to be servants in this new regime.

To poetically describe Father, Warren wrote many hymns. He also changed the words of existing hymns and of popular songs from the radio. The new lyrics described Father with his body renewed as a young man, running and jumping on the gold-paved streets of Zion. The lyrics said he would sire many children and enjoy a great posterity. Father's wives sang these songs for professionally recorded CDs, with Warren lending his voice to about half the songs. Whenever a new CD came out, Warren required members to buy it for twenty dollars or be cast out. Wherever you went in town, you heard this music. People were constantly singing lyrics such as, "He will be renewed. He will run and jump on the golden streets as a young man."

In meeting, Warren made us raise our right hands as he said, "Do you believe our prophet will live three hundred and fifty years into the millennium?"

The entire congregation raised their hand and swore, "Aye."

We believed Father would somehow be transformed in the twinkling of an eye. He would instantly go from a decrepit, elderly man to a handsome man in the blossom of youth. I tried to remember stories from the Bible or the Book of Mormon when someone had been completely renewed, but I couldn't recall any. Father was so feeble—how would he become like a twenty-five-year-old again? Still, I believed it would happen.

Though nothing was ever said publicly about Father's health, the gossip mill was just as strong in the FLDS culture as in any other. We kept hearing that Father was not doing well. At this point, Warren began instructing Father's wives to read every book they could find about holistic and natural healing. Father had eighty-five wives, and many started having "revelations" about what would heal Father. One night when I visited him at dinnertime, he took a little bite of fish and then swallowed a handful of fifty or sixty pills. The wives were trying every natural remedy they could think of to renew their husband.

Father said to me, "These damn women are washing my eyes with cayenne, trying to get them to heal."

His regimen also included three vinegar enemas each day.

Strangely, Mother Marilyn had little to do with Father's care. Instead, she focused solely on advising Warren. She distanced herself from the rest of us, behaving in secretive and subtle ways.

To me, Mother Marilyn was always a terrible enigma. She reminded me of the stepmother character in *Cinderella*. Though she could be cruel to us "frozen seed," however, I never saw her get after her children for anything, not even something as minor as fussing with each other or arguing loudly. In some ways, she was the epitome of the word *matriarch*: a mother who is head and ruler of her family and descendants. Yet she never cared about her children's physical or personal safety. Her only concern was that they become great leaders.

Mother Marilyn was a master of deflecting sins onto others—all the Steeds were. Her children were consummate tattlers, but if you tattled on one of her children, she would say, "You shouldn't tattle, because you're the one who sinned." When Warren did something wrong, even a sexual sin, she would say to the person who confronted her about it, "You did this or that. You are not worthy of the priesthood."

Father always said that if a man allowed a wife to rule over him, he lost priesthood and could even be kicked out. Yet I'd witnessed Marilyn exercise authority over Father and, through him, exploit thousands of adults and children. I wouldn't have been surprised if she had some secret on Father that she used as blackmail.

Warren exercised complete control over Father's life. He authorized what Father ate, where he went, who accompanied him, and who could visit him. Warren stayed by Father's side continually, refusing access to any other sons. Usually only Warren and Father's younger wives would be around him. We would hear things, but then we'd be told, "Father's just ill with the flu."

Father had always loved car rides. So, every day of the week, Warren would organize an outing with a group of Father's young ladies. Acting as chauffeur, Warren would drive them to Zion National Park or other scenic locations. One day, I saw a car pass me on the street. Warren was at the wheel, accompanied by Father and several young wives. The man in the passenger seat with a glazed expression was not the commanding prophet I'd always known.

To make matters worse, Warren increasingly isolated Father and his wives. He controlled Father's calendar, so it became almost impossible to make an appointment. Only a few elites got in to see Father. Prior to this, we could make a phone call and arrange an immediate meeting. I called and called because I wanted to visit my elderly father. But they rarely answered the phone anymore. When they did, they evaded my attempts to make an appointment.

Since my mother was a registered nurse, she helped provide round-the-clock care for Father. She would trade off with another wife who was also a nurse. My mother believed in traditional medicine: doctors, hospitals, and surgery. In her mind, herbs were not a cure-all, though they could supplement medical care. She pushed for Father to go to the hospital, but we were told to live by faith. God would heal. If you went to a doctor or hospital, you didn't trust God.

Mother started saying, "They're going to kill him with all these remedies." She continued to push for more traditional care for Father. Warren eventually fired her and put Mary, a much younger wife and nurse, in charge. But Warren controlled which medicines and methods were used in Father's care.

One treatment was bentonite clay, a powder that could help with regularity. However, too much could cause severe constipation and obstruction issues.

It could also be deadly.

ON SATURDAY, SEPTEMBER 7, 2002, AT ABOUT EIGHT O'CLOCK IN THE morning, we got word that Father was gravely ill. He was being transported to the hospital with a serious bowel obstruction. No one was invited to go to the hospital, but we were told to exercise our faith to fast and pray for his healing. We all spent the day pleading with the Lord for his recovery.

On Saturday evening, we were told that Father would be coming home. The news was met with great rejoicing, except not by my mother. She said vaguely, "They feel they've cleared out the obstruction." But she seemed concerned and preoccupied. She refused to talk further with me.

In Sunday meeting the next morning, we were told that Father would not be in attendance. Strangely, neither Warren nor Adrian were there either, so Uncle Fred took charge. He was normally a kind, soft-spoken, and funny gentleman. However, today he seemed unusually serious. Standing before us, he gazed down at the pulpit, not at us.

About halfway through the meeting, my brother Seth walked in with a phone. Interrupting a meeting like that was unusual, and a ripple of concern went through the congregation. Seth handed the phone to Uncle Fred. He sat down, listening intently. Even after he ended the call, he continued to sit, staring at the floor.

Finally, he got up and said, "Our beloved prophet, Rulon Jeffs, passed away at two o'clock."

The room fell into utter, silent shock. My first thoughts were *Why wasn't I told? Why didn't I get to say good-bye? Why couldn't I see him?* Though I was deeply hurt, I tried to dismiss these thoughts. They did not seem like a faithful reaction to what had happened.

Ending the meeting, Uncle Fred tried to give us a message of hope. "Uncle Rulon is just in the other room. He's still with us. We still have access to his spirit."

People returned to their homes and hid in their rooms to cry. The Crick took on an atmosphere not only of shock and despondency but also of fear and worry.

WE'D ALL COMPLETELY BELIEVED THAT FATHER COULD NOT DIE. EVEN though I'd watched his decline, I'd never feared that we would part in this life. We'd been told that his sickness was a test. If we could rally our faith, he would become well.

As I came out of the meeting, Mother rushed to me, sobbing. "What are we going to do?"

All I could say was, "Let's wait and see."

A depressed pall came over the people. It was our fault the prophet had died. We were not faithful enough to help him be renewed. We were rife with wickedness. We knew the destructions would happen at any moment, and we would be helpless. Now there was no one to carry on the church.

In the FLDS faith, a man had to become an apostle prior to becoming the prophet. But Father used to say, "I will never ordain another apostle. I am the last prophet. I will lead the people to Zion." At the same time, he'd talked about Warren being his right-hand man, as if Warren were next in line as prophet. But Warren had never been ordained an apostle, which was necessary to continue the line of prophets. Neither had anyone else.

To the people of the FLDS Church, Father's death equated the death of the priesthood, which was the power to act on God's behalf. The priesthood was the pillar that held up the church. It was vital to even the most fundamental tenants of the FLDS belief system.

Without the priesthood and with the destructions imminent, how would we survive as God's chosen people?

No one had an answer.

FATHER'S FUNERAL WAS TO BE HELD THE NEXT WEEKEND. WARREN phoned all of Father's sons. To me, he said, "You are invited to Father's viewing, and you may stand in the reception line to represent his family."

Father's body was placed in the large living room of his home. Warren and all of Father's wives stood near his head. As I approached the casket, I was jarred by the sense that Father didn't look dead. The last time I'd seen him, Father had been relatively healthy, with good color. He now looked the same, as if he were just asleep and would soon wake.

As I shook Warren's hand, I wondered why he seemed so calm. I expected to find Father's guardian heartbroken, wringing his hands in grief. But Warren behaved as if this were no big deal. I thought I could also discern a little arrogance and fear in him.

I took my place in line with the other sons. Over two full days, thousands of people attended the viewing.

As the last mourners left, Warren finally sat down with the family to account for Father's death. He said that on Saturday, they'd taken Father on a drive to Cedar Pocket, Arizona, a scenic red-rock location between St. George, Utah, and Mesquite, Nevada. During the drive, Father became violently ill and vomited nearly a pint of fluid. Warren gave him a blessing and then rushed him to the hospital. After medicating him for the bowel blockage, the doctors sent him home later that night.

The next morning, Father began vomiting again and turned completely white. He was once again rushed to the hospital. The doctors said that surgery might solve his problems, but he was too weak and would never survive it. Father slipped into a coma. He awoke briefly to utter his final words, "Oh, my God."

Warren had known that Father was dying, but he and Adrian were the only ones present when Father passed away. Warren assured us that the passing was peaceful. Right before Father died, Warren took his hand and said in prayer to God, "Take me and leave him."

In my mind, I thundered, *No!* This seemed like a move for Warren to begin ingratiating himself with Father's wives and others, setting himself up as a martyr who was willing to die for Father.

It was also a way to start taking control of the church.

Destroying Their God 135

My father, the prophet Rulon T. Jeffs, is buried in Colorado City, Arizona.

FATHER'S FUNERAL WAS HELD ON SUNDAY, SEPTEMBER 15, 2002. The choir area behind the pulpit was filled with Father's family, about two hundred people. The meetinghouse overflowed with about three thousand mourners. The funeral program listed Rulon T. Jeffs as presiding and Warren S. Jeffs as conducting. Warren kept saying, "Father is just in the other room."

At Father's burial site, Warren and two other brothers sang a song that Warren had written. I was allowed to help lower Father into the grave. As we did so, I felt overcome with sorrow. *Why did I not know? Why was I not allowed to say good-bye?*

Several of my brothers expressed the same sentiments. Whenever Father had been hospitalized before, we were all told to rush over and wish him well. Why had that not happened this time? So many questions plagued our minds. Why was this instance so different? Why did we find out about his death while we were in meeting? Couldn't our family have been told before the rest of the congregation? Why couldn't we, as Rulon's sons, take more part in Father's passing? And why hadn't Warren authorized an autopsy?

The whole event seemed unreal. I kept waiting for the coffin to open and Father to jump out. It didn't seem possible that he could really be gone.

But as that first shovelful of dirt thudded on the coffin, I began believing this might really be happening.

Father is buried in the Isaac W. Carling Memorial Park in Colorado City, Arizona. His modest headstone says Rulon T. Jeffs, Prophet of God. He lies buried next to his first wife, Kathleen, who died many years prior.

Because Father had been ordained an apostle, it was only natural for him to assume church leadership when Uncle Roy died. Father would say, "Uncle Roy is still leading the people from behind the scenes, but because I'm an ordained apostle, I am the prophet."

Warren seemed to pick up right where Father had left off. By constantly saying, "He's just in the other room," Warren groomed us to think we still had access to our prophet. The whole community believed we would see him again in some form, even if only spiritual. We felt a sense of waiting for him to return. Before long, Warren began implying that Father *had* ordained him an apostle.

Only seven months after Father died, one of Father's wives had twins. The healthy babies were seemingly full-term. Warren was the only person who had direct contact with Father's wives those last few months.

Chapter Sixteen

Marrying My Mothers

In Deuteronomy 22:30, Moses sets forth a law: "A man shall not take his father's wife."

The FLDS people took this commandment seriously. However, back in the early 1990s, a man by the name of Woodruff Steed, who happened to be Mother Marilyn's father, died. His eldest son, Allen, was a prominent man, well liked and relatively humble—for a Steed. When Woodruff passed away, my father gave some of Woodruff's wives to Allen. This action was completely unprecedented and shocking. It went against everything we'd been taught.

Because Father gave Allen only his father's older wives, the incident blew over quickly. The wives were in their seventies or eighties, well past childbearing age. Father reassigned Woodruff's younger wives to other men. He said he'd given the older wives to Allen only for convenience, so these widows would be cared for. Little did we know, Warren would use this charitable act many years later as a precedence for his perversity.

Something called "Saturday work projects" had become constant in our lives. We were told that we needed to consecrate every Saturday to the church. We'd spend the day performing service such as harvesting crops at FLDS farms or building new homes for people in the community. Participation was mandatory to maintain church membership.

Each Saturday, we gathered at the meetinghouse promptly at 7:00 a.m. Warren sat up on the little raised stage with the members seated below. Once we'd congregated, Warren assigned each of us a task for the day. Instead of joining in, he and his young wives went home. His older wives stayed with us to work.

While we labored hard in the FLDS community, Warren stayed secluded in his house suffering for us, with his wives watching over him. His mental anguish over our unworthiness was much more difficult than the physical labor we performed. As members of the church, we felt privileged that Warren would direct and guide us in our daily affairs. We felt sincerely grateful to him for all the suffering he endured on our behalf.

In September 2002, within a week after Father died, Warren stood up at one of these work meetings and began with his usual rhetoric. "I am here to do the will of my father. Father is in the next room and is still leading the people." These rehearsed words had become so common, we barely paid attention. However, what came next caused us all to sit up in our seats. Glaring down with a face full of disdain, Warren said, "I want you to know that Father says to leave his wives alone."

He said this as if every man in the room had been chasing after Father's wives. We were completely baffled. As far as I knew, no one had even thought of behaving inappropriately toward any of Father's wives. An action like this would go against everything we'd been taught. Besides, many people were still watching for Father to be renewed in some manner. If this happened, all his wives would rejoin him.

Why would Warren accuse the men of something so sinful as coveting Father's wives?

WEEKS PASSED, AND WARREN CONTINUED TO HOLD MEETINGS, USING his familiar wording about Father still leading the church. However, I noticed that his wording began to change. Though subtle, the shift was definite. "I am here to do the will of my father. He is gone in the other room. He is working through me."

It felt like Warren wanted us to believe he was in constant communication with Father, who was now leading the church through Warren. However, just when we needed stability and direction, Warren began to disappear. Increasingly, Adrian and Uncle Fred were put in the position where they needed to advise us.

The prophet was personally essential to each individual member of the church. If you had a confession to make, if you wanted to know whether you were worthy for another wife, if you wanted to know your standing, or if you wanted to question your ability to attain salvation, you had to go directly to the prophet and seek his counsel.

But now the people had nowhere to get their questions answered. I called several times to speak with Warren, but I was always told to call back next week. Warren's appearance at meetings became spotty. He would be gone for several weeks at a time. He completely avoided making himself available to the bewildered people.

Adrian, Uncle Fred, Merril Jessop, and all Mother Marilyn's sons—basically the elect few—could still gain access to Warren. But the rest of us were left stranded, wondering where he went with such frequency.

After several months of this limbo, Warren stood up in a meeting and changed everything.

In his droning monotone, he said, "I am just here to do the will of my father. Father is in charge. I have three witnesses who have stories to tell. They will now stand and bear testimony."

The three witnesses were Naomie, Isaac, and Mary. Naomie had been Father's favorite wife in his later years. About thirty years old at that time, she was loyal to both Father and Warren. Isaac was a devoted full brother to Warren, Father and Mother Marilyn's youngest son. Mary was Father's wife who'd assumed his full-time nursing care, basically getting my mother kicked out of that job.

In their own words, each witness bore testimony that Father had specifically told them Warren was next in line. Although Father had never ordained another apostle, he'd told these three witnesses that they should follow Warren if Father somehow died.

Staring at Warren in complete adoration, Naomie said, "I know Warren received the keys to the priesthood. One day, Warren went into Father's office. When he came out, his face glowed with a brilliant light." Her voice was sickeningly sweet, and she gazed at Warren like he was a god. "It was a heavenly glow! That's how I knew he'd been given the keys. To make sure, I went to my room and prayed. God gave me a vision. Father appeared and told me I should marry Warren."

There was a stunned silence.

"Warren and I are married."

When Naomie said how long they'd been married, we knew that on the day Warren warned us to leave Father's wives alone, he and Naomie were either already married or soon to marry.

But that wasn't all. After Naomie, Warren had already secretly married six more of Father's wives, and he would eventually marry about three-quarters of them. When Father died, he had around eighty-five wives. During Father's later years, Warren had personally handpicked many beautiful, thin women for the prophet. He now took these same women as his own spiritual wives. He kept all the attractive women who knew how to keep sweet, all of Father's favorite ladies. Other wives were eventually given to other men.

WE DID NOT GET TO VOTE FOR WARREN AS THE NEW PROPHET. "You have heard the stories of these witnesses," he told us. "It is up to you to accept it or not. I will lead you to Zion. If you are of little faith, you are of little worth. You will be destroyed if you don't follow me."

For many people, this unprecedented event came as a relief. They finally had a prophet! Now the church could move in a defined direction. Warren had known he could use the people's hopelessness to get them on his bandwagon, and it worked. Those close to Warren felt excited because now they could move up in the church hierarchy faster than ever before.

However, some left this meeting—including me—feeling confused and apprehensive. Our religion had an established order for designating a prophet, a proper chain of authority with the successor named and ordained beforehand. This just didn't feel right. Warren didn't have the required priesthood authority, but if any members didn't accept him, he could still cast them out.

So, just like that, with no fanfare, an immoral bastard became the next prophet of the FLDS Church.

Chapter Seventeen

Yearning for Zion

WITH WARREN NOW OFFICIALLY AT THE HELM OF THE CHURCH, THINGS began to rapidly change. The religion's message blared twenty-four hours a day, not only Warren's recorded music but also tapes he'd dictated about key FLDS principles. Meetings became a bigger part of our life. Now we had Sunday morning meeting, Sunday meeting, Friday meeting, priesthood meeting, and pre-priesthood meeting. I think people believed FLDS doctrine just because they'd heard the information repeated so many times.

We were at the Short Creek meetinghouse so often that this building became the church's hub. It was named the LSJ Meetinghouse, short for Leroy Sunderland Johnson—Uncle Roy, the prophet before Father. With balcony seating above the chapel floor, the large building could hold just over three thousand members. The builders had installed grand-looking—but fake—organ pipes to mimic the world-famous LDS Tabernacle in Salt Lake City. LSJ also contained an impressive array of high-tech equipment for spying on the people.

The FLDS leaders wanted secrecy. However, LSJ stood on land controlled by the faith's United Effort Plan (UEP) trust, which meant the land was public. To get around this, the leaders broke the trust and deeded the LSJ's land to Adrian's name, making the LSJ private property. This meant no one could step foot on the land without an invitation.

Since the 2002 exodus, security had become a real issue. Warren put measures in place that continue to this day. A man was posted at every door of the LSJ. With huge lines of people waiting to enter, we had to arrive a half-hour early to church. Greeters would shake our hands and

The Leroy Sunderland Johnson (LSJ) Meetinghouse in Colorado City, Arizona.

feel our spirits. If they detected that a member did not have a good spirit, that individual would not be allowed inside.

I often thought, *What the hell? Isn't this supposed to be a public meeting?*

Warren had a revelation one day: "Any person who comes to meeting and records it will lose the use of their right arm."

This was another form of extreme fear. We totally believed that if we brought in something that could record, we would lose the use of our arm. The greeters started asking us, "Do you have a cell phone, recording device, or any guns?" If we did, we had to leave the item at the door and pick it up on our way out.

Later, I found out that a camera was hidden in the chapel. During meetings, the head of security would sit in an office and scan the audience to see if anyone started to record the speaker or do anything suspicious. This was allowable because LSJ sat on private property. Sometimes we saw kids or adults pulled out of meeting because security thought they were trying to record. One friend said a security guard came after him because he'd reached inside his coat pocket for something. It was a pen.

DURING ONE OF HIS INCREASINGLY RARE APPEARANCES IN A SHORT Creek meeting, Warren instructed the priesthood, "Brethren, it is time to bow our backs again and give anything and everything we have. I have special projects that you must fund through increased contributions."

Other than saying they were to "build Zion," he didn't inform us as to what these "special projects" were.

Was he serious? We were already giving a full tithe of at least ten percent of our income to the church. With our large families and the financial losses we incurred when we moved to Short Creek, funds were tight. Now he wanted more?

But no one questioned out loud, to do so would be to lose our salvation; we just dutifully obeyed and started contributing even more of what we didn't have to Warren.

MEN WERE NOT THE ONLY ONES WHO WERE ASKED TO MAKE EXTREME sacrifices. When Warren took over, he really wanted the mothers to live the Law of Sarah closely, to increase our harmony as a people.

Following the example of when Father took Esther, one of Mother Marilyn's twins, and gave her to my mother to raise, Warren began to take babies away from their mothers at birth and give the infants to a fellow sister-wife to raise. She, in turn, would eventually receive someone else's child to care for.

This was key because children were not supposed to know their own mothers and were to treat all the mothers equally as their biological mother. Living the true Law of Sarah, children in the community would be raised, never knowing who their real mother actually was. Warren started this plan with his own wives, because the prophet's family needed to be perfectly obedient. However, the scheme never really worked. Mothers know and grow attached to their own babies long before they're born.

UNBEKNOWNST TO NEARLY THE ENTIRE FLDS MEMBERSHIP, IN November 2003 Warren purchased property just outside Eldorado in west-central Texas. A small ranching and wool-production community, Eldorado was located about two hours north of the Mexico border. With fewer than two thousand residents at that time, Eldorado was an ideal location to build a secret FLDS community.

Warren bought the property using an FLDS member, David Allred, as a front man. The sale was completed under the name of Allred's company, a manufacturing arm of a corporation called SnugZ USA. Warren purchased seventeen hundred acres for roughly $1.1 million in cash, funded entirely with our "special projects" donations we'd been told would be used to "build Zion."

The property was top secret. With all the eventual press coverage about the FLDS in Texas, it's difficult for outsiders to believe that almost no Short Creek members initially knew anything about the Texas property's existence. With a prophet who thrived on keeping most of his actions and decisions in the shadows, how could we?

Texas was meant to be a sacred place where Warren would build the Yearning for Zion Ranch, or YFZ for short. Here, the elect people of the true church would receive special training and ordinances to become the chosen of God. To go to YFZ, you had to qualify with the prophet and receive his express permission. Later, people not chosen to go to this consecrated land would be considered scum.

Texas was where we'd prepare before moving to the center place in Jackson County, Missouri, where Zion would eventually be established. Following the destructions and rebuilding by the faithful, the people of Enoch would meet the survivors at Zion. The FLDS needed to get ready for this wonderful event.

The prophet called men on "missions" to begin the building process in Texas. If you were called, you were warned not to tell anyone, not even your wives or children. Short Creek residents would just disappear in the middle of the night, and we were to ask no questions about where they went or when they'd be back. The only people who knew you were at YFZ were people on the ranch and Warren.

YFZ was so hush-hush that Warren created a code name for it: R1, with R standing for refuge. It was Warren's place of refuge, but not the people's. For them, YFZ became a place of cruel slavery and, eventually, depravity.

ALLEN STEED AND ERNIE JESSOP WERE THE FIRST TO BE CALLED ON missions to YFZ. Allen was generally a humble man, but he carried a hint of Steed arrogance. He was president of a large excavation company called Steed and Son, which he owned with his brothers. Ernie was a cool kid who'd grown in favor with Warren. At age twenty-eight, he was made the presiding elder of YFZ. This gave him authority over Allen, many years his senior.

Although Allen didn't have any particular standing in the religion, he had five or six wives and thirty to forty children, and the community held him in high regard. He walked away from everything, however, abandoning his family and business to start excavating for homes on YFZ.

For the first year, Warren seemed pleased with Allen's work. Allen kept up the pace required of a construction manager over an entire project with abundant dirt and rocks and few other natural resources.

One day, Warren called to instruct Allen that he needed to have one particular property—I believe it was for Adrian Morgan, Warren's first counselor—done by a certain time and date. Warren often gave unrealistic deadlines. He warned Allen, "If you're not done by the deadline, you will be considered unworthy and lacking in fervency. God will strike you down."

Allen had one piece of equipment with hydraulic hoses. It was the only machinery that could finish the job in time. During the excavation, one of the hoses broke, making the machine inoperable.

Because of YFZ's secluded location, it was not possible to buy a new part. Once safely on the ranch, people were forbidden to leave. If you had an issue, you were required to call one of a select few trusted members, all of whom lived at least one hundred miles away. They could not physically come and help you, but they could try to sneak something to you in a shipment already headed to the ranch.

This could take weeks, if not months.

Much later, once the existence of the YFZ Ranch became public knowledge, Allen told me, "When my equipment broke, I knew I was in terrible trouble. I had six hours until my deadline. As soon as it broke, I got on my knees and prayed, asking the Lord to fix this machine no matter what it took. I prayed for six straight hours."

True to his word, Warren called the minute the deadline expired and asked, "Is the project done?"

Sweating under the intense Texas sun, Allen answered, "No, I'm sorry. My equipment broke, and we can't get it done right now."

Warren replied, "You are immediately cast out. You are not worthy of the priesthood or your family for the rest of your life."

One of Warren's loyal men promptly arrived in a truck, took Allen off the ranch, and dumped him out in the middle of an untraveled road. He had no money or food. His only possessions were the clothes he wore.

This experience destroyed Allen. His family had no idea where he was because he'd left on a secret mission. With no one to turn to, he walked forty-five miles to San Angelo, Texas, and began looking for a job. Still loyal to Warren, he never tried to call his family. From that point forward, Allen blamed his own lack of faith and fervency for everything bad that happened at the ranch.

Allen lived alone for four years while we all assumed he was safely protected on the ranch. In the meantime, his family had been reassigned to other men. Warren never bothered to inform his wives or children that Allen had been kicked out.

Whenever Warren ordained someone for a YFZ mission by the laying on of hands, he would say, "If you fail, you will lose all your blessings." This created tremendous pressure on people. If a man worked for seventy-two hours straight and then lay down for even a few minutes, Warren or someone would wake him up and say, "The Lord sees your lack of fervency."

During this time, we later learned, Warren had gone into hiding because he thought the government was trying to kill him. He was traveling around the country having sex with his wives.

IN MAY 2004, LOCAL SHERIFFS CONFIRMED THE PRESENCE OF FLDS people living in Eldorado. Before this, they'd been told the property would be used as a corporate hunting retreat. By the time the truth was discovered, the property already contained many homes for those involved in the construction efforts.

The Texas authorities began to be concerned about what was truly going on at the Yearning for Zion Ranch. However, they could never have imagined that soon a building would be constructed in which the vilest atrocities against innocent children would take place.

In early 2005, Warren ordered that a temple must be finished by the end of the year. He even came out of hiding to dedicate the temple's foundation.

Long after, I talked to several men who worked on the YFZ property and temple. They considered it a great honor to help build something so monumental. But these men worked three-day shifts with no sleep. Twice a day, they were allowed fifteen minutes to eat. Some became so exhausted that they could sleep standing up. Formerly robust men became emaciated and barely able to function.

This suffering was all because of Warren's edict that the temple must be finished before the conclusion of 2005. He said the end of the world was coming and the faithful must be gathered there to be "taken up."

During this harried time, Warren had a revelation. The Lord gave him specific instructions on how to make concrete with new ingredients. This was to be the concrete of the new millennium. First used on the ranch, it would eventually be sold into the world and make millions of dollars for the FLDS Church.

Ray Jessop was set apart to perfect the new concrete. Warren gave exact specifications, but they didn't work. Ray reported the problems back to Warren. The prophet then returned to the Lord to get new specifications. Everything had to be produced from materials already on the ranch, such as rock and sand. One of the ingredients was pumice—Warren said it was stronger than rock. Anyone in the construction industry knows that pumice is porous, so there's no way it can be used to make concrete.

Of course, this new concrete never worked. Warren kicked Ray Jessop and four other men off the ranch for lacking faith. Ray would later go to prison for having an underage wife.

Accidents began to happen. People suffered grave injuries due to overwork and unacceptable living conditions. Children were neglected by distracted and exhausted parents. Lacking sleep, my half-brother Isaac's wife lost control of their van while driving her two young children. The vehicle slammed into a rock. One child was killed instantly, and the other was crippled.

Merril Jessop's son William fell off a building while working. The accident basically made him retarded, and he died five years later.

The people sacrificed millions of dollars to build the Yearning for Zion temple. Too many also sacrificed their health and even their lives.

IN THE SUMMER OF 2004, ABOUT THE TIME THE TEXAS AUTHORITIES were investigating what was actually happening on the YFZ Ranch, I received a call from my half-brother Lyle. He said he had a message from Warren. I grabbed the nearest chair and sat, sensing this might be something huge. I'd heard nothing from Warren since Father died on September 8, 2002, nor had I seen him much, as he was in hiding from the government.

Lyle told me that our prophet had a mission for me.

Twenty years earlier, Father had placed my younger sister, Vanessa, as second wife to a man I thought was weird. He just seemed off, so I was against this marriage from the beginning. Vanessa didn't like him either and did not want to marry him. At the time of the marriage announcement, I brought my concerns to Mother and asked her to stop this from happening. Though Mother felt the same uneasiness as Vanessa and I did, she refused, saying that we needed to support Father. Even though Vanessa was in tears, Mother told me to let it go. So, I did. Against our wishes, the marriage proceeded.

Over time, Vanessa learned to live with this man, and they now had five children.

Warren's message instructed me to go and "gather up" my sister and her children and take them into my home. Warren was releasing her from her marriage, though she was not being corrected. In addition, Warren gave me some specific counsel to deliver to Vanessa's husband: he had lost his priesthood and his second family, but his first wife and children could remain with him while he repented, and he would be allowed to stay in Short Creek.

However, he could not have any contact with Vanessa or her children.

I did as I was told. When I gave the news to Vanessa's husband, he was surprisingly gracious, with no tears or anger. He basically said, "Okay, whatever Vanessa wants to do. It's fine with me."

I gathered up Vanessa and the children and moved them into my home in Short Creek. Vanessa appeared to have mixed emotions—though she'd learned to love her assigned husband to a certain degree and had settled into her life, she seemed neither happy nor sad to be taken away from him. There was no close bond between them; it was more like they'd both learned to tolerate each other.

I assumed this separation would last only while Vanessa's husband repented, and then the family would be reinstated. Not knowing how long it would take, I installed Vanessa and her children into a comfortable living situation in our home. However, after they'd stayed with us for only one week, with no warning a man close to Warren showed up on my doorstep and said Warren had sent him to gather up Vanessa and her children again. He took my sister and immediately sent her to be spiritually sealed as the eleventh wife of another man.

Seriously? After their twenty years of marriage, I thought that surely, following a period of repentance, Vanessa and her children would be reunited with her husband. I was wrong.

In the FLDS, when a woman is reassigned in marriage, it's as if the first marriage never occurred. The children are considered born anew. The wife and her children become the property of the new husband, and the biological father has no rights or access to his own children. It's as though he never existed. The new wife and her children immediately change their last name. We were even told that such children would go through some type of transfiguration, literally taking upon themselves the image of their new father. However, it was never explained whether this would happen in this life or the next.

This unsettling situation left me feeling troubled. I thought, *What if something like this happened to me?*

Four months later, it would.

Chapter Eighteen

Mission

WARREN CONTINUED TO DISAPPEAR FROM SHORT CREEK. THE PEOPLE were told he was out of town, with no further explanation. Occasionally he would show up for meetings, but other than that, we did not see him.

In his stead, Warren left Fred Jessop as the bishop of Short Creek with three assigned counselors: William Timpson, first counselor; Nate Jessop, second counselor; and Lyle Jeffs, third counselor. We were instructed that these men had full authority and that they were one with Warren. Uncle Fred was to be considered Warren's mouthpiece. These priesthood men could do whatever was needful at the prophet's behest, and we were to treat their words and actions as if they were Warren's.

Though Warren was physically removed, his words grew even more impassioned via phone and his chosen spokespeople. He intensified his fear-based preaching about world-ending scenarios. Every sermon exhorted us that only days or weeks remained. Warren was our sole means of survival—if we did not stay in his good graces, we would die. These messages left the people even more concerned. Where was our prophet as the end of the world approached? Shouldn't he be here to guide us when the destruction came? Why was he deserting us?

Then, as if Warren's absence wasn't enough, the first counselor in his presidency, Adrian Morgan, also disappeared. Even Bishop Fred Jessop seemed confused about what was going on. Still, the propaganda continued. "Warren is on the Lord's errand, doing the will of God. Warren is preparing the way for us to survive the destructions. They are only weeks away."

One day, Adrian Morgan visited Short Creek and stood up in a meeting. He told the people that this was a critical time and whatever we did, we were not to make any rash decisions. He became highly animated, impressing on us all that only a few weeks were left before the destructions came. What if we made a foolish decision now that would soon impact our entire salvation? I listened, but I couldn't help questioning his message.

I wasn't alone in my thinking. Some formerly pious worshippers stopped going to church altogether.

Two months after Vanessa's marriage reassignment, another shocking event happened at one of our Saturday work project meetings. Warren, making a rare appearance in town, did something unprecedented. Normally he addressed the crowd from an elevated stand. On this day, however, he came down from the stand and began moving through the assembled group. He held a tablet of paper with writing on it. Never before had he left his elevated position when speaking to the people.

In the audience, Warren shook hands and spoke with three of my half-brothers, Brian, Spencer, and Hyrum, as well as four of the Barlow boys, Dan, Louis, Nephi, and Joe. The Barlow family held influential status among the people and in the church. Dan was mayor of Short Creek. Joe acted as one of three church patriarchs and was among those who sat on the stand with Warren during Sunday meetings. Nephi was charged with all the construction projects. These were the four men who'd pressed Father to make one of them an apostle after his stroke.

We all thought that perhaps these men had been chosen to perform special callings. Why else would Warren come down off the stand and shake their hands?

After returning to the stage, Warren said, "I've had a special revelation that certain men have lost priesthood and must move from priesthood lands and away from their families. They are to have no contact with the priesthood, including their families. They are to go and repent from a distance." Then he named the seven men he'd just shaken hands with.

The breath caught in my throat as the entire room went stone-cold silent. Words cannot describe how utterly devoid of sound it was—no rustlings of clothing, no shuffling of feet, not even the sound of breathing could be heard. The tension sucked all air from our lungs.

No one said a word. What could we say? Every one of these men were high priests, leaders in our church and community. We'd had no inkling that anything was wrong. They were all devout followers and loyal to Warren and the priesthood. Now they'd all been exiled.

I kept asking myself what they'd done. I snuck a glance around the room. I had to see if others were as stunned as I was.

They were.

Not a soul moved. Most eyes were fixated on Warren, but others looked down at the floor in disbelief. We'd seen Winston Blackmore get chastised and punished in public, but never before had we witnessed a large group be publicly corrected.

Warren told the entire crowd to get on their knees and pray that no other people would suffer this same fate. We all immediately humbled ourselves to the floor. Warren offered the words of the prayer with a hopeful tone, but a dark, cold spirit infused the room.

Our prophet seemed to want to make a public point: *I now have power to cut off any person.*

Later, my mind kept going over what had happened. I was still on edge, with a sense of dread. I sensed that Warren's unprecedented action was only the beginning. Something big was on the horizon—I just didn't know what it was.

Amazingly, all seven men complied without a fuss and were soon gone from the Crick. They were told they had to write confession letters to Warren, and their letters must match the revelations that Warren had received on their behalf. He wouldn't tell them why they'd been cast out; it was their responsibility to determine, on their own, what they had done wrong and confess it to Warren. Until their confessions matched what Warren claimed were their offenses, they could not come back to their families.

Now Warren had another excuse to never be seen personally in Short Creek. Not only did he think the government was out to kill him, but I was told he believed that other people, primarily the Barlow boys, were after him because he'd kicked them out so publicly and cruelly.

It was a ridiculous notion. The Barlow boys could be assholes, but they were not murderers.

For instance, Louis Barlow once wasted five hundred thousand dollars of the people's money in a Nigerian email scam. He believed we would receive a tanker of oil by contributing to this supposed shell organization. Louis would come to our priesthood luncheons and say things like, "Thirty-two tankers can leave the docks now because I just paid a hundred thousand dollars, plus lawyer's fees." Finally, either the scammers decided they'd taken enough money or the authorities caught them—we never did find out, but they stopped answering Louis's emails.

As mayor, Dan Barlow decided at one point that Short Creek needed to be self-sufficient. He secured $35 million of government funding so he could build our own self-sustaining power plant. The local power company offered to lower our rates, but Dan pushed forward with his plant. He promised us the new plant would be seventy-five percent more efficient. Once the plant was finished, however, our power bills exploded.

One year, the Barlow boys collected five hundred thousand dollars from the people of Short Creek to pay taxes. They paid themselves two hundred thousand of this money as salaries for their tax-collection work.

As self-serving as the Barlows could be, however, they weren't dumb enough to kill Warren or anyone else. At the same time, I'm not sure they would've been smart enough to pull it off.

Lyle began hinting to me. "Warren has been thinking about you," he'd say. "Warren is concerned about you," I began to feel impressed that I'd soon be called on a mission.

One weekend evening in late August 2004, the phone rang at about eleven. The noise startled me. I hurried to answer the call before it woke anyone. It was Guy Allred, one of Warren's three errand boys who called church members on missions.

"Warren wants to see you," Guy said. "Do not tell your children, wives, or any family members. Just after midnight tonight, sneak out of your home and meet at the cemetery. Do not bring a phone or any electronic device. Leave your wallet at home. Do not carry any identification with you. You are not to use a vehicle. Walk, but don't go directly to the cemetery. Walk a distance. Stop. Look behind you. Go north. Go east. Switch to south. Then walk west. Make no pattern as you go. Be there at ten minutes after midnight."

As I was trying to process these instructions, Guy dropped this bomb: "Don't expect to ever return to your family."

I knew those called on missions never saw their families again unless their family members were deemed equally worthy to be called on the assignment. Until then, a family could never question where their loved one had gone. How would my family cope without me? How long would it be before I saw any of them again, if ever? Even though we had a happy family life, I doubted my wives would stay together if I was gone for a long time. If my family got discouraged because they weren't worthy to join me on my mission, would they all just scatter to the wind?

I realized I must put my trust and faith in the priesthood leaders and believe they would take care of my family for me. I must not hesitate to accept a mission call.

Before I left my house, I walked through it as silently as possible, mentally saying good-bye to my wonderful family. I wondered if I would ever see them again. At the same time, I could not keep the smile from my face. Jubilation filled me until it seemed I would burst. There was hope for me yet! Through all my rebellious teenage years, not once did it occur to me that I could qualify to serve the prophet or the Lord in this manner. But now the Lord found me worthy. I hoped and prayed my family members would soon qualify to join me wherever the prophet felt directed to send me.

After saying my one-sided good-byes to my wives and children, I did as I was told. I wove my way through town, constantly checking for anyone following me. I felt grateful that most people were in bed this late. Even though I was worthy to serve a mission, if I was found out on my way to the cemetery, I would be cast out of the church. I would lose everything. Wondering about what lay ahead made me feel almost feverish, though the brutal southern Utah sun had gone down.

When I finally reached the cemetery, four men walked toward me. My nerves quieted—whatever was going to happen was here and now. Though we all knew each other, we went through the formality of identifying ourselves. We'd been told to wait for Guy, but time slowly passed with no sign of him. Just as I prepared to leave, a Suburban pulled up. We all jumped in.

"Do not pay attention to where we go," Guy instructed. "Do not speak to each other. Lay back and sleep, if you'd like. I'll inform you when we get to our destination."

Leaving Short Creek, we drove about sixty miles southeast to Arizona's Kaibab Plateau, next to the Grand Canyon. Then we took off south toward Phoenix, only to abruptly turn around and go back through Short Creek to St. George, Utah. We traveled on everything from dirt roads to freeways. Sometimes the only lights we saw were very far away.

I thought to myself, *There's no freaking way anyone could follow us! This is a little silly.*

We finally stopped in Flagstaff, Arizona. Normally this trip took three and a half hours, but we'd driven for five hours. By then, it was about six in the morning. When we pulled off the freeway, Guy told us, "You all need to pray fervently that we weren't tracked or traced and that our prophet can find us. Do not speak to each other. Focus on prayer and faith."

We all obediently complied, keeping our heads bowed in constant prayer.

After a half-hour, Guy received a call. "Yes, sir," we heard him say. "Okay, sir. Yes, sir."

He turned to us. "Our prophet has detected we were followed because of your lack of faith. We are unable to meet with him."

Guilt smothered me. I could barely breathe. It was all my fault! I'd actually thought all that extra driving had been silly. Amazingly, I wasn't the only one who felt this way. Other men in the car began to weep.

There was nothing we could do but go back home.

Guy turned the car toward Short Creek, but he took another five-hour random route. About noon, he dropped us off at a secret location, and we walked back to our homes.

When I came through the door, my children surrounded me. "Father," they cried, "where have you been?"

I just smiled at them, because I knew I couldn't say anything. We were sternly warned that we were not to mention a word of what happened to anyone. Being called on a mission stayed between you, God, and the prophet.

TWO WEEKS LATER, I WAS SUMMONED AGAIN. THIS TIME, WE MET AT Guy Allred's house at one in the morning. Walking to Guy's, I hid in different places, as instructed. Guy hurried me inside and warned, "If you wish to see the prophet, pray constantly. Only faith will allow us to see him."

The men in my group were different than before. We solemnly loaded into Guy's car. This time, we headed north and then south. We went to Mesquite, Nevada, then to Las Vegas. We ended up in Cedar City, Utah. During the five-hour drive, no one said a word—we were too busy praying. I did not feel at all skeptical about the excess driving. Eventually, we pulled off the highway and waited an hour until the phone rang. We did not stop praying.

After the call, Guy said, "Our prophet has revealed it safe. We are to go to Kolob by Navajo Lake."

Relief and excitement washed over me. This was really happening!

We drove up the canyon, stopped at a campground, and waited fifteen minutes before the phone rang again. After Guy hung up, he said, "The prophet has detected we were followed from Cedar City because you weren't fervent enough."

Again? I couldn't believe it. I was so close! What was wrong with me? As Guy turned the car around, I mentally beat myself up. He meandered four or five hours to reach the Crick, which was only an hour away from Cedar City. I paid no attention to where we went. I felt like I was a failure. It was one of the most discouraging times I could remember ever living through.

THE THIRD TIME I WAS SUMMONED, I WAS SURPRISED TO SEE MY SON Seth in the new group. We had no idea we'd both been called until we saw each other in the car. This time, our drive took us from Short Creek to St. George, north almost all the way to Salt Lake City, and then back south to Fillmore, Utah. Again, Guy pulled off the road and asked us to pray. When the phone rang fifteen minutes later, a familiar message came. "The prophet has detected you've been followed because of your lack of faith and fervency."

Once again, we turned around and started home. Dejection hit me hard. However, this time Guy apologized to us. He claimed he hadn't been fervent enough, so it was his fault we couldn't go on. Then almost every other man in the car claimed he was the one who wasn't fervent enough.

All I knew was that I'd given my best and it wasn't good enough. During the entire drive, I hadn't said one word. I'd prayed with every ounce of my being so I'd be fervent enough to receive the call to go on my mission. Woman and children as young as fourteen could be called on missions, but it wasn't going to happen for me. On the long drive home, I accepted that someone as worthless as me would never be able to serve.

WHEN WARREN FIRST BEGAN TO DISAPPEAR, HE DEMANDED MORE donations from the people in Short Creek. Warren told each elder to donate a thousand dollars per month, in addition to the ten-percent tithing we already paid. We were never told why we needed to make this additional financial sacrifice, only that it would help build up the kingdom.

We found out much later that, during this time of hiding, Warren was out traveling. He mostly took along his favorite wife, Naomie, but occasionally he'd choose another wife to accompany him. He used our donations to buy properties not only in Texas but also in South Dakota. Our donations paid for developing these properties so those chosen by revelation could live in places of refuge, and we even paid some of their living expenses. It felt like we were slaves supporting the elect in their glorious lifestyle.

True, the chosen could not leave the YFZ Ranch to earn a living. Once you were there, you had to stay. The ranch tried to be as self-sufficient as possible with large gardens and their own dairy. The cattle grazed on cactus and spit out the needles. Eventually, the goal was to make YFZ completely self-sustaining. Even so, they needed money to pay taxes on all those properties.

The people in Short Creek paid for YFZ and other places by the sweat of our brows. We were told to borrow against our cars and max out our credit cards. The rising generation had good credit, and Warren wanted to take advantage of it. While all people in the Crick were required to donate, those who eventually moved to sacred lands were no longer obligated to pay increased donations.

Though absent, Warren continued to marry Father's younger wives. He never married Father's older wives. All total, he probably married over sixty of Father's ladies. Warren made it seem like the men of the church were not worthy of Father's wives. Because of his extreme worthiness, Warren was the only one who could take them. And because Warren was so holy, he could not stand in the presence of anyone but these exalted women.

However, as I found out later, Warren wasn't marrying just Father's wives. As his desire grew for younger and younger wives, he would ask men to give him their underage daughters. But first Warren assigned them an underage girl to marry themselves. Remember, if a man denied a placement marriage, he was cast out and lost everything, so of course they all accepted. This way, the men were less likely to inform the authorities about the prophet's underage wives, since they had underage wives too.

One of Father's wives understood what Warren was up to. She escaped from our community before she could be forced to marry him. After she was gone, we were told she left because she'd committed adultery with a man. Because of her sinful nature, Warren didn't want her, so he cast her out. But I felt sure it wasn't true.

SINCE OUSTING THE BARLOW BOYS, WARREN HAD CAST OUT SOMEONE every weekend. He would call on his faithful followers and say, "Go and tell this man he has lost priesthood and must repent."

The men lived in constant fear. We all wondered, *Am I next?* If a man lost his family, the bishop took charge of all his wives and children. Banished men were instructed to send whatever child support they could, but they could not call it tithing. These men worked hard, earning as much as possible to donate to the church for the care of their families. So in essence, even banished people were required to contribute toward the building up of the sacred places.

Warren's banishments would stop for a month or two after his arrest in 2006. But then they would start again until the YFZ Ranch was raided in April 2008, when they would stop for another two or three months. At this writing, the banishments are still happening, even though most adults older than twenty-seven are now gone, except for the top hierarchy. As I understand it, today basically only people twenty-six and younger are active in the FLDS community and church.

Chapter Nineteen

Sadist's Game

IN THE FALL OF 2004, I BEGAN WORKING WITH JOHN NIELSEN, MY stepbrother. John's father had committed adultery and been cast out of the church, but he was still allowed to live in the Crick. In 2000, my father had married John's mother, mostly out of pity—he never treated her like a real wife. John owned a door-and-window company and brought me on as a marketing specialist and business development manager.

I woke one morning with a depressed and foreboding feeling that I could not shake. Since I was awake, I went in early to the office that I shared with John. When I arrived, John greeted me. We were both soon absorbed in our tasks.

Next thing I knew, William Timpson, Nate Jessop, and Lyle Jeffs walked in. They asked John to leave so they could speak to me alone.

With no preamble, William Timpson said, "I have a message from Warren. You have lost priesthood."

These words rocked me to the core, but there was more. "You are called to move out of town and repent from a distance. You and your wife Stacy and her children need to move immediately off priesthood land. Jessica and her children will stay with her brother Samuel under the direction of her father, Adrian. She is no longer your wife—she is taken from you and will remain in the church. You, Stacy, and her children are all cast out."

In amazement, I waited for an explanation of what I'd done wrong to justify such a brutal punishment. But all I got was another admonishment to stay away from priesthood land and have no contact with Jessica.

Swallowing hard, I asked these men, who held my life in their hands, "How long do I have to move my family?"

"You need to leave as soon as possible."

But I had nowhere to go and no financial resources. When you lost priesthood, you could no longer live on priesthood property or work for a priesthood business. The church owned my home, so I couldn't sell it to buy another house. John's company was considered a priesthood business, so I would also lose my job.

Before they left, I gave each man a hug and said, "I will comply."

I drove home slowly, trying to think how to phrase this devastating news and imagining how each member of my family would react. I wasn't sure I'd be able to go through with it, but I had no choice. I gathered my family in the living room. The words were the hardest ones I've ever had to speak, but I mustered up the courage and told them. The older boys tried to remain stoic, their eyes focused straight ahead, but the girls and young children were overcome with tears.

Stacy's children cried, "Why? What did we do?"

Jessica's children cried, "What did Stacy's children do wrong?"

The kick in the gut was that my children were truly superior. They were angels. They'd done no wrong; they did not deserve this banishment. I felt guilty that my kids with Stacy were being punished for no apparent reason other than their association with me. Some of them weren't even old enough to have been baptized yet and become members of the church.

When Adrian arrived to pick up Jessica and her children, I said a tearful good-bye, numb with the realization they were no longer mine. Now Stacy and I and our children would have no further contact with our friends or most of our family.

I FOUND A HOUSE ABOUT TWENTY MILES NORTH OF SHORT CREEK IN Dammeron Valley, Utah. It was a small rental home in a subdivision by the mountains.

We were gone within a week.

THIS WAS THE FIRST TIME A MAN WAS CAST OUT WITH A PORTION OF his family, and it never happened again. Though grateful I could keep a wife and some of my children, I could not understand why I was sent away with half my family. I had no idea of the cruel mind game Warren was about to play to cover up his own sins and desires.

It's difficult to describe how traumatic this experience was for my children. Many of them have yet to overcome it. We believed with all our hearts that we were members of the chosen people, that we would be lifted up and survive the judgment. Now, we had no hope. With the destruction only weeks away, how would we prepare if we weren't part of the church? The horror of the situation caused brutal scenarios to replay over and over in our minds. Believing we'd be dead within weeks, we resigned ourselves to hell.

To survive, we focused on getting by day by day. In Short Creek, we'd begun homeschooling with Warren's curriculum, so we continued this education. However, Stacy soon began to fall apart. She'd been emotionally challenged before, but now she came absolutely undone. In her grief, she turned into a cruel and vicious mother to the children.

I'd started a trucking company with my older sons. We worked in St. George, hauling loads of dirt. I would come home from work in the evenings and find Stacy alone in the house sobbing her eyes out.

"Stacy, where are the children?" I would ask.

"I don't know," she would choke through her tears. "Why are they always running away? They hate me."

So, every evening I had to go out behind the house and up into the lava trails, walking about half a mile to gather up my children. When I asked what was going on, they said, "All Mother does is yell at us all day!" and "Mother says we're all pieces of shit."

I begged Stacy to learn some control and stop being so hard on the children, reminding her they'd done nothing wrong. But Stacy continued her hysterical behavior, saying she had no control because they wouldn't mind her. To escape their mother's verbal abuse, the kids began running away first thing in the morning, as soon as I left the house.

I became desperate. After I'd been kicked out, I was told I could communicate with Warren through a post office box. I started writing letters of repentance. I wrote every day. I didn't know what I'd done wrong, so I'd confess to anything I could think of, hoping we could come back so my family could heal. I poured my heart into each of these letters, often confessing things I'd never done.

After a month of writing and mailing my confessions, I still had no calls or contact from anyone in the priesthood. My kids were not eating and had completely changed. I knew I must do something.

I sat Stacy down and expressed my concern that her behavior would ruin our tender children. I suggested we get her a place of her own where she could just focus on taking care of herself. She agreed, so we rented her an apartment in St. George and moved her out.

We'd been legally married as teenagers, so I proposed we consider divorcing so I could have custody of the children. Again, she agreed.

My daughter Celeste was our oldest girl living at home, only fourteen at the time. With her mother gone, she took over the homeschooling and did a good job. Despite the trauma, the children seemed to stabilize. I bought them pets—no cats or dogs were allowed in Short Creek—and tried to think of fun things to do, like weenie roasts in the backyard every night. They seemed to get a bit happier.

The divorce process moved along. There was no alimony to consider because I would have full custody of the children. I took care of Stacy's costs, but I encouraged her to get a job just so she'd have something to do and not go stir crazy. She found part-time work cleaning homes. She loved having people to talk with outside the family.

Stacy began to stabilize, but only for a short time.

Soon, she began suffering from hallucinations. She had visions of Father and Uncle Roy instructing her what to do. When I took the kids for visits, I always stayed as a monitor.

One day, Stacy called our son Luke, who was a responsible sixteen-year-old, and asked him to immediately come get her. He asked her why, but she refused to tell him.

As soon as Luke picked her up, she said she needed to go to Short Creek. He reminded her we weren't allowed to go there, but she replied that she didn't care. During the drive, he repeatedly asked his mother why she wanted to go to Short Creek. Finally, he stopped the truck and said he wouldn't drive any farther until she explained what was going on.

With a far-off look in her eyes, Stacy said, "Warren visited me in a vision and told me to go back to Short Creek. He's going to restore me!"

Luke immediately turned around and took her back to her apartment in St. George.

Stacy continued going on about visions of the prophet Warren telling her what she should do. I pushed her to complete the divorce paperwork. In December 2004, the divorce was finalized and I took full custody of our children.

And thus began a three-year ordeal for me.

In this house I bought near St. George, Utah, I hoped we could settle into our new lives outside the FLDS.

AFTER SIX MONTHS, THE EARTH'S DESTRUCTION HAD NOT COME. I still wrote confessions every day, trying to gain repentance so my family could return to the church, but I never heard anything back. I felt utter discouragement. There was no hope for us. Though I'd done everything I could think of, I had no idea when I could regain my fellowship in the church.

I decided we needed to settle into our new lives outside the FLDS.

I bought a home in Winchester Hills near St. George. It was forty-five hundred square feet on a one-acre lot, with plenty of open areas for the children to play and with sand dunes and hiking behind the house. The property had a barn, so I bought the children some horses. We also had a swimming pool on our land.

One day as I was working in March 2005, William Timpson, the prophet's first counselor, called. He asked if I was sitting down. I said yes because I was driving.

He said, "I have a message from Warren. Now that you're divorced from Stacy, you're to gather Jessica and her children and legally marry her. She is to move out with you and be a mother to Stacy's children."

I immediately turned around, raced to Jessica, and drove her to Las Vegas. We were married at a drive-up wedding chapel. I still had no priesthood, which was why I was instructed to get a civil marriage. It was in no way romantic, not even really a wedding—it was just a piece of paper. But it was an important step to get my family back in the church, and I wanted to show my obedience.

Jessica was an excellent mother to Stacy's children. They finally started to appear happy. We settled down and decided that this was our life. We all tried to be as obedient as we could, including dressing in the FLDS manner. I continued to write repentance letters every other day. However, we received no priesthood communication.

I WAS NOT THE ONLY MEMBER TO BE HURT IN SUCH A CRUEL MANNER.

After Father died, my half-brother Leroy had been ordained patriarch of the church. Until then, the church had never had a patriarch. Warren called Leroy the "father of the church." He was well-liked, known for being jovial and funny. After Father died, Leroy was given some of Father's older wives. He had about twenty wives when he was called on a mission to the YFZ Ranch and disappeared.

Warren decided to make an example out of our brother. In around May 2005, Warren called a Saturday work project meeting to tell the people, "Leroy failed his mission and is guilty of seeking Father's wives. He has been cast out, never to return."

As I thought about it, I felt that Leroy had posed a threat to Warren's authority. Either Adrian Morgan or Leroy easily could have taken over the church because they were so admired. Also, Leroy was fully aware of the blood atonement that almost happened in Canada with Deborah. He'd been commanded to go with Deborah's father to Winston Blackmore and make sure the act was done properly. Leroy had fully supported this "saving" punishment, but I thought it might be another reason why he eventually got kicked out, along with Winston and Deborah's father. Warren needed to discredit everyone who knew about blood atonement because if the people found out he'd authorized it, there could be a mutiny.

Leroy moved to Oklahoma City and got a job as a CPA. He was eventually served papers requiring him to give information regarding Warren's whereabouts. He remained so loyal and faithful to Warren that he didn't show up in court. Instead, he spent three or four months in jail to protect the prophet who'd so casually cast him aside.

In his private dictations, Warren stated that he'd received a revelation that Leroy was guilty of homosexual tendencies. Warren never said this in public, only in private. I knew Leroy well, and he didn't have a homosexual bone in his body.

Even after Leroy lost everything—his family, friends, job, and church membership—he never lost his faith in Warren. Because we were told never to disclose anything about the YFZ Ranch, Leroy never did. He embraced the warning, "If you talk, you could suffer."

IN MARCH 2006, A YEAR AFTER OUR LAS VEGAS WEDDING, I CAME home and found Jessica sobbing on the couch. I asked her what was wrong.

"I received a call from William Timpson with a message from Warren. He says I'm to leave you and go back to the Crick with my children."

I felt as if the world had stopped spinning.

"What are you going to do?"

"I'm afraid for us, so I want to go back."

Seemingly only moments later, Jessica's brothers were at the house. I watched helplessly as they began the process of packing up my wife and our children.

During this chaos, Stacy's and my son Luke got a call from William Timpson. William instructed Luke that he could gather up Stacy's children, including himself, and if they chose to come back, they would be welcome on priesthood land. They could live with their Uncle Lyle.

Luke came to me in distress. He didn't want to be the one who gave this choice to his siblings. I couldn't believe the priesthood would burden an innocent teenager with this awful decision, instead of speaking to me directly.

Because I believed the end of the world was coming soon, I knew it would be better for the children if they went back to Short Creek. But I knew my older children should be free to make their own choices. I sat the children down and told them they were welcome to go back if they wanted. Luke said he didn't want to go. He was happy living with me. But the other children were young, and they wanted to go with Jessica, the mother they'd become attached to.

Everyone was sobbing. "We don't want to leave you, Father!"

Then Jessica's brother David, who was packing up her belongings, received a call. Another message had come from Warren. David was ordered to gather all my children, regardless of their wishes, and take them back to Short Creek.

Now with no choice, the children were beside themselves. I tried to put on a brave face for them. I gathered them up and said, "Go with Uncle David. I'll be back soon, and we'll all be together again."

This seemed to alleviate their fears. Stacy's children joined in the frenzy of gathering their belongings. Far too soon, the packing was done and the children and Jessica all sat in the trucks, tears overflowing.

Trying to look strong for my children's sake, I watched as half a dozen trucks with hitched trailers drove off with my whole world. I stood there long after the trucks had gone over the horizon, hoping this was just a test or a sick joke or a nightmare.

But they didn't come back. My whole family was gone.

I finally understood why I was banished with part of my family and later allowed to regroup all my kids with Jessica. Warren was doing what he did best. He'd found the ultimate way to punish me. Just when we were finally rebuilding a peaceful life, he'd snatched away what I held most dear. No doubt he enjoyed the sadistic thrill.

I wandered back into that now-oppressive home, stripped of toys and happy laughter, resounding with emptiness.

And began the process of trying to live alone.

Chapter Twenty

Heavenly Sessions

Jessica and the children were gone, but I still had no idea what I'd done wrong. In despair, I clung to the belief that I could repent and come back to the people.

For the next six months, I holed up in the Winchester Hills house. It was forty-five hundred square feet, but I rarely left my bedroom. Any time I roamed the house, went to the store, or ran some other errand, I stirred up a fresh memory of one of the children. Fortunately, I still owned my trucking business, and I could schedule my drivers via computer or phone. But if I tried to go into work, grief paralyzed me.

This area of St. George, Utah, was beautiful in a wild, otherworldly way. People traveled from across the globe to hike Snow Canyon, just a few miles from my home. The landscape featured red-rocked cliffs, jagged sandstone formations, and desert shrubs. However, the scenery only added to my sense of isolation and bleakness. I'd never felt so alone. I wanted to die.

My pain went beyond emotional. Unable to sleep, I prayed constantly like I'd never prayed before, beseeching the Lord on behalf of my family. I'd doze off for a few minutes and wake up restless and distressed. I had no appetite, so I survived on minimal snacks. Within two weeks after my family was taken, I'd lost twenty pounds.

For the first few days, I received no word from anyone. About a week after my family left, one of my daughters and a couple of my sons began sneaking phone calls to me. I loved hearing from my children, but it was excruciating when we hung up and I knew I couldn't call them. I would sit by the phone in agony all day, waiting for it to ring.

I continued writing to Warren, confessing anything that came to mind. I begged him to allow me to come back. I kept paying the mortgage on the house, truly believing we'd all live there together again at some point. I wanted to keep the pool and the animals, all the things the kids loved.

And I prayed. Day in and day out, I prayed.

ONE DAY, ONE OF MY SONS CALLED. "I NEED TO TELL YOU SOMETHING," he said. "I asked Uncle Lyle why you can't come back with us." He hesitated for a moment. "He says it's because we've been talking on the phone."

I'd never heard my son sound so angry.

That night, I pled with the Lord to tell me what I needed to do to go back. I felt like I should cut off all contact with my family. The next day, I asked my children to stop contacting me. We all cried during these conversations. I reminded them that if we were obedient, we would be back together again someday soon. But I felt even worse, if that was possible.

The ousted Barlow boys were living in St. George. They often called me to ask if I'd like to get together. But I did everything I could to avoid the Barlows, as well as anyone else I'd ever known who was no longer in the church. FLDS leaders believed that if you were seen with an apostate, you were an apostate. You could not have any kind of relationship with what were called "correctees."

I honestly believed the destruction would come any day. I'd resigned myself to being obliterated with the wicked and living in hell for the rest of eternity. But I decided to get fully involved again in my trucking business. Driving a truck would give me something to do until the destruction came. My friends at work would help me get my mind off my troubles and feel some connection with humankind.

I scaled back my letters to Warren to only about once a week. I estimate that I wrote over five hundred letters during my time out of the church, but I never received a response.

A FRIEND CALLED AND ASKED ME IF I'D LIKE TO WORK WITH HIM IN Cedar City, Utah, about fifty miles north of St. George. I jumped at the chance to get away from my awful memories. He gave me a contract to haul dirt from a gravel pit to a development he was working on.

My truck had a sleeper, so I lived in the truck during the week and returned to my St. George house on the weekends. Many FLDS lived in

Cedar City, but I wanted to avoid all priesthood people. I felt ashamed if they even looked at me. To avoid contact, I would park my truck as far outside the city as I could.

I made pretty good money. Each month, I kept the bare minimum to support myself and Stacy and sent many thousands of dollars for child support. I figured if I worked hard, turned over all my extra money, and kept praying, I'd eventually get my family back.

One day my son Joshua called me. I felt incredibly relieved to talk with him—it had been such a long time. He'd been working for my half-brother Lyle, the bishop of Short Creek, which meant he was basically working for the church. Joshua owned a truck and trailer, and he asked if I knew of any available work. I invited him to help with my contract in Cedar City.

Joshua had put himself at risk by contacting me, but Lyle agreed to let him work with me. However, Joshua was required to travel between Short Creek and Cedar City every day. I thought this was a big waste of time and money—the drive was about sixty-four miles each way. But Lyle had always been a terrible businessman.

It was such a pleasure to work with my son. We'd see each other at the pit and talk all day on the CB radio. We bantered as father and son but did not discuss religion. We were both still loyal to Warren.

Even with Joshua back in my life, however, I ached with the constant, physical pain of loneliness. Every morning, I would wait with intense anticipation for Joshua to get within CB range. Hearing his voice and seeing his face became almost my entire reason for being.

WHILE I LIVED ALONE, WRITING MY LETTERS AND PRAYING TO SEE MY children again, Warren invented a new way to convince the FLDS people that his actions were of God. He called it the heavenly session.

During a heavenly session, Warren's soul left his body, traveled to the spirit world, and communed with God to receive instruction for the church. While his spirit was gone, his body suffered atonement for the people's wickedness. This suffering was so extreme, Warren claimed, that the Lord often took him close to death.

At the Yearning for Zion Ranch, the temple contained a room designated for heavenly sessions. Warren requested a four-inch foam mattress for the bed so his convulsing body wouldn't injure itself during atonement.

Three-inch padding covered the floor and walls to further protect the prophet's body as it thrashed around.

Warren deemed six of his wives as worthy and qualified to witness his heavenly sessions and officiate over this sacred ordinance. Generally, only one wife at a time was with Warren in the room, and he allowed no other witnesses. The chosen wife acted as guardian of Warren's body, making sure it didn't get hurt. She also recorded what happened during the heavenly session. Once the session ended, the wife enticed Warren's spirit to reenter his body by providing "heavenly comfort."

I later heard a recording of Warren training some of his wives. "The Lord has selected which one of my ladies can be with me," he tells them. "While you are in attendance with me during these sessions, you have the great honor of being in the presence of God."

Of course, no instruction from Warren could come without chastisement and fear. "You could be struck down by the heavenly powers," he warns the wives. "Be careful when you touch me. You can feel the fire, a blood atonement, as a symbol of the excruciating pain of the spirit." He chides: "If you don't qualify to be with me, you are just concubines, not wives. To be a full wife, you have to be able to be in the presence of the heavenly legion."

As the recording continues, Warren explains that sexual desire allows his spirit to reenter his body, with renewal achieved through sexual comfort. A previously trained wife teaches the wives how to prepare for this comfort, including shaving their armpits a certain way. They were to shower before the session and put on a white robe provided by Warren.

"All you have to do is set your bathrobe aside," Warren instructs. "You can just take it off and step over to me." He pauses. "I counsel you to trim your pubic hair to three-quarters or one inch. Long hair gets in the way, and it is abrasive against me as you are rubbing. As you rub your sexual parts against me, it should not be with hair. It should be with . . . I'll call it the lips."

Warren encourages the wives to prepare for his spirit's reentry via "heavenly sensual, sexual excitement," meaning masturbation. "Get the inside fluids outside, so I can have some lubrication" to exit the heavenly session.

Witnessing heavenly sessions, wives reported seeing light emanate from Warren's body and angels hover around him. They described how Warren would lie in bed and begin shaking, arching his back, and violently contorting. After some time, he would go limp, as if dead. Following the heavenly comfort, Warren would wake up as if startled and report, "I'm back."

Of course, Warren had no idea what happened during heavenly sessions, so attending wives would tell him everything they'd witnessed. Many of the sessions were taped, allowing Warren to review them time and again.

AT FIRST, HEAVENLY SESSIONS HELPED WARREN JUSTIFY HIS BEHAVIOR. Before he announced something big, he held a heavenly session. Then he claimed he was simply conforming to instructions given from above. This gave him more freedom to do things like excommunicate members not in line with God and promote less-than-worthy men to important church positions.

In time, however, heavenly sessions started to seem like just another weak excuse for Warren to harm innocent people. The FLDS community began questioning the validity of these communions with God. To prove their legitimacy, Warren invited a few of the most elect to view him as he left his body to go speak with God.

This session took place in one of the church's heavily guarded sacred refuges. Warren stood up and said, "So you can see how I suffer for you people, the Lord will allow you to witness one of my heavenly sessions."

Warren immediately dropped to the ground, shaking and thrashing. A beloved member known as Uncle Fred jumped out of his seat, ran over to Warren, and yelled, "Call an ambulance! There's something wrong with him! He's having an epileptic fit!"

Uncle Fred grabbed Warren, attempting to help his prophet. With the spell broken, Warren ceased his shaking. Because of the inappropriate interruption, the connection with heaven was severed. No heavenly session occurred for those gathered to witness.

Two months later, Uncle Fred was excommunicated from the church for questioning the heavenly session. Six months later, he died of natural causes while in exile, virtually alone.

Chapter Twenty-One

On the Lam

OTHER DARK RUMORS SPREAD ABOUT WARREN'S YFZ RANCH. ONE mystery involved Warren's second wife, Barbara. She was the full sister of Annette, who held the coveted position of Warren's first wife. In the FLDS, full biological sisters often married the same man. First wives encouraged their husbands to marry their younger sisters so the first wife would know what to expect and could more easily control the new wife.

After Warren married Annette, her father had apostatized from the FLDS and started his own religion, taking Barbara with him. When Warren needed another wife, Annette and Warren persuaded Barbara to come back to the FLDS and marry Warren. He didn't seem to like her, but taking a daughter away from an apostate was a win for him.

Barbara had worked for me at HydraPak, so I knew how negative and miserable she was. She was always grumping around with a bitter look on her face—in truth, she was bitchy. Even though she hated polygamy and often spoke out against it, she stayed in her relationship with Warren, and they began to start a family. Even more surprisingly, Barbara somehow qualified to live on the YFZ Ranch.

After a year on the ranch, Barbara became ill with breast cancer. She rushed to her husband, but he brushed aside her concerns. "This is a test," Warren told her. "If you have faith to be healed, even from a terminal disease, you can be. You must stay on the ranch and test your faith that God will heal you without worldly intervention. No doctors."

Barbara prayed fervently to be healed. After several months of beseeching the Lord, however, she got worse and went into a coma. Warren didn't want outsiders—Gentiles—coming onto his property, so he instructed that Barbara be transported to the hospital. No matter what happened, she could not die on the ranch.

Along with my son Seth, my mother had been taken down to YFZ. Mother drove Barbara to the hospital. The doctors said that Barbara's disease had spread too far and they couldn't do anything for her. They told Mother to simply make Barbara as comfortable as possible.

Mother called Warren. "She is rebellious," Warren said. "Let the Lord take her. Take her to a hotel, and let her die."

Mother checked Barbara into a local motel and maintained a nursing vigil. After two or three weeks of agony, Barbara passed away with Mother and her sister Annette by her side. My mother later told me that if Barbara had been allowed to go to the doctor sooner, they probably could have healed her.

"It is God's way of getting her redemption," Warren said when he heard the news. "God gave her what she deserved."

Warren had Mother transport Barbara's dead body back to YFZ, where she was presumably buried. But no one knows for certain—Warren didn't want any outside influence, including morticians, getting involved. As Warren's sacred place of refuge, YFZ was kept shrouded in secrecy. Only the special elect could step foot on the property, definitely not anyone outside the faith.

With Warren as prophet, the FLDS rules became stricter and stranger. Father had reintroduced the possibility of blood atonement for grievous sins such as murder and adultery, but Warren said it could also apply to lesser transgressions such as fornication and even something as simple as disbelief. Under his rule, any sin could be cause for blood atonement.

I believe Warren created the YFZ Ranch—at least in part—as a secret blood-atonement center for killing and burying people. I believe Warren wanted not only to be a leader but also to be worshiped. What better way to inspire a worshipful attitude than by saving people from their sins and keeping them from eternal damnation? With sole power over the privilege of blood atonement, which qualified individuals through confession and restoration, Warren became the only possible path for their salvation. I think he wanted to see how far he could push the people to accept his power over life and death.

Essentially, Warren became their god.

The YFZ property contained two unmarked graves. Their identities were never verified. Most assumed the bodies belonged to Barbara and the boy who died when his exhausted, overworked mother crashed her car during YFZ's construction. But others whispered that both bodies were unknown people who suffered blood atonement.

WHILE THE FAITHFUL CONTINUED TO FULLY GIVE OF THEMSELVES TO build the YFZ Ranch and the Short Creek members sacrificed their money to support the chosen, Warren traveled in style, primarily with his favored wife, Naomie. She acted as his scribe, assisting him to keep a daily diary.

Warren told the members that the government was out to kill him. He likened himself to the LDS prophet Joseph Smith, who was martyred for his religion. Warren told us that he suffered for us by staying in tents "in the weeds" and driving junky cars.

The truth was so far from this, it was ridiculous.

In one dictation, Warren suggested that since he had so much money, he should gather up select wives and go hobnob with the wealthy in England. But he decided he needed to continue as God's witness of America's wickedness. Over a year's time, Warren visited every capital city in the continental United States. Standing on the steps of each state capitol building, he declared to heaven, "I dedicate this state to the Lord for destruction."

During his travels, Warren stopped wearing his weekday uniform of button-down shirts and slacks and his Sunday uniform of stuffy blue or gray suits. To blend in with the world, he donned shorts, T-shirts, and tennis shoes. When he roamed on motorcycles, he wore full leather gear. To keep the authorities guessing, Warren had his cronies buy him a new car every three months. They paid cash and never used Warren's name. He drove Porsches, Mercedes, BMWs, and Land Rovers. Whenever he felt he needed to enter Canada, he hiked in to avoid the border check. He and Naomie varied their accommodations from cheap motels to posh five-star resorts.

In Las Vegas, Warren decided to attend *Zumanity* at the New York-New York resort. This adult-only acrobatic Cirque du Soleil spectacle focused on sensuality, bisexuality, and cross-dressing. When Warren sent a courier to buy tickets, the man returned with a pale, sickened countenance.

"Really, do you want to see this?" the courier asked. "Do you know what it is?"

Warren answered, "Yes, I have to be a witness."

During their time in Vegas, Warren also went to strip shows. In his dictations, he mentioned the homosexual acts he'd viewed. In his quest to find the world's most wanton places, he and Naomie traveled to New Orleans during Mardi Gras. He witnessed the world's evil by visiting adult stores throughout the country and renting pornographic movies. After carefully choosing which films would help him best understand humanity's evil ways, he would take Naomie back to the hotel and watch the movies with her.

Tiring of all the porn, Naomie started pushing back. Warren was disgusted at her lack of loyalty. He kicked her out of the church for a month or two, but then he brought her back. He could not live without her.

On May 6, 2006, the FBI placed Warren on their Ten Most Wanted list, with a one-hundred-thousand-dollar reward for information leading to his arrest. He was charged with two counts of sexual conduct with a minor, rape as an accomplice, and unlawful flight to avoid prosecution.

Chapter Twenty-Two

The Fullness of the Law of Sarah

During my childhood, several events made me believe my father was a truly holy man. On one occasion in family class, Father commanded all his sons to stand up, raise our hands, and swear we'd give our lives to protect the virtue and purity of our sisters. He didn't mean just our biological sisters—he meant all the women in our church.

I took this covenant very seriously, and I assumed all my half-brothers did too.

As prophet, however, Warren said the time had come to unite his wives with him—and with each other—through a new expansion of the Law of Sarah. Previously, my family had lived the Law of Sarah when Father gathered together all his wives and admonished us children not to treat any one woman as our biological mother.

Warren selected a group of his choicest wives to receive this new revelation, some as young as age twelve. He explained that when Sarah gave Abraham her handmaid, Hagar, to wife so he could conceive children, Sarah was with them sexually. "The Lord has shown me that, in heaven, the Gods are with a quorum of their wives when they conceive," Warren said. "I need quorums of wives to be with me and assist me—yes, even physically. A quorum can be three, six, or even twelve wives. This is the ultimate in loving your sister-wives as you love yourself. You help them conceive."

According to Warren, the new covenant was called the Fullness of the Law of Sarah. The wives must "yearn for each other equally," accept each other sexually, and watch as other wives performed heavenly comfort on him. Representing the fullness of celestial law, the ordinances of this covenant were to take place inside the temple. Warren put the women under an oath and covenant to keep it secret.

LIKE THE HEAVENLY SESSIONS, THE FULLNESS OF THE LAW OF SARAH required training sessions. One session of almost three hours was taped and later made available online. Warren gives sermons, scripture readings, and prayer circles. His favorite wife, Naomie, takes the ladies to the bathroom to cleanse themselves and dress in white robes. She shows them how to trim their pubic hair into a certain shape favored by Warren. She instructs them how Warren preferred to receive the administration of heavenly comfort.

When I heard Naomie directing the other wives, I couldn't help remembering something from her past. Many years before in Short Creek, a little five-year-old girl was found tied to a tree naked, with human bite marks all over her body. The child said Naomie had done it. Naomie admitted harming the child, but she gave no explanation why. She was twelve at the time.

Shaved, trimmed, and dressed in their robes of white, the wives rejoin Warren. "Leave your robes where they are," he instructs, "and come join hands in a circle of prayer."

Once they've disrobed and formed their circle, Warren explains, "Many ladies think the Law of Sarah means, 'I agree my husband can have another wife, but I won't think about them in bed together.' In the FLDS, you assist. When I am down and out, you help each other come alive, which makes me come alive."

Warren's next command brings giggles. "Look at each other, don't just look at me. Can you see how this makes you equal? When you got married, you gave yourself, mind and body. With time, you'll feel just as comfortable and natural around each other unclothed as clothed."

Warren then tells the women to go off and pray to the Lord, so they can receive a personal testimony of the Fullness of the Law of Sarah. "If any ladies reject this," he warns, "they will be rejected of God."

As the wives leave for their praying rituals, Warren says, "This is not like the world where they have sexual relations for selfish pleasure. Greater comfort comes in heavenly comfort, beyond what the world can give. You ladies don't know how the men in the world are."

One woman replies in a soft, childlike voice, "We are so glad we don't have to know. We are so grateful for the priesthood."

When the women regroup after prayers, Naomie teaches them where and how to perform the "heavenly touch" on each other. Warren then witnesses this ordinance as they perform it on each other. On the audiotape, he can be heard saying, "You perform heavenly comfort on her" and giving other specific directions.

After watching for a while, Warren picks a wife to pleasure him with heavenly comfort.

Before long, Warren wrote letters to all his wives describing the Fullness of the Law of Sarah. If his ladies didn't accept it, they could not be with him in this life or in the afterlife. The new law was the only way these women could qualify to be mothers in the celestial kingdom, the highest order of afterlife in the FLDS Church. When a few wives refused to be involved in such depravity, he expelled them.

At one point, Warren received a letter reporting that some ladies were performing heavenly comfort on each other without his knowledge. He gathered the ladies together and chastised them. They were not to engage in heavenly comfort without Warren present to provide his direction and approval. While in hiding, he sometimes called from out of town to direct, and his ladies recorded these sessions for his later enjoyment.

FBI agents later allowed me to read a fifteen-year-old wife's letter to Warren. Apparently, he'd given this wife approval to masturbate whenever she wanted. She wrote that one day she went into the bathroom and became wet, but not with urine. She thought of Warren as she had several orgasms. When she couldn't climax anymore, she started crying. Another wife knocked on the door and asked if she was okay. This wife administered oral heavenly comfort on the fifteen-year-old so she could climax again. In the letter, she expressed how beautiful it was that she and her sister-wife could share this together while thinking of Warren.

When I found out about the Fullness of the Law of Sarah, ice filled my veins. I knew I had to protect my daughters from it. I found it ironic that Warren instituted this law after he'd witnessed the world's wantonness in Las Vegas, New Orleans, and elsewhere. Until then, the FLDS had taught that sex was solely for procreation. No one ever explained how acts of homosexuality and group sex could be sacred if children couldn't be conceived. According to the Bible, homosexuality is sinful.

My family, most of whom remain faithful to the FLDS religion, do not believe this happened or that it's even possible. Ninety percent of the FLDS people still don't know about the Fullness of the Law of Sarah, though the information in Warren's own voice is available to anyone online. If I hadn't listened to it myself, I'd probably still be faithful to Warren.

Some FLDS believe I speak out against Warren as revenge for getting kicked out of the church. This is untrue. I've been propelled into action by disturbing additions to the FLDS religion, like the Fullness of the Law of Sarah. I believe this law will eventually be required for all members.

Chapter Twenty-Three

Ripping Away Innocence

WITH A DOZEN WIVES AND OVER FIFTY CHILDREN, MERRIL JESSOP HAD already given at least eight daughters to Warren as plural wives, including Warren's favorite, Naomie. One week after Merril's daughter Merrianne turned twelve, Warren approached Merril and said he wished to marry this young girl too.

Merrianne was sweet and innocent, the essence of purity. But Merril did not hesitate or offer any resistance. He simply scheduled the wedding for two weeks later. Warren couldn't officiate over his own marriage, so he temporarily ordained Merril to perform the sealing ceremony, as he'd done in the past with Merril and others.

On July 27, 2006, the day her father married her to the prophet, Merrianne had not yet started her menstrual cycle. Merril later claimed he didn't think the prophet would have sex with her until she was old enough to have children.

Right after the ceremony, Warren left without Merrianne and was gone for two days. When he returned, he gathered some of his wives—three of them Merrianne's biological sisters—and told them to prepare Merrianne for a special ordinance that night at the Yearning for Zion Temple. It would take place on the temple's top floor in the holy celestial room, which was impeccably decorated with all-white furniture, carpeting, and accessories.

Warren ordered a custom-made bed for this ordinance. "It will be covered with a sheet," he said, "but it will have a plastic cover to protect the mattress from what will happen on it." He also specified what kind of

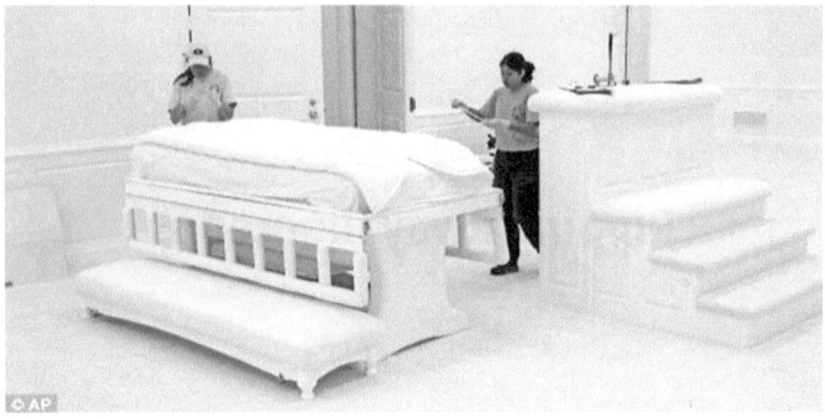

Texas authorities examine the YFZ temple's "training bed," where Merrianne Jessop was raped while some of her sisters assisted in the "ordinance."

wood to use. "This has to be built with such construction that while I do what I do in it, there are no creaking noises."

What happened to Merrianne is documented in an audio recording, which I later heard. The tape is not high-quality, so it's sometimes unclear which wives are present or speaking. Warren's voice is often too muffled to understand. The Texas Rangers and the FBI had to use specialized equipment to analyze the tape.

Warren begins by giving his child-bride a blessing, his toneless voice without human warmth or compassion. "Sister Merrianne Jessop, I put my hands on your head and bless you, by the power of God, for heavenly gifts as a heavenly comfort wife, to be able to come into the heavenly sessions with your spirit eyes open to heavenly visions and angels. Merrianne, you have been chosen. You are a holy vessel of God. We perform this ordinance between the prophet, the ladies, and Merrianne."

In the middle of the blessing, Warren begins panting. "Does that feel good?"

The girl answers softly, "Yes."

"I perform this ordinance in the name of Jesus Christ, amen."

Merrianne's tiny voice affirms, "Amen."

Warren resumes panting. A slamming, thrusting noise begins. His new bride faintly squeals.

As his passion mounts, Warren calls out to a wife, "Untie her!"

Continuing the violation, Warren prays and gives instructions to the other women. He pants. His voice remains robotic-sounding when he asks, "How do you feel, Merrianne?"

There is no discernible answer.

After about fifteen minutes, Warren prays, "Show thy servant what to do next." Then he stops praying and just has sex. Merrianne keeps quiet, but other women's voices can be heard.

Warren has a vocal climax. He says, "In the name of Jesus Christ, amen."

After some rustling, Warren asks Merrianne if she's okay.

In a faint voice, the girl says, "Thank you."

WHILE WARREN WAS BUSY INITIATING HIS CHILD-BRIDE, I KEPT TRYING anything I could think of to get my children back. In one of the last correspondences I received from Warren, he said, "In order for you to see your family, you have to constantly pray."

He wasn't talking about having a prayer in my heart or thoughts. He meant physically praying on my knees in fervent supplication to the Lord. I didn't know how to follow this directive. I kept asking myself: *How am I supposed to support my family if I'm praying all the time? How do I go bid jobs if I need to stay on my knees?* I did the best I could, dropping to my knees whenever it was feasible.

Thoughts of my family never left me. Though I wasn't allowed any contact, I knew where Jessica and our children were. Every weekend, I drove to the Crick and parked far away from the house where they stayed. I would sit for hours in my car watching for them, yearning for just one glimpse of my children. The only thing that kept me hanging on was working with my son in Cedar City. Obediently, I did not listen to any news.

One day over the CB radio, Joshua asked, "Did you hear the news?"

"What news?"

"Warren was arrested."

My heart dropped. I thought, *Wait, that's not supposed to happen.*

Joshua and I met face-to-face to discuss this startling turn of events. FLDS Church leaders had told us Warren would never be caught because God's revelation kept him four or five steps ahead of the government. How had he been found?

Though watching the news was forbidden, we had to know.

We were standing inside a truck stop, and soon the TV news came on. Warren's capture in Nevada was the lead story. I felt the reporter had to be wrong—it had to be some kind of mistake or false reporting. But then Warren's image flashed on the screen. I saw his lanky frame ambling into the Las Vegas courthouse. No doubt it was him. It *was* true.

My stomach tied in knots. Blackness crept into my vision, and my skin tingled with sweat. I had to sit down before I passed out. One thought repeated in my mind: *How will I ever get back my family now?*

Deep down, I fervently prayed that Warren would soon be freed. All my dreams of getting my family back rested on him. To see my children, I would need to be resealed to my wives. Sealings not only had to be approved by Warren, but it was his duty as prophet to keep a record of every sealing, which required him to personally witness each one.

With Warren in jail, I feared I'd remain alone for the rest of my life.

One week after Warren's arrest in August 2006, I traveled to the Crick and drove around looking for the gold Ford Expedition I'd given Jessica. If my family was still in the Crick, I should have been able to spot the vehicle somewhere. I went back several days in a row, but no sign of my family existed. I wanted to ask someone, but they would just say it wasn't my business. I knew in my heart Jessica had gone elsewhere with the children.

Eventually, I stopped looking for my family and refocused on earning income through my trucking business. I believed that if I donated enough money to the church, they would give my children back. On weekends, I returned to the desolate Winchester Hills house. With no contact from Joshua, Saturdays and Sundays crept by. I felt curious about Warren, but I used all my willpower to avoid news reports—in the FLDS Church, curiosity can cost you everything. I looked forward to Mondays when I could talk to my son again.

I found out later that when Warren was captured, he was on his way to Short Creek to marry Jessica, even though she was still legally my wife. The moment he was caught, he'd put his cronies into action. They took Jessica and our children to a house of hiding in Colorado.

I trucked all through that winter. Eventually I sold the Winchester Hills house. I figured with Warren incarcerated, I had no need to keep it, as I'd probably never get my kids back to live with me. But even though things looked bleak, I never gave up. I clung to a small hope that things would still somehow work out.

With my contract in Cedar City completed, I moved the two trailers I owned to separate RV parks in Leeds, Utah, north of St. George. I still took care of Stacy financially, so I installed her in one park and myself in the other. Though we lived only a few blocks apart, Stacy and I spent little time together. She was difficult to be around, always rambling about her dreams and visions of Father and other former prophets. But I felt obligated to take care of her.

Since I lived right next to a grocery store, I decided it was time I learn to cook. I also educated myself on how to do laundry and other basic household chores. My family would be impressed, once we were all together again!

That winter and spring, I kept hearing about a strange confession Warren had made. Again, I forced myself to stay away from any details about it. Instead, I continued writing my letters, hoping for some kind of contact.

I watched in dismay as Stacy's quality of life slowly deteriorated. She was not taking care of her personal hygiene. She did not sleep and looked horrible. She claimed to have constant visions. She seemed extremely agitated. I suggested she see a psychiatrist, but she ignored me.

One night, she called, sobbing. "I can't take it anymore."

I ran over to her trailer and found her lying on her uncomfortable couch in a daze. She had a bed, but she'd stopped using it. As she raved, I could tell she didn't even recognize me. I begged her to let me take her to the hospital, but she wouldn't listen. "I'm okay," she said. "I'm just in a vision."

I called our son Jeremiah. He was cold to me, but I told him he needed to call his mother and convince her to go to the hospital. After I explained her symptoms, Jeremiah agreed and made the call. Stacy asked him to come down to drive her to the hospital—she didn't want me to take her. Thinking back, I wonder if some of her behavior was intentional so she could get attention from the FLDS people.

At the hospital, they performed a psychiatric evaluation. The doctor diagnosed her as schizophrenic and borderline suicidal. He gave her a prescription, but she refused to listen to his advice. She declared that her visions were real and she would not take medication.

The next day, I pleaded with Stacy to fill her prescription. I feared she'd completely lose her mental health. Even Lyle emailed and said she should take her medication and would be blessed for it. Unbelievably, he instructed Stacy to listen to me. But this didn't help. She said she wanted a second opinion, so I made an appointment with a female psychiatrist, thinking Stacy might respond better to a woman. This psychiatrist said Stacy was completely fine and had been misdiagnosed.

The new diagnosis buoyed her up. I didn't know what to do, so I backed off. We went weeks at a time without contact. I occasionally checked on her to see if she needed food. Meanwhile, I settled into life in my own trailer, working hard to make it as nice as possible.

Chapter Twenty-Four

Returned to the Fold

"I HAVE A REVELATION FROM WARREN," LYLE INFORMED ME ON THE phone in June 2007. "You are to go gather up your children with Stacy, including Danielle and Celeste and their children, and move to Colorado."

I couldn't stop a smile from spreading ear to ear. Five of my thirteen children with Stacy were still underage. My adult daughters Danielle and Celeste were both married to the same man, but he'd been kicked out of the church. He was the son of my sister's first husband and one of his other wives. Between the two of them, Danielle and Celeste had seven of my grandchildren.

Even Lyle's next words couldn't wipe away my grin. We were required to live in a remote location and go into hiding. Under no circumstance was I to be found. The government was amassing as much ammunition against Warren as they could, including family members they could force to testify against him. The government wanted us to turn traitor against our own prophet.

Lyle told me to find a home in Colorado and pick up Stacy's children in Short Creek by July. What relief! What happiness! Lyle said nothing about Jessica or where she and our seven children were, but at least now I had something to look forward to. Lyle instructed me not to say anything to Stacy. She would stay in her trailer. Our son Jeremiah would watch over her, and I would continue taking care of her financially.

Within a few hours, I'd hooked my travel trailer to my pickup and was on my way.

Anxious to see my kids, I set a goal to find a place within a week. As I made the long drive to Denver, I felt loneliness and relief mixed together. I still worried about Jessica and wanted to get her back, but for now I'd start a new life in Colorado.

When I arrived in Denver, I camped in a Walmart parking lot. The first thing I did was look up *remote*, so I could be exact in my obedience. The word meant "little or no habitation." I got online—this was okay for a priesthood purpose—and searched for places to rent, but nothing around Denver fit the criteria.

I broadened my search and found an old bed-and-breakfast in Sterling, a small town in Colorado's northeast corner, about one hundred and twenty miles from Denver. The log-cabin-style home was adjacent to an old elk farm. With seven bedrooms and many bathrooms, it was a perfect plyg home. I used Google Maps to make sure the home was remote. The closest house was one mile to the east.

I met my stepbrother John Nielsen for dinner. He'd already moved to Colorado with his four wives and forty children. Lyle had said the only church members I could contact were John and himself. No one else could know where I was going.

John asked if Jessica was coming back with me. When I said no, his whole demeanor changed, as if he felt despair for me. My heart sank. Did John know something I didn't? I wonder now if he knew Jessica had been slated to marry Warren. Maybe he'd hoped that, with Warren in prison, Jessica would be returned to me.

Fewer than a thousand people lived in Sterling, but the town had a Walmart where I could park my trailer.

The only way to reach our potential new house was via a five-mile narrow dirt road. My GPS couldn't find the road, so I spent several hours driving around. When I finally reached the house, I saw that the property had a small barn but no trees. I called the owners and found out the house was completely furnished. I signed a lease the next day.

After hauling my trailer to the new house, I headed out to get my kids. As I drove toward the Crick, Lyle called. He told me to stay in Denver, and they'd bring the kids to me in a truck. The next day, however, Lyle called and asked me to go to Vegas, where for some reason the church had moved Stacy's five underage children.

I drove my pickup to Vegas and parked at a Petro truck station. After some time, a local FLDS member called me. He said he'd bring the kids to me, as they were in hiding and I couldn't know where they lived. My stomach churned—I never thought I'd feel so nervous to see my own children. I worried my kids were more righteous than me and wouldn't want to be with me.

As I sat in my pickup, a van drove up. I got out and just stood there. Five children piled out of the van, smiling and giggling. My fear vanished. As one, they ran over and gave me a hug. My heart soared! It felt so good to wrap my arms around them again—I never wanted to let go. I'll never forget how happy we were talking and laughing in that gravel parking lot. Feeling thrilled, I told them about our new place. They were excited to see it. I couldn't believe how much some of them had grown. After three or four hours, I reluctantly let them go back to their hiding place, as they hadn't yet packed for our move.

In my trucking business, I'd bought a couple of refrigerated semitrailers, known as "reefers." I didn't have anywhere to store them in Colorado, so I'd offered to donate them to the church. They instructed me to bring the reefers to Vegas the next day.

I drove my pickup to St. George, where I kept my semi and the reefers. Then I hauled the reefers back to Vegas. While I was traveling, Lyle called me. "Two men will pick you up and take you somewhere to be rebaptized into the church. Do everything they say."

I experienced a moment of utter bliss. My years of prayers were finally being answered!

The two men arrived at the Petro station in a Ford Expedition. They blindfolded me and helped me into the backseat. They instructed me to lie down and not say or do anything. We drove around for about two hours so they could make sure they weren't being followed. When we stopped, I heard the rumbling of a big gate being wheeled open. Then the car drove up a steep incline.

They led me stumbling into a building, still blindfolded. When they let me take off my blindfold, I was in a changing room. I put on white baptismal clothing, and they escorted me to an indoor swimming pool. Lyle walked out, also clothed in baptismal garments.

My five children were there to watch. I wanted to rush to them, but Lyle told me not to. I obeyed, not wanting to jeopardize my return to the church in any way. Lyle rebaptized me and gave me back my priesthood, ordaining me an elder. He told me that I could now have my kids back, but I could do nothing with my wives. Then I was blindfolded again and taken back to the Petro station.

I was instructed to meet at the Crick the next day, where my five underage children had been returned. That night, I was so full of energy that I barely slept. I drove back to St. George and swapped my semi for my pickup. With fourteen people and their luggage to transport, I hitched a trailer to my pickup, and John drove one of his vans down from Colorado to help.

When I arrived at Lyle's house in Short Creek, fourteen people ran out and gave me a hug all at once. As I felt their arms wrapped around me, my soul cried out that I was home. Judging by all the squeals and laughter, the children were equally thrilled.

We loaded everyone up. Before we left, Lyle made me swear I'd take every precaution on the journey, as secrecy was imperative and no one could follow us. I followed his advice. We drove back to St. George to get my semi, which my son Luke drove, and we headed to Colorado. With all our diversions, the trip to our new home took about twenty-four hours.

When we arrived, we didn't unpack the vehicles. We just talked and caught up all night long. I found myself reaching out and touching my children over and over. I needed to convince myself I wasn't dreaming.

The next day, we moved the children's things into the house. I wanted to spend every waking moment with them, but I knew my next priority was finding work.

Even though he was almost twenty, my son Luke lived with us in our new home. He had his commercial driver's license, and he helped me relocate my trucking business to Colorado. Because the Jeffs name was all over the media, I worried we wouldn't get any work. I also knew that if people realized how closely related I was to Warren, that's all they'd want to talk about. To avoid these problems, I dropped *Jeffs* and used my middle name as my last name.

It took us about a week to find contract jobs. Luke and I would leave for Denver at 4:00 a.m. In the city, we'd haul dirt for about ten hours.

Then we'd drive two hours back home. These days were extremely long, but this was one of the happiest times of my life. At the same time, I missed my other children terribly. I never gave up hope we'd all be together again.

Our Sterling house was so remote that we could see the lights on windmills forty miles away. I took the smallest room on the third floor. Sitting out on the balcony, I'd look at the prairie's emptiness. Even though things were going well, I had feelings of misgiving. Something wasn't quite right.

We took what Lyle said to heart and kept our curtains closed always. It was difficult for everyone to stay inside all day. My young grandchildren were going a bit stir-crazy. But the government was spying through the windows. If they caught us, they'd force us to give evidence against Warren. If this happened, we'd be banished forever.

ONE DAY WHILE I WORKED IN DENVER, MY DAUGHTER CALLED ME IN a panic. She said a helicopter was flying over the house, hovering about a hundred feet above. She sounded terrified that we'd been discovered. I told her to take a picture of the helicopter, if she could. I called Lyle, and he told me to get out of that house as soon as possible.

This was in December. The winter weather had been unusually harsh. With no trees to block the wind, the driving snow flew across the flat land, causing whiteout conditions.

And now I needed to move my family out of our house.

Luckily, John knew of a place in Bennett, about thirty miles east of Denver, right off Interstate 70. The home sat on forty acres. We moved during a huge snowstorm, hoping it would conceal us. Right after we settled in, I became gravely ill with pneumonia. I called Lyle and asked if I could go to a doctor or hospital. "No," he said. "You must trust God to heal you. No one can know where you are."

My illness got so extreme that I couldn't lie down, as I was drowning in my own fluids. I spent the night sitting in a chair, slipping in and out of consciousness. I was too weak to call out for help. In the morning, my daughter Danielle began to scream. I looked so pale and drawn that she thought I'd died overnight. My body was completely limp—I couldn't even move my arms. She told Lyle I was literally dying, but again he said no doctors or hospitals. My poor children feared Lyle enough that they were willing to watch me die.

A friend named Dutsun came over with his wife. They sang me a song and gave me some ginger water. As soon as I drank it, I felt much better. But it was still two or three days before I was out of the woods.

Later, I found out my mother had been living near us, running a birthing center. I drove past her place every day, but we were so secluded that I never knew. It would have been nice if Lyle had told me. She could have nursed me while we remained in hiding.

After my recovery, I worked several jobs. I continued to do trucking with Luke. I worked for Phaze Concrete, helping them expand their business into Colorado. And I worked with John in his door shop. He desperately needed help because his unpaid church calling consumed most of his time. He distributed food to all the FLDS living in Colorado.

In our new home, we blacked out our windows and never allowed the children outside. We continued following the rules of absolutely no TV, newspaper, or radio. I used the Internet only to find jobs to bid on for Phaze Concrete. While online, I never looked at the news. We had zero contact with members from Short Creek or any other location.

Apparently, however, not all FLDS members followed the rules. In February 2008, John told me that, while delivering food, he'd heard more rumblings about Warren's weird confession in prison. But I knew that if I investigated any claims against our prophet, I would be considered apostate. I felt it was more important to keep improving my standing so I could get Jessica and our children back.

We continued as a family in hiding, isolated with no word about our status or future.

Chapter Twenty-Five

YFZ Raid

By April 2008, our large family had overflowed the septic system and broken the sewer line at the Bennett property. I didn't want to alert the owner that a polygamist family lived in his home, so I tried solving the problem myself. Spending two weeks redoing a septic system wasn't my idea of a great time, but the warm spring sun felt nice after our long winter of hiding.

One afternoon, I heard a vehicle approach the house. I paused in my work, ever wary.

It was John, his face grim. "We need to talk. There's been a raid at the YFZ Ranch. They've taken all the kids."

I could barely breathe. Why would they take our children?

John wasn't done. "Warren claims God will destroy the people involved, and the children will be returned." He looked around. "We need to become hypervigilant so we don't get caught. The government is after us more than ever."

Over four hundred children had been taken off the ranch, John said. This news stunned me. I had no idea so many people lived on the ranch—I didn't even know it was big enough to accommodate that many. At the time, all I really knew about YFZ was that Adrian and Merril lived there and had built some kind of temple.

"What can we do?" I asked John. "Can we go help?"

"I talked to the bishop. He said we should stay at our posts and avoid any contact with the media. He said to pray, and the Lord will handle it."

With our media blackout, we heard little for several months. Our leaders claimed that, when the government realized the church had moved its headquarters to the ranch, they'd raided it to manufacture charges against Warren. They wanted to cut off the church's head and wipe out the FLDS religion. They'd leaked a false story to the media, saying a girl on the ranch called police and claimed her older husband was sexually and physically abusing her. Our leaders assured us the government paid the girl to make this accusation. The government would find no incriminating information at the ranch, as there was none.

We heard terrible stories. The government wanted to adopt our children out to Gentile families or perhaps even kill them. They were holding FLDS mothers in horse stalls, beating and starving them. The Texas Rangers had hit and kicked the men who'd peaceably gathered to protect the temple. Police had put guns in their faces, and snipers had aimed high-powered rifles at them. Warren said the YFZ temple was now desecrated and could never be used again.

The reports about the raid filled me with horror. At the time, I still had no idea where Jessica and our children were. Was my family at the ranch, enduring this harsh treatment? My mother was now living at the ranch. Was she hungry or hurt? Hiding in Colorado, we felt powerless to help our loved ones.

All this persecution was likened unto the day of Joseph Smith, when people were driven from their homes and murdered. Like Joseph Smith, Warren was incarcerated. We were never told he'd been charged with being an accomplice to incest and engaging in sexual conduct with a minor. According to the church, Warren was a good, clean man.

Bill Shapley was a spokesman for Warren and the church. If a reporter contacted us, we were to refer them to Bill for any information. Ironically, Bill was the one who admitted Warren had married a twelve-year-old girl. He said Warren was like Joseph with the Virgin Mary before she gave birth to Jesus Christ. Warren was not having sex with this wife. He was simply protecting an innocent girl from evil men seeking to take her.

When I heard this explanation, I felt relieved. I'd heard a rumor that the media published a photo of Warren kissing the twelve-year-old girl. I didn't see the photo, but now I knew the media must have manipulated it. In response to the media hype, the church issued another end-of-the-world warning. Because of all the false information about Warren, the planet would be torn asunder in 2009.

Lyle called us again in October 2008. He told me that William Timpson, the bishop of Short Creek, had been corrected and sent away. Lyle had been placed as the new bishop, and he wanted to meet with me. Also, we'd been discovered again and needed to move. I found another place about twenty miles from Bennett. Neighbors lived fairly close, so we constantly feared discovery.

I was summoned to an assembly in Short Creek. Church attorneys had drafted a document claiming Texas violated our religious rights. They laid this document on a table and told us to sign it. We did so, in complete ignorance. The church used the document to file an emergency motion. The court of appeals found that Judge Barbara Walther did not have enough evidence to remove all the children from the ranch, and she must order their return. With more time, prosecutors could have prepared enough evidence to permanently remove the children. However, it ended up taking two hundred people two years to go through everything.

It haunts me that, trusting completely, I personally signed the document that returned FLDS children to that abusive environment.

I LATER LEARNED THE TRUTH ABOUT YFZ AND THE RAID. THE CASE yielded thirteen terabytes of evidence, including millions of documents. For eight months, I spent all my spare time going through documents, audiotapes, and video recordings. Even after seeing for myself, I could scarcely believe what had happened while I was in hiding.

Warren wasn't dumb. At first, Texas was the perfect place to locate his new Zion. Texas law stated that a fourteen-year-old girl could legally marry without parental consent. However, soon after Warren started building YFZ, Texas happened to raise the age to sixteen. The revised law also stated that if a man was ten years older than a minor, they could not marry even with parental consent. Only another minor could have sex with a girl under sixteen. Breaking this law was a felony.

When the new law came into effect, Warren said that because they'd performed ordinances, having sex with multiple underage wives was not illegal—it was their religious right. In my view, the men at YFZ were not extra holy; Warren chose them because they would give Warren their young daughters and take underage wives themselves. Many women said

YFZ was like living in a brothel. It was about sex, not religion or morality. Warren even had sex with his wives in the temple baptismal font.

Everyone living on the ranch must have known what was going on, but some were more culpable than others. Lloyd Barlow was called on a special mission to become a doctor and practice at the ranch. He knew about the underage marriages, and he facilitated underage births. Lloyd eventually lost his medical license, but he did not go to prison.

My mother was a birthing nurse. She took a secret oath to not tell what was going on. When I asked her about it later, she looked me in the eye and said, "It's all lies. The government made it up. Warren is justified and right." I believe this is why my mother won't talk to me—she knows she lied to me, and she knows I know she lied. Even when she got kicked out of the church twice due to her lack of faith, she never contacted me.

Many others knew men were taking young girls as wives, but they were too cowardly to stop it. To this day, the church maintains they were only doing the Lord's will; the government persecuted the good people of the FLDS, and they fabricated the evidence. But I've seen it, and they couldn't have fabricated it. I know the accusations are true.

The Texas Rangers raided the ranch looking for evidence of underage marriages. To their surprise, they found more than four hundred children, along with two or three hundred adults. More than half the teen girls were pregnant or had babies. The Rangers took the children into protective custody. Many mothers left the ranch to stay with their children, but the men couldn't leave while the investigation continued. When I visited Texas before and during Warren's trial, I saw where the women and children had been housed. The facilities were clean, safe, and comfortable.

While searching Warren's house at YFZ, an investigator noticed a funny crack in a cabinet's back wall. Behind the cabinet, he found a well-hidden door to a secret room. Inside, they found a cache of Warren's sacred records, which led them to search the temple. I believe this discovery was inspired.

As a SWAT team approached the temple, FLDS elders stood outside the fence. They formed a prayer circle, kneeling to exercise their faith to keep the SWAT team out. The elders said they would fight to the death. They threatened that if anyone approached, the Lord would strike him down with lightning. The SWAT team pleaded with the elders to open the gate. After waiting several hours, the SWAT team battered down the gate and smashed open the temple's front door.

Aerial view of the YFZ temple in Texas.

In the temple, the authorities found a bank vault. They had to use drills to penetrate the vault's three-foot concrete walls. Inside was a stash of Warren's child pornography. He'd taken nude pictures of twelve underage girls, alone in their prepubescent shame and in a group photo. They also found a transcription of Merrianne's rape. When Warren was first arrested, the FBI had seized a laptop that contained this recording, but they didn't know who the girl was. Now they knew.

Armed with this evidence, Child Protective Services asked one of our leaders, "Do you know a girl named Merrianne?"

"Yes," he answered.

"Did you know she married Warren Jeffs?"

"Yeah."

"We want to be allowed to test her and see if she's a virgin."

The leader went to Merrianne's father and asked his permission. Merril Jessop swore sex had not occurred between the prophet and his daughter. Warren was on the road, and he was captured just two weeks after the marriage. After much stalling, Merril finally said, "Sure, go ahead."

Of course, Merrianne's exam proved she'd been violated. But she never did testify against Warren. An anonymous person adopted her. Merril eventually went to prison, where he served only two years of his twelve-year sentence.

Chapter Twenty-Six

Forever Banished

After I'd settled my family in our third place in Colorado, Lyle called me in July 2009. Warren had received a revelation that, because of the Texas raid, all Father's sons needed to move back to the Crick with their families. The Lord was displeased. A new gathering was needed in Short Creek to unite our faith so Warren would be released from prison. Only then could our prophet redeem Zion.

I had mixed emotions about this. I did not look forward to moving again, but we wanted to return to Short Creek. Hopefully this would be our last move.

Once we arrived, we were told to prepare for a mission call to the YFZ Ranch. The Crick was just a stepping-stone. The ranch was designated as a holy place for the elect to gather. Those not selected would stay in Short Creek, and the city would eventually be destroyed by fire.

After the raid, the people still living on YFZ were considered even more sacred and holy. Their suffering, sacrifices, and endurance had made them extra special to the Lord. The children of YFZ had been raised up like calves in a stall. Many had never seen the outside world, making them extremely holy and special.

While we waited in the Crick, we were assigned to share a large home with another family. This home had originally been built in the 1950s or 1960s, with an addition put on later. A couple with four children lived in the newer part, with ten bedrooms and eight bathrooms. Lyle placed my family of fifteen in the home's old, decrepit part, which had five closet-sized bedrooms and three bathrooms.

I kept expecting Lyle to switch the smaller family with ours, but it never happened. Even worse, the house was filled with mold. My daughter Danielle's asthma got worse. I called Lyle to ask what he could do to help my daughter.

He did nothing. I thought, *This is how you take care of the needs of the people?*

I'd never lived in such horrible conditions. I tried cleaning the place as best I could, and I replaced all the plumbing, carpet, and electrical. Still clueless why I'd been kicked out, I began wondering if I'd been given bad housing because I still wasn't as worthy as other Short Creek members.

Or was it a test? I'd been told to expect a YFZ mission call. We believed the end was coming. If we united in our faith for Warren's freedom, he would soon be released.

WHENEVER I WENT TO THE STORE OR TOOK ALL MY KIDS TO CHURCH, people gave us strange looks. "There's that weird family," I imagined them whispering to each other. "He doesn't have any wives." It felt almost like we were being shunned.

My half-brother Leroy had it even worse. He'd been restored to the church, though we'd been told he would never be allowed to return. However, he did not regain his family. Within a week after Leroy was cast out, his wives and children had been reassigned, mainly to my father-in-law Adrian. Now Leroy lived alone in a tiny house, too ashamed to let anyone visit.

I missed Leroy. It had been a long time since we'd spoken. Growing up, Leroy was the brother who'd made us laugh about split-pea soup and peanut butter and honey sandwiches.

One day, my friend Jacob and I stopped by Leroy's house. After we knocked, Leroy took a long time to answer. He was so embarrassed to see us, he practically cowered. He was broken and crushed. He'd been emasculated.

This was my brother! I thought to myself, *How does God do this to someone? God wouldn't tear people to pieces like this!*

THOUGH LUKE AND I STILL RAN OUR TRUCKING BUSINESS, MY STEP-brother John asked for my help. He wanted to start a new business harvesting potatoes and freezing them for sale. He needed me to help set up the manufacturing plant. So, for the next three months, while Luke drove trucks, John and I traveled around the country buying freezing equipment.

Warren and our church were still in the news, so I continued going by my middle name. I spoke to Gentiles only when necessary, never with any idle chitchat. I worried about the consequences if I ever offered my opinion and it got back to the FLDS. I did not want to be kicked out again.

During church meetings, Warren would call us from his prison cell. "Do not believe anything you read about me," he often said. "It's all lies. Don't listen, or you will be an apostate and be damned." Then he would give us more of his verbose "keep sweet" training.

We were told that the government continually attempted to kill Warren. He was alive thanks only to the grace of God. However, we also kept hearing rumors about Warren's strange confession, which was available on the Internet. I was curious, but my fear of losing my family kept me away from the media.

IN LATE OCTOBER 2009, LYLE ANNOUNCED THAT WARREN HAD received another revelation. The Lord had created a special rebaptism ordinance so members could prove their personal worthiness to live on YFZ. If you qualified, you would be invited to participate. If you didn't get invited, it meant you were cast out.

We were told that this rebaptism gave members an opportunity to back out of the church, if they wanted. If you did get rebaptized, it was a final baptism. If you later committed a sin and tried to repent, you would never be allowed back into the church. Before rebaptism, you had to become absolutely clean and pure. You had to make sure you'd confessed everything you'd ever done wrong. If not, you would be detected and cast out forever. You would never receive salvation.

The new revelation meant that over two thousand rebaptisms needed to be done within two weeks. Certain men were set apart and ordained to perform these special baptisms. To meet the deadline, they worked in shifts twenty-four hours a day.

I thought the concept of rebaptism was weird. I'd always believed our ordinances followed a certain sequence: get baptized, get confirmed, receive the priesthood, and then marry. These were special, one-time ordinances. But I still wanted the new baptism. When several days went by without an invitation, I felt extremely nervous. I wondered, *Am I going to get kicked out again?*

Finally, I received a call from someone who worked with Lyle. He told me when to report for rebaptism, and he instructed me to wear all-white baptismal garments.

Rebaptism had nothing to do with Christ. Standing in the water, I uttered the words of the new ordinance: "I know Warren Jeffs is a prophet of God, and I will follow him at all costs." Then I was immersed.

Still in my wet clothes, I went to another room to be reconfirmed with the gift of the Holy Ghost. This ordinance included a personal blessing spoken by inspiration.

The man who performed my confirmation knew me. He laid his hands on my head. During his blessing, he said, "I restore all your former ordinances and blessings, including your marriages."

I left the room in complete shock. *How is this going to work?* I wondered. *Are my wives really mine or not?* The man knew my wives had been taken from me. Did he have authority to give them back to me? Was I supposed to go and gather them up?

As I changed out of my wet clothes, I heard a knock. I was asked to return to the confirmation room.

"Do you have wives?" inquired the man who'd confirmed me.

"Well, I don't know. Do I?"

"Do you have wives who live with you?"

"No."

"Do you have wives that belong to you?"

I couldn't help a little sarcasm. "Well, I guess after this baptism I do."

"So, as far as you know, they were taken from you?"

"Ask Warren," was all I could say.

They decided they'd better redo my confirmation, this time "with inspiration." In the revised blessing, the man said, "We restore your former baptism and priesthood, but not your former sealings."

I should have felt at peace because my sins had been washed away. But I was questioning church authority again. I felt nothing but confusion.

IN DECEMBER, WARREN SAID THE LORD HAD TOLD HIM HE'D BE released from prison by year end. The people were to build him a twenty-thousand-square-foot house in Short Creek. For complete soundproofing, all the walls would have six inches of airspace inside. Warren would commute from the Short Creek house to the YFZ Ranch, where he would do special work.

Near Warren's new house, the church was to construct an endowment house, a holy edifice where special ordinances could be performed. Only those who'd been ordained and set apart could work on building the endowment house. I was not among them.

To drown out my concerns about my reconfirmation, I worked hard on Warren's home. I tried to clear my mind of questions, but I couldn't help wondering why Warren needed a huge, new home if Short Creek would soon be destroyed.

During this time, our leaders taught us more about the United Order, in which members would have all things common, with no one person owning anything. We'd heard about this higher law before, but we'd never been given specifics. In late December, Lyle announced that because we'd completed our new commitment and were washed clean and pure, Warren now commanded us to live the United Order.

A different story of destruction began to be preached. As recounted in Acts, Ananias and his wife, Sapphira, sold a piece of land. They gave the money to the church but kept some for themselves. After lying about it, both were struck dead. This story served as our constant reminder that anyone who held anything back from the Lord would face immediate and total annihilation.

The United Order became everything. All things belonged to God, and he could do anything he wanted with his possessions. We were instructed to make a list of everything we owned and consecrate it to Warren and the work of the Lord. I felt so anxious to get back into good graces that I had my family do a painstakingly thorough inventory of our home, even every pencil we owned. I inventoried my trucks and equipment, valued at around two hundred and fifty thousand dollars.

After church each week, we'd go up and shake hands with all the influential men. On the last Sunday of 2009, I brought a large folder containing my inventory list and the titles to my trucks and equipment. I walked up to Lyle and handed him my folder.

"Lyle, I give you my all. This is everything I own."

I felt elated. I truly hoped that now I could fully rejoin the church and be with my family forever.

A FEW DAYS LATER, I GOT A CALL FROM A MEMBER OF LYLE'S GOD Squad. "We can't find your titles. Did you turn them in?"

"Yes, I gave everything to Lyle."

"Okay, we'll keep looking."

After church the next week, I went up to shake Lyle's hand. I asked if he'd found the titles. He said no. I reminded him that I'd personally given him the titles. He said he remembered, but he didn't say anything else to comfort me. I had a gut-wrenching feeling.

Fifteen minutes later, after I'd arrived home, Lyle called. He said I needed to come back to the meetinghouse and meet with Adrian Morgan. As I walked down the short passage to the leadership offices, twelve men stood along both sides. Forming a human hallway, they gave me ominous stares.

When I passed the head of security, he shook my hand. "Dear Brother Wallace, I love you and bless you."

Inside the office, Lyle and Adrian shook my hand, and then Lyle left.

"I have a revelation from Warren," Adrian said. "I'm going to read it to you."

Adrian held a stapled document of about five pages. He began reading, but he flipped back and forth between pages instead of reading from start to finish. I couldn't understand what he was doing.

"The Lord has found you wanting," he read at one point. "You are not giving your all. You are commanded to leave your family. You are to leave priesthood lands. You must repent from a distance. You have not lost priesthood. You can come back once you repent."

Finally, after all my long years of wondering, Adrian told me what I'd done wrong. "The Lord says you are guilty of seeking your father's wives."

I thought, *Holy cow, that's the one thing I never confessed!* It had never entered my mind to go after any of my father's wives. I didn't even know most of them. It would have been a huge taboo, like marrying my own mother. The thought sickened me.

Adrian repeated that I needed to leave immediately. Wanting to read the entire revelation for myself, I asked for a copy. He told me to ask again later and he'd give me one.

I returned home, gathered my children, and told them the new revelation. I felt like this might be a new beginning, something I could do to finally make everything better. The revelation said Jessica and her children were to move into the house with Stacy's children, so Jessica could care for them. I hoped we'd all be reunited there soon.

I went to a hotel in Beaver, Utah, and wrote another confession to Warren. Although I'd never considered marrying any of my father's wives, I fully confessed to this sin. I sent the letter to the same post office box I'd used earlier to communicate with our prophet.

The next day, I called the children and asked how things were going. They said Jessica had not come. She refused to be with them. I wondered how this was possible. An FLDS cannot refuse a revelation and remain faithful. Refusing was grounds for expulsion. FLDS like Jessica survived by being like robots, never expressing opinions or showing any emotion except the false smiles of keeping sweet. Was she leaving the church?

Eventually, the kids learned that the church had moved Jessica back to Colorado.

A few days later, I called the FLDS office to see about getting a copy of the revelation, as Adrian had promised. "Adrian is a liar," Lyle said. "We never give copies of revelations to anyone."

Knowing I'd have to wait a while, I checked out of the motel and started living in my truck cab. After another week, Adrian called me from the YFZ Ranch on January 10, 2010.

"I have another revelation from Warren," Adrian told me. "The Lord God has judged you. You have no priesthood. You are to live your life in repentance, but you cannot be part of the priesthood people. You are never allowed to come back or have any contact with your family. You are now excommunicated."

Adrian and I had been good friends. I'd married his daughter Jessica. We often golfed together. But Adrian's voice was cold and emotionless as he delivered this pronouncement that would forever change my life.

Thinking about it later, I realized Adrian had lied when he first read me the revelation, flipping back and forth between the pages. They'd never intended to allow me back into the church. But they needed to lure me away from my family before they fully excommunicated me. They knew that if I'd known the truth, I would not have voluntarily left my children. Now it was too late because I couldn't physically enter the Crick again. Posted on the bluffs and plateaus in an eight-mile radius of the city were men with binoculars and cameras. As soon as they saw a questionable vehicle, God Squad members came in their trucks to follow and hassle it. If they saw me trying to enter the city, they would delay me while hiding my children. My only chance to ever see my kids again was to stay away, for now.

My last phone call with my family had taken place a week before my final excommunication. "Father, I love you," my adorable little granddaughter said. My grandchildren called me Father because I'd helped raise them after their father was cast out. "When are you coming back to get us?"

All these years later, I've never heard from most of my grandchildren again.

One week after telling me I was excommunicated, Adrian was cast out of the church. He would later receive an eight-year prison sentence but serve only eighteen months.

Chapter Twenty-Seven

False Prophet

I felt all was lost. My devastation after losing my family, church membership, and personal connections was indescribable. At this time, I didn't know the reality about Warren—I still honestly believed he was the true prophet. Of course, I felt increasing doubts, but I'd been taught since birth never to turn against the prophet.

I figured I had about one year left until the world ended and the Lord took me. I busied myself driving across the country, trying to think as little as possible. About three weeks after my excommunication, I received a call from my adult daughter Danielle.

"We need to know what's going on."

"What do you mean?" I asked.

Danielle explained that they'd been living all this time with no information. Lyle never told them anything—they hadn't heard from him since I'd been kicked out. Danielle expressed concern about their living situation. The family had recently received some food from the storehouse, but they didn't know how to pay the power bill, which was due soon.

Anger flooded through me. Why weren't they taking care of my children? They'd promised! I never would have left my children without knowing they'd be cared for while I repented. When I was permanently exiled, I was again told they'd be provided for. I suspected Adrian had never told Jessica about the revelation that she was supposed to care for my children. I believe they added it just to reassure me, so I'd leave peacefully.

I tried calling Lyle many times, but he refused to take my calls. Frantic about my family, I tried calling Adrian. His family said they'd been told to burn everything connected to him.

Lyle finally responded to my email. He agreed to talk to my family and make sure they were provided for. That was the last I ever heard from him.

Before long, Danielle called me again. Choking back tears, she said Lyle had visited the family and told them I'd been permanently exiled.

"Father, what did you do?"

I said I didn't know.

"I love you," she said before we hung up. "I'll take care of the children the best I can. I hope to see you again someday."

When I tried to check in with Danielle a week later, she didn't take my call.

In April 2010, I stopped at a California truck stop to fuel up. As I walked past the newspapers, I saw a picture of Warren kissing Merrianne. The headline stated, "Warren Jeffs Marrying Underage Girls," but the picture told me all I needed to know. At every one of his weddings, Warren would kiss his new bride while someone took a picture.

This was my first indication of what Warren was really doing. He'd truly married extremely young girls. I didn't know how to process this information. Father had spent his life telling us Warren was a pure man. I struggled against knowing the truth—it was extremely difficult to overcome a lifetime of teachings. I tried to put it on the shelf.

The two prophets before my father, Leroy S. Johnson and John Y. Barlow, had both married girls as young as twelve. But we'd always been told it was to remove them from abusive households or save them from fornication. No marital sex happened while they were young. It was just a preparation period.

I wanted to believe the same of Warren. The only reason he'd married Merrianne was to save her from falling into temptation. No way would he have sex with a twelve-year-old girl, especially not this one. Emotionally and physically, Merrianne seemed more like a nine-year-old.

Why, then, was Warren kissing her in the picture? It had to be fake.

In June 2010, I received a call from my friend Jacob Morton. He'd been kicked out of the church on the same day as me. He asked if I knew about Warren's confession. I'd heard rumors, but I told him no. He asked if I wanted to see the video recording. Chiding Jacob, I said I wanted nothing to do with it. I would remain loyal to Warren.

For the next two weeks, however, Jacob's invitation grated on my mind. We'd always been told that anything about Warren in the media was manufactured. But I was already excommunicated from the church, which meant I was going to hell. If I saw this confession, what could it hurt?

I finally called Jacob to apologize for being so rude. He accepted my apology and emailed me the link to Warren's confession. As I sat in my truck, I began watching it. The video had been taken three years earlier at the Purgatory Correctional Facility in Hurricane, Utah. Wearing a green-and-white-striped prison jumpsuit, Warren communicated with our brother Nephi via prison phone. I'd been expecting an imposter, but he acted and sounded exactly like Warren, speaking in the familiar, boring-as-hell monotone.

Internal warnings went off in my head. This was a real videotape! Lifelong instincts told me to immediately stop looking. But my thoughts answered, *I'm damned anyway. I can't go any farther down, so what the hell?*

I continued to listen and watch.

"I am not the prophet," Warren said. "I never was the prophet. I have been deceived by the powers of evil, and Brother William E. Jessop has been the prophet since Father's passing."

As Warren spoke, Nephi furiously scribbled. "The Lord came yesterday—no, two days ago—and bestowed upon me the gift to understand his words. Then he spoke to me, without the powers of evil interfering, so that I could—" Warren took the phone from his ear, as if listening, then continued, "—have this opportunity to undo what I have done. And, I ask for everyone's forgiveness and say farewell forever, you who are worthy for Zion, for I will not be there. The Lord has promised me that I would have a place in the telestial kingdom of God if I had my brother Nephi write these words down."

Warren paused a moment. "I am the greatest deceiver since the days of Adam. I have also been immoral with a sister and daughter." He had to catch his breath before he could continue. "The Lord told me if I would confess to the church and the world, I would be saved. Last night Satan appeared to me as an angel of light, but at this time, right now, God is speaking through me."

Throughout the confession, Warren cried. He seemed genuinely stricken and humble. Nephi assured him, "We love you. This is a test. You are the prophet—"

"Just a minute," Warren interrupted, "the Lord is still dictating. This is not a test. This is a revelation from the Lord God of Heaven, through his former servant, who was never his servant, who is dictating these words at this time. That you may know this is not a test."

Warren admonished Nephi to get a copy of the tape from the jail and make it available to all people, "even apostates and Gentiles." He concluded barely audibly, "I say farewell again, to all who qualify for Zion. Farewell."

Even after Warren left, Nephi blurted into the phone, "We love you. We love you. We love you." He kept the phone to his ear, but eventually he hung up. Breathing hard, he reread the confession he'd just transcribed. He finally stood up, wiped his eyes, and leaned against the wall, his hands clasped as though in prayer.

Meanwhile, Warren returned to his cell and attempted suicide by hanging himself. Later, he threw himself against his cell walls and rammed his head into them, until he was tranquilized.

MY INITIAL REACTION TO THIS CONFESSION WAS COMPLETE SHOCK. I watched it repeatedly, trying to wrap my brain around it. When I finally accepted its truthfulness, I was filled with a mixture of relief and pain. I'd been right all these years! Why had I doubted myself? I'd given everything for this man, and he was a liar. Knowing I'd lived a lie was bad, but knowing I'd perpetuated this lie in my family was worse.

My next thought was, *How am I going to get this information to my family?* I assumed that since Warren had commanded Nephi to make the recording public, the church must have announced it. Since 2007 I'd been kicked out or hiding, so I hadn't heard the announcement. I called my family to see if they knew anything, but the phone numbers had been disconnected.

I called some friends in Short Creek who were still members of the FLDS Church but not particularly loyal. Sometimes they acted as moles for me, such as when I'd searched for Jessica and the children. But they'd never seen or heard about any confession video.

Apparently, the leaders had suppressed Warren's confession, even after Warren told them to make it known. What else were they keeping from us? How many lies had they told us over the years? I had to know.

I began looking for information about Warren and the church. I also started actively searching for my children, no longer trusting the church to take care of them. When I wasn't driving the truck, I studied everything I could find. A Texas man had posted some of Warren's dictations of priesthood records on the Internet. When I heard the tape of Merrianne's rape in the YFZ temple, my body and soul flooded with revulsion and sorrow for what she had to endure.

As I gained insight into what Warren had been doing, I felt more and more shocked. I resolved to save my kids from the abuses I learned about. In fact, I became so frantic with worry that I could hardly work, drive, sleep, or keep down food. I followed the FLDS story in the media. I tried contacting anyone I'd ever known, but no one else admitted hearing the confession.

OVER A FOUR-MONTH PERIOD, WARREN ACTUALLY CONFESSED THREE times. In addition to his videotaped confession at the Purgatory Correctional Facility, he tried to hand his written confession to a judge. He also audiotaped another confession for the people living on the YFZ Ranch, but it never reached them.

I later found out that two days before his Purgatory confession, Warren had received unsettling news from his lawyer. Because Warren was classified as a federal fugitive, all the terabytes of evidence against him would be made public, including the rape of Merrianne. Warren couldn't do anything to suppress the details of his deviant and perverted behavior. In my opinion, fear drove him to confess. No wonder he tried to kill himself.

After Warren's confessions, however, Merril Jessop called him, as documented in prison records. "We still believe in you!" Merril told him. "What have you done that's so bad? You are still our prophet." Then Warren found out the judge had ordered the tapes not to be made public, as they would unduly influence a jury. In response, Warren recanted his confession. He said he'd been testing the people to see if they'd stay loyal.

I lost any shred of respect I still held for Lyle and Merril. If they were good people, they would have shown the confession to the FLDS members, as Warren commanded. Yes, it would have rocked the foundation of their faith, but they had a right to know so they could make their own decisions. Instead, Lyle and Merril hid the truth because it would have exposed them, too. In my opinion, everyone who covers up for Warren is just as guilty as he is. To this day, the people of the FLDS Church still have not heard Warren's confession.

For me, realizing Warren was not a true prophet also raised doubts about earlier prophets. Even more painful than knowing the truth about Warren was knowing my own father perpetuated the deceit. I still have not come to terms with this.

Chapter Twenty-Eight

"I Am Smiling. Are You?"

After Warren's arrest in late August 2006, he was jailed in Las Vegas and then moved to Hurricane, Utah. While awaiting trial, he developed ulcers on his knees from praying for hours on his cell's cement floor. In court, he was convicted of two counts of felony rape as an accomplice. He'd committed these crimes by marrying fourteen-year-old Elissa Wall to her nineteen-year-old cousin.

Sentenced to two consecutive terms of five years to life, Warren was moved to the Utah State Prison near Salt Lake City, where Father had forbidden his beloved Warren ever to return, due to the city's impending destruction. After about six months, however, Warren's conviction was overturned. When the judge instructed the jury, he'd said that accessory to rape was the same as rape, which was not true under Utah law. The Utah Supreme Court decided the judge's confusing instructions had biased the jury.

Warren was then sent to Kingman, Arizona, where he was charged as an accomplice in four counts of sexual conduct with a minor. The state had spent years building the case, but the key witness decided not to testify. By this time, Warren had already served two years, which would have been his sentence if convicted. Arizona did not pursue further legal action.

Utah considered retrying Warren, until Attorney General Mark Shurtleff traveled to Texas and saw their evidence. The Utah judge had not allowed the tape of Merrianne's rape, but Texas could use it in court. With the stronger evidence in Texas, Utah decided to let Texas try Warren.

After Warren moved to Texas, I called the county sheriff and asked if I could speak to Warren. I wanted his help locating my children, and I wanted to hear his side of the story. Sheriff Dave Doran agreed. However, when he handed Warren the phone through the prison bars, Warren hung up on me. If he'd taken my call, my subsequent course may well have been different.

My connection with Sheriff Doran led to my advising the Texas Rangers. I gave them information about Warren's character, what he was capable of, and what he would do in certain situations. I also worked with Warren's prosecutors. They asked what Warren would do when confronted with certain information, and they asked whether certain witnesses would be credible if called to testify. Warren's prosecutor subpoenaed all of Warren's wives, but they didn't show up for their depositions. He didn't prosecute them for failure to appear.

While I was in Texas, one of my Short Creek moles kept me informed. As we prepped for his trial, Warren was given phone privileges. He often called Short Creek to preach in meetings. He was generally limited to five minutes at a time, so he'd continually have to hang up and call back.

"Are you being a sweetener?" Warren asked during one of his phone sermons. "Are you sweetening other people?" I still laugh when I think about that.

As his trial neared, Warren requested that his court-appointed attorneys refute all evidence on the grounds of religious discrimination.

After the 1953 Short Creek raid, Uncle Roy had found something in the Arizona law against taking children and adopting them out without parental consent. He showed his attorneys, and they successfully used the law to argue that the raid had amounted to religious discrimination.

Warren's attorneys, however, said they needed to defend him on the merits of the case, or they would lose their licenses. They refused to follow Warren's religious discrimination strategy. The day before the trial started in July 2011, Warren fired his attorneys. They tried to convince him that they'd built a solid case and could get him cleared, but he refused to listen.

Judge Walther didn't want anything to go amiss with this trial. She forced the fired attorneys to sit and listen to the entire trial, in case Warren had any questions and needed their counsel. However, they would not be paid unless and until Warren rehired them.

The trial lasted two weeks. I was there for every minute of it.

During the trial, Warren continued to phone in to Short Creek meetings. "I am smiling," he would say to the people. "Are you?" Lyle was the only FLDS member Warren authorized in the courtroom. In his reports to the church, Lyle dutifully depicted the prophet as smiling and happy—always keeping sweet, as he commanded the people to do.

However, it was all a lie. I hadn't seen my brother in five years, and his behavior surprised me. He was argumentative and openly defiant, sometimes rebuking the court in the name of Christ. Other times, he would sit with a blank, almost catatonic look on his face. Warren acted like he was above Judge Barbara Walther. She suffered a limp from childhood polio, and he told her God would soon send her a crippling disease and end her life. She put him down whenever he ranted, but she never held him in contempt of court.

When court recessed one day, Lyle stood at the door and handed every person a written warning that they should not come to court the next day. Warren had received a revelation that the walls would come crumbling down and everyone would die.

I believe Warren was bored in prison, and the trial let him show off his self-righteousness and indignation. I never saw him smile once.

During the trial, the prosecution played an audiotaped heavenly session. The witnessing wife had been one of Father's favorites before Warren married her. She was beautiful and highly sexual. As a child, she'd been sexually abused by a brother, and both Father and Warren knew about it.

Near the end of the recording, Warren asks the wife to describe what happened.

"You were lying there peaceful," she begins in a soft, sweet voice. "Then you started to shake and contort. Then you started screaming, 'Oh, my God, what are you going to do? I can't do this. Why do you have to do this to me?' Then you said, 'Thy will be done.'"

After a few moments of silence, the wife continues, "Oh, my dear, beloved Warren. You suffered so greatly. I saw God take you. I'm so sorry. I give my life to you."

Soon the wife starts panting. "You are so beautiful," Warren tells her. "You turn me on so much."

Sex commences with much moaning, groaning, and panting. The wife is extremely vocal—we could hear everything in graphic detail. The recording ends with Warren and the wife experiencing loud climaxes.

In the courtroom, the audience remained silent. Sensing we all probably needed a breather, the judge called for a recess. The bailiff instructed all to rise.

"I can't," a news reporter shouted. "I've got a boner!"

As Warren tried to justify himself, I sensed he knew he was in the wrong. He did little in his own defense. He lamely cross-examined a few of the prosecution's witnesses. He called only two witnesses and basically asked them to give their opinions about various scriptures.

During closing arguments, the judge gave Warren his allotted thirty minutes. But he just stood there and said nothing. The judge counted down the minutes. "You have twenty more minutes, Mr. Jeffs." "You have ten more minutes." With about five minutes left, Warren said, "I am at peace."

When the sentencing phase began, Warren chose to leave the courtroom, probably to avoid hearing what people said about him. But he didn't want his court-appointed attorneys—who still sat waiting—to take over. The judge informed him that some type of counsel must be present. So, he allowed the court-appointed attorneys to take over, and he left the room.

On August 10, 2011, justice was handed down for many sexually tormented young girls and women. Warren was sentenced to life in prison plus twenty years for sexually assaulting two girls he claimed were his spiritual wives.

It seems to me that Warren gave up. I think he wanted to be in prison—I think he's happier there. He didn't file for an appeal, so now he has no chance of appeal.

In prison, Warren often stands for hours lost in his own world, almost like an autistic individual. A Texas jailer told me that, when Warren is awake, he masturbates every forty-five minutes, right in front of the guards. It's as if he's saying, "Look what I can do, and my people still love me." They've tried putting him in a straitjacket to get him to stop.

I believe Warren is the evilest man on Earth. Even in prison, I think he constantly asks himself, "How much can I get away with, and for how long?" Jail suits him well. He can be the crud that he is and still run the FLDS Church as its revered prophet. Because they're not allowed to watch or listen to any media reports, the FLDS people are kept from the truth.

In November 2011, Merrianne's father, Merril, finally went to trial. In my view, he's the lowest form of cowardly scum. He delivered his twelve-year-old daughter to Warren so he wouldn't be cast out and lose his position, money, and family. People say Merrianne married Warren willingly, but how could a twelve-year-old make such a decision? If she was a willing participant in the temple, why did Warren tie her down?

For marrying Merrianne to Warren, Merril received the maximum possible sentence: ten years and a ten-thousand-dollar fine. I felt glad about this small justice for Merrianne, but then Merril got early parole after serving less than four years.

Chapter Twenty-Nine

Moving Against Evil

According to my Short Creek source, Lyle posed an alarming question during a general church meeting: "How do you know Warren can't direct celestial marriages through me?"

If Warren passed his priesthood keys to Lyle, celestial marriages would begin again, fast and furious. Like Warren, other men in the church had been marrying younger wives—some had even been charged for it. My seven precious, young daughters could become prime targets. It terrified me not knowing where my daughters were or what was happening to them.

I had to save my children. I had to do something—no one else was going to. When I was young, I took an oath to protect the virtue of my sisters and all women, and I still hold true to this oath. I could not stand by and see men prey upon another innocent girl to satisfy their sexual lust. There was nothing good or righteous about the Fullness of the Law of Sarah.

I knew I didn't have enough influence to take on the church myself. I wondered about Roger Hoole, an influential Utah lawyer who'd helped other former FLDS members score convictions against Warren. Warren and Lyle continually slandered Hoole as a sexually deviant man whose real purpose was to rape our girls.

With my lingering doubts from FLDS brainwashing, I found it difficult to consider trusting this man. But I believed I needed to at least check him out. I found Hoole's phone number but then spent many days contemplating my next step. This would be a turning point. Once I contacted Hoole, my children would say I'd turned traitor. I risked forever losing their love.

As I weighed what to do, I kept coming back to my disgust for Merrianne's parents and sisters. They'd refused to be her advocates. What kind of father would I be, knowing what I knew but doing nothing, hoping others would challenge Warren?

Nothing meant more to me than my children's love. However, thinking of my girls getting raped felt worse than having my children hate me.

When I picked up the phone to call Roger Hoole, I knew my family would despise me.

"You're a Jeffs?" Roger asked.

"Yes."

"Lyle and Warren's brother? Why are you calling me?"

I explained how I'd been expelled and didn't know where my children were. I wanted to hear Roger's side of the story, and I hoped he could help me.

Roger didn't want to talk on the phone because Lyle was tapping phone lines. He said he'd think about it and get back to me.

AFTER I'D SPENT MANY DAYS IN FITFUL ANTICIPATION, ROGER FINALLY called me back. He wanted to meet me at the Matheson Courthouse in downtown Salt Lake City. I went through security and proceeded to the small room Roger had identified.

To calm my nerves, I took deep breaths. I expected Roger to be a wretched, dirty old man. But I'll never forget his warm smile and his round, burly physique. All my doubts fled. I immediately felt comfortable. I've never known someone with a calmer demeanor.

When I asked Roger why he requested we meet at the courthouse, he said he'd wanted me to go through security. Since I was Warren and Lyle's brother, he feared I'd been sent to kill him. But now that he'd seen my face, he knew that wasn't the case.

For an hour, I told Roger all about my dilemma with my family. He remained guarded, as if he didn't know what to think. He said he needed to further ponder the situation.

About two weeks later, we met again. Roger suggested the only way I could find my children was to force Lyle, Adrian, and Merril out of hiding by filing a lawsuit alleging fraud. We would base our case on Warren's voluntary testimony that he was not the prophet. Though Adrian had been excommunicated, he was still Jessica's father, and we hoped drawing him out would bring Jessica and my children out of hiding as well.

We spent several months preparing the lawsuit. We filed it in July 2011, right before I went back to Texas for Warren's trial. Because I was still legally married to Jessica, I couldn't claim custody of our children. But my divorce from Stacy had given me full custody of our children. Three of them were still underage, all daughters.

The hardest part of this plan was serving the papers. Warren was in prison, so he was easy, but Adrian, Lyle, and Merril were all deep in hiding.

However, we had a secret weapon.

Roger had helped a boy who'd lived with Lyle and eventually left the church. The boy's mother still lived in Lyle's home in Short Creek. Roger asked the boy if he would visit his mother and serve her the papers. Legally, if you serve an adult member of the household, you have served the recipient.

Amazingly, the boy agreed.

IN MID-AUGUST 2011, RIGHT AFTER I RETURNED HOME FROM WARREN'S trial, Roger, the boy, and I drove separate vehicles down to Short Creek. The God Squad knew our cars, so we all borrowed cars from people who weren't on the FLDS radar. We left from different locations, and we met in a designated place in the Crick. In addition, we'd hired a private investigator to help us.

From a nearby hill, we used binoculars to survey Lyle's home. Fences as high as twelve feet surrounded the property, with guards at every gate. However, the boy knew about a backyard gate often left unattended. As we looked closer, we realized this gate was indeed unlocked and unmanned. The boy bolted down the hill, ran through the back gate, and knocked on a door.

To my surprise, one of my own daughters let him into the house, no doubt assuming he was visiting his mother. A few minutes later, his mother chased him out. We could hear her screaming at him. When the boy rejoined us, he told us he'd served the papers to one of Lyle's adult daughters.

The papers gave Lyle twenty days to answer. If he didn't, he would be called for a deposition or a warrant would be issued for his arrest.

One week later, Jessica called me, annoyed. "What are you doing?"

"I want to see the children."

"Not until the court forces me," she replied.

"Okay, have it your way."

I didn't know where my underage daughters with Stacy were, but I assumed they were at Lyle's house. To help me regain custody, a convoy of ten police cars and five FBI cars drove with me up to Lyle's property. As we approached, my mind kept flipping between worry and fear. I wasn't concerned about the church or the God Squad, except that they might run off with my daughters before I could take custody of them. My biggest concern was how my kids would react. Would they give me the silent treatment, or would they scream at me?

An FBI agent accompanied me to the front gate and asked where Lyle was. The guard said he didn't know. When I asked where my daughters were, he said he didn't know that either. The agent told the guard that if the children were not produced, the FBI would go through every home in the Crick to find them. We felt confident this threat would work—no way would Lyle let the FBI go into everyone's home.

A few minutes later, two of my sons drove up. They started angrily questioning my motives. I felt sad to see them so furious, but I was not surprised.

Once my sons saw that anger wouldn't work, they begged me to reconsider.

"Lyle is not the father of my children," I replied. "I am taking them."

One son asked, "What can we do to make you stop?"

"There's nothing you can do. You need to bring my daughters to me right now."

I gave them one hour until we started searching the other homes. Thirty minutes later, my phone rang. The caller told me to go to the city park. When we arrived, the Short Creek town marshal drove up and asked me what was going on. This man was in Lyle's pocket, and I felt no respect for him whatsoever. I told him he knew exactly what was going on. He said I needed to produce the divorce decree, which I did.

The FLDS were doing everything I'd expected: stalling, claiming innocence, sending my sons to question me, and so forth. Nevertheless, I was now struggling to keep my frustration from showing. Staying calm, I reminded the marshal that soon we'd start searching all the homes. The FBI backed me up.

A half-hour later, a truck drove up with my three underage daughters. They were fourteen, sixteen, and seventeen. My heart skipped a beat, knowing this was the moment of truth. How bad was it going to be?

As I walked up to the truck, their voices burst out of the vehicle. "We hate you! We don't want to be with you! We want to stay with Uncle Lyle! You can't take us against our will! We will never love you again!"

My two sons watched, arms folded.

"I'm doing this for your own good," I said to the girls. "I know you don't understand."

Crying now, they refused to make eye contact. They kept saying they hated me. "You are not my father," one daughter said. "You have no right to do this."

One son demanded to see the document proving my rights. I showed him the divorce decree, and he stormed away.

The FBI had to physically remove the girls from the truck and put them in my Suburban. They sobbed as we drove to Mesquite, Nevada, where I'd arranged housing. Whenever I tried to speak, they put their hands over their ears.

Chapter Thirty

Betrayal

My son Luke joined us in Mesquite to help his three sisters. We tried to settle into a routine. Though the girls remained bitter toward me, Luke was able to care for them and keep them safe while I worked. This eased the transition for all of us into our new life together.

However, the FLDS Church still held Luke's loyalty. He'd been working toward getting accepted into the United Order, but his association with me put that on hold. As with many things in the church, the United Order was still evolving. I'd been required to inventory everything we possessed and consecrate it all to the church. Now members also had to give the bishop every paycheck they received, and the bishop gave them back what he felt they needed. They also had to promise never to speak with anyone outside the church.

Even though Luke was conflicted between the church and me, I always felt like he supported me. When the church kicked me out the first time, Luke was the child who took it hardest, not wanting to leave me. Though Luke's ultimate loyalty still seemed to lean toward Warren, the girls were tied to him, and I hoped my relationship with my son would pull the girls toward me.

I admired Luke for his selflessness. He sacrificed his personal desires and his membership in the United Order just to help his sisters. To me, he typified the greatest love one could have for another.

When I first moved to Mesquite, my friend Jacob Morton offered me a place to live. Jacob had been kicked out on the same day as me, and he was the one who'd told me about Warren's confession tape. I worked for Jacob's company servicing water conditioners, and I lived in his six-bedroom house. I offered each of my three daughters their own bedroom, but they refused—they wanted to room together.

My intent was to slowly ease my family away from the FLDS Church. They knew I'd filed a lawsuit against Warren, but I did not speak out openly against their prophet. I didn't want to further alienate them. I hoped we could get close again, like we once were. I hoped they would start asking questions and eventually figure things out on their own.

However, the girls kept their distance from me. Occasionally they relented and we'd go to the park to play Frisbee and football. But they refused to go anywhere else with me, even a simple dinner out. They completely shut me down when I offered them a fun trip to Las Vegas. In the past, we'd enjoyed going on rides together at places like the New York-New York Resort.

To help my girls feel comfortable, I joined them in their religious practices. I prayed with them daily, both morning and night. The church required members to read a sermon of Father's or Uncle Roy's morning and night, so I read the sermons with them. I allowed the girls to continue their homeschooling with the curriculum originally designed by Warren.

"I want to help you, not hurt you," I often told them. "There are things you don't understand, but hopefully one day you will."

When they lived in Short Creek, they'd had no computer. I left my computer on all day with the Internet open. Since they never went anywhere, I thought they might get bored and start poking around. But they didn't touch the computer. They spent their days mostly in the backyard pool I'd installed.

My daughters never did open up to me. They treated me like I was the devil. I would come home in the evening hoping to play foosball, air hockey, or pool with them. When I walked through the door, I would go wherever I heard their voices so I could be with them. But more often than not, they would immediately disperse.

Luke made halfhearted efforts to help. From the way he'd initially spoken, I felt a glimmer of hope that his mind could be opened. However, Luke didn't dare delve into the complexities of my excommunication or the truth of the FLDS religion.

To my delight, three of my married sons often came over to visit my daughters. I enjoyed reestablishing our relationships. Not only did I appreciate getting close to them, but I also hoped to keep them out of the United Order. Once they joined the Order, all relationships with me would be completely shut off forever. As with Luke, I felt touched that they were willing to delay their salvation to keep in contact with their sisters and me.

The boys offered me a sense of hope. I felt I could stick this out because I had nothing but time on my side. However, it was really only the beginning of the end.

THROUGH MY MOLES IN SHORT CREEK, I FOUND OUT THAT LYLE HAD become extremely angry with me. He openly told church members to think of me as a master deceiver and the worst enemy of the priesthood, because I influenced other exiled men to go after their children.

At first, I'd tried to persuade only Jacob Morton, but now I talked to every man who'd been kicked out, begging them to get their children at any cost. I left no doubt about the true danger for their children—particularly daughters—who lived in Short Creek.

Partially in response to my actions, Lyle sent this letter to the church membership:

> Dear people, our prophet is on the firing line. He is the One Man on earth that receives the word of God for us to be able to make the changes in our lives to justify His hand lest allow greater tribulation to further humble us. Let this people rally NOW for our Prophets delverance, by abiding his words for your very lifes sake. Loyalty to Priesthood by coming out of the world. Zions camp is being gathered. Choose to be chosen at this late hour.
>
> [sic] but only to those who stood up for him by living as they were taught. I pray for this people to be found acceptable to the Lord today, I pray in our character to enable us to be able to become like Him. God is fighting this battle, but is requiring the oneness and purity of His people to and principles. Perfection is the call. Purity is the standard that we must be to be Zion. No more half heartedness. Rally to the standard of Zion
>
> May the Lord now see He now has a pure and loyal Priesthood who will stand for His servant on earth at this critical hour. He will be delivered, in the name of Jesus Christ. Amen
>
> Uncle Lyle

My sources also reported that Lyle and Warren had begun saying they'd do whatever was necessary to stop my vocal opposition. I was their greatest enemy and threat to their mission.

I became aware that I was being followed. When I made phone calls, I could hear clicking and static, and I experienced delays. Later, my girls admitted that Lyle had told them about a tap on my phone.

Luke began spying on me and reporting back to Lyle where I was going and what I was doing. My heart sank, but I made sure Luke didn't know everything. He didn't realize I was in constant contact with the FBI and also speaking to Arizona and Utah authorities. Sadly, after that initial time when Luke had seemed to warm, he eventually became cold again.

I COULD SENSE SOMETHING BIG COMING, BUT I HAD NO IDEA WHAT. I kept my eyes open and waited.

I learned that Jessica had returned to Short Creek, but she no longer lived with Lyle. I often traveled to the Crick to spy on her house, hoping for a glimpse of my children. A member of Lyle's God Squad would always alert the powers-that-be when I approached priesthood land.

My every action felt scrutinized. I could feel Lyle's and Warren's presence everywhere I went. But I still hoped that eventually at least my sons would leave the FLDS community. If my prayers were somehow answered, I wanted to provide a way for my boys to support their families. So, I worked hard at growing my trucking business. I traveled to Vegas to purchase trucks and trailers so my sons could step right in once they turned away from the FLDS.

IN SEPTEMBER OR EARLY OCTOBER 2011, JACOB FILED THE SAME LAWsuit to regain his family that I had. I hoped this added to Lyle and Warren's angst.

Before the church kicked me out, I was close with Jacob's family, including his beautiful twin daughters. Warren had said these sisters were chosen to marry a special man. They knew they'd already been secretly promised in marriage, but they did not know to whom.

One twin fell in love with my son Luke. I knew Luke was getting attached to this girl, and I secretly supported them. But then Lyle Jeffs caught Luke texting this girl. Worried about the girl's promised placement, Lyle called me in to discuss the situation. I didn't want to get cast out, so I agreed the budding relationship was wrong. I told Lyle I would take care of it.

When I spoke with Luke, I said I didn't believe he'd done anything wrong, but I asked him to be more careful. It was too late, however.

Everyone already thought my son was a terrible person for texting a girl. For a time, they ostracized him.

My relationship with Jacob's kids soured after he filed his lawsuit. My friends in the Crick confided that his children blamed me. With so much preaching about the United Order, these twin girls wanted to qualify for it. As their ticket to salvation, they became vocal against me. Though I'd been outside the church for only just over a year, suddenly I had few friends left in Short Creek.

AFTER I FILED MY LAWSUIT, PEOPLE STARTED ASKING ME ABOUT WARren's younger years and if he'd committed any sins against little girls. I'd promised my mother that I would never reveal Warren's molestation of Vanessa twenty years earlier, but I decided I would no longer cover Warren's sins.

I began telling a few people what had happened to my sister. Jacob asked me to tell his daughters. After I told the twins, one twin went to Mother to see if what I'd reported was true. At that time, Mother still lived in the Crick, but she was completing a repentance mission because the FLDS had kicked her out. The twin came back to me and sternly chastened me. She said Mother told her I'd made up everything out of anger to scare people away from Warren.

My own mother had called me a liar. That cut me to the bone—I'd never knowingly or maliciously lied to anyone. After she called me a liar, family members refused to believe me. To make matters worse, the twin went directly to my sister, and Vanessa agreed I'd made up the incident with Warren.

I knew it was FLDS brainwashing, but I still couldn't believe it. Not only was my credibility shot, but I began feeling like I'd truly and finally lost everything. Mother and I had never been close, but I'd hoped we shared some kind of mother-son bond. I'd honestly believed my mother would stay loyal to me, but her loyalty to Warren was more important than the truth offered by her own son. Ever since the church first kicked me out, Mother had believed I was apostate and evil.

The last time I saw my mother was in October 2009. Serving the FLDS as a midwife, she'd saved the lives of many women and children. In 2010, however, the church permanently excommunicated her for administering birth control to women who needed it for health reasons. The church viewed birth control as a form of murder. Not only did they kick out men and women who used birth control or had sex during pregnancy, but they'd even expelled women who miscarried their unborn child.

I doubt I'll ever see my mother again, and I've accepted this.

As I soul-searched, my conscience remained clear. My only purpose in fighting Warren was to alert people and help save children. With nothing left to lose, I strengthened my resolve. Regardless of the consequences, I was going to keep telling people the truth. It's hard to describe, but I felt a strong burning inside of me. I would not be guilty of withholding what I knew and what I'd seen. Warren's victims needed a voice.

I wanted to help FLDS fathers be men, stand up to Warren, and protect their children. I began telling my few remaining friends in the Crick that they had to get their children away from Warren, no matter what it took. But nearly all of them resisted, saying that Lyle and Warren would never do anything to harm their children. They trusted their prophet and bishop. I was a boat rocker, a jaded man who wanted to hurt my brother.

A few listened, however. One of my Crick friends was not allowed to see his children because his wife had been reassigned to another man. He filed a lawsuit demanding visitation with his children, and eventually he got full custody. In subsequent years, more men filed lawsuits to get their children back.

A pit opens in my stomach whenever I think that, even today, FLDS people still think their children are safe. To maintain his reign as prophet, all Warren needs to do is control the children. No wonder he and Lyle have kicked out so many adults.

Normally, Warren and Lyle did everything on a timeline of only one year, because the world was going to end. However, I heard that Lyle had begun gathering millions of dollars, paying cash for RVs valued at over seven hundred thousand dollars, and secretly buying homes under other people's names. He appeared desperate to prepare in case he and Warren lost control and the FLDS crumbled, instead of the world.

Outside Jacob's house, I started noticing a truck parked off to the side. The God Squad was careful when watching me, but they also made sure I knew I was being watched. I felt uneasy, almost paranoid. The feeling that something bad would happen soon continued to grow within me.

My moles confirmed that something huge was on the horizon, but they weren't sure what.

I kept looking over my shoulder but didn't otherwise try to protect myself. Sure enough, in late October 2011, my so-called accident put me into a forty-five-day coma.

Based on evidence and witness reports, I believe Warren and Lyle, my half-brothers, ordered the tampering on my car. It's no coincidence that on the night of my accident, Lyle commanded my sons Seth and Jeremiah to go to Mesquite and gather up my daughters and confiscate all my property, including my vehicles and computers. They also came to the hospital and took my phone, which was full of evidence against my brothers.

They wanted me permanently silenced, but I survived.

Chapter Thirty-One

My Children Begin to Escape

After my release from the hospital, I went back to living in Jacob's home. I couldn't walk more than a hundred yards without getting completely exhausted. When I shopped for groceries, I had to use an electric cart.

I applied for temporary disability income, but I was denied because I could do sales work on the phone while my broken leg healed. I tried to find a rent-free home in the Crick, but nothing became available. In St. George and Hurricane, I searched for work that was not physically taxing, but I found nothing.

This was a time of intense isolation for me. My boys had delivered my possessions to Lyle. My cars, motorcycles, trucks, boats, and other vehicles were now hidden away from me. After two months of calling, I managed to catch my son Seth by surprise. I asked him where my things were, but he gave me only a vague answer.

When I pressed, Seth confessed that Stacy was using my Volkswagen Jetta. She'd been accepted back into the community as a mother, but she was not reinstated in the church. I didn't mind Stacy using my car, but I told Seth that I needed the rest of my belongings. He agreed to bring them to me, but then he went incommunicado again. I couldn't figure out why he wasn't doing what he'd said he'd do. He'd always been so responsible.

I contacted my moles in Short Creek. They said Lyle was telling my family and the community that I'd been branded by God, and it was just a matter of time until I died. No wonder Seth wasn't responsive.

Before I was kicked out of the church, I'd owned a company called Phaze Auto Yard. My son Jeremiah was now running this business. After much time and effort, I found out that my sons had parked several of my vehicles in Jeremiah's auto yard, including two Corvettes, a Jeep, a boat, and the two trailers Stacy and I had lived in before I moved to Colorado. Over the next few weeks, I constantly nagged and threatened to do whatever it took to get back my property. Finally, Jeremiah started bringing my vehicles to me.

As I tried to recuperate, I suffered an embolism and then a kidney stone. My doctor expressed concern about my ongoing physical condition. These problems might be only the beginning of recurring health issues. At age fifty-one, I tried to face the fact that I'd never be physically normal again. I might be sickly for the rest of my life.

A sense of depression settled over me. If I was going to be an invalid, I didn't want to live anymore. But thoughts of my children kept pressing on my mind. I wanted them back. However, I wondered who would be their mother. For the first time in my life, I felt no desire for a relationship with a woman. After the damage caused by the accident, I didn't even know if I could be physically intimate again. I had no means or energy to do anything. Why would any woman want to be with me? How could I take care of a family?

Determined to beat my dismal prognosis, I began pushing my body to heal and become strong. I kept trying to contact my kids in the Crick, where I knew they lived with my sons Seth and Jeremiah. Occasionally I spoke with a child, but Jessica was afraid to talk to me because she was still loyal to Warren and Lyle. I made sure the FLDS leaders knew that I knew where my kids were. I started looking for a place away from Short Creek. If any of my children saw the light and left the FLDS Church, I wanted to provide them with a refuge from the inevitable shunning.

Around this time, William E. Jessop tried to take over the FLDS Church. He'd seen the video in which Warren declared himself a false prophet and named William as the true prophet. Using this recording as evidence, William petitioned the State of Utah to become president of the FLDS corporation. However, he did not succeed.

Some FLDS believed that when my father ordained William as bishop, he'd also ordained him an apostle and given him all the priesthood keys. If this claim were true, William would have been the only apostle ever ordained by my father, which would have made him the rightful next prophet. However, there was no record of such an ordination. When I asked William, he admitted he had no recollection of it happening.

My housemate Jacob was loyal to William's new church, and I attended a few times. After surviving my accident despite the prophecies against me, I'd regained some community status. Several FLDS declared that whichever leader I chose to follow, they would follow as well. So, when I decided the William situation stank and removed myself from the controversy, some people got mad at me. At the same time, I worked hard to avoid getting pulled into the ex-FLDS group, which caused me further ostracism.

Two of my grown sons, Sterling and Casey, lived together in Salt Lake City. In June 2012, I received an emergency call from Casey. They'd been riding four-wheelers at the sand dunes, and a motorcyclist had launched over a dune and landed on Sterling's head. Airlifted to a Salt Lake hospital, Sterling was now in a medically induced coma with his head and neck in a halo.

I immediately picked up Sterling's mother, Stacy, and drove to Salt Lake. The doctors told us Sterling would probably suffer permanent brain damage. I arranged a place for Stacy so she could stay near Sterling. Then I returned home to keep my own doctor appointments. I followed Sterling's progress via phone, and I travelled to Salt Lake every other week to visit.

Around this time, I received a call from my daughter Constance. My children all knew I'd begun a fight against Warren. When Constance said she wanted to leave the FLDS and come live with me, I was elated. Unfortunately, I soon realized she had ulterior motives.

Constance had connected with a boy. She wanted freedom to meet up with him whenever she liked. He was a jerk, but she loved him. I hated him. As soon as she arrived, she also became a big partyer. This was typical of children who left the FLDS. Once freed from so many restrictions, they wanted to experience everything they'd been denied.

Two days after Constance arrived at my house, I got a call from Jessica. "Do you know where Constance is?" she asked.

"She's with me," I said. "If you were worried, why'd you wait two days to call?"

"You know why. I can't talk to you."

This was typical of how well Jessica and I communicated.

Constance began sneaking out all the time. I made sure she knew I didn't approve. I suppose my wording could have been better, but I was so worried about her ruining her life that I couldn't keep my mouth shut. As she continued to ignore my wishes, a rift grew between us. Eventually, I felt I needed to get a restraining order against Constance's boyfriend. She was furious. I pled with her to do something with her life, to get an education and become a productive citizen. However, she ignored me. Before long, she met another guy.

I was in a tough place. How hard could I push Constance without going too far? When I had all my children, we were such a happy family. We didn't fight. But now I was at a loss. I loved my daughter and wanted only the best for her. How could she not see the mistakes she was making? I would lie awake in bed, worried sick over her, trying to come up with a solution that we could both live with.

Sadly, none of my efforts paid off. After staying with me just shy of two months, Constance went back to Jessica.

Sterling spent two months in the hospital, finally returning home in August 2012. He healed well except for some minor brain damage. Around this time, I found out four of my children had decided to leave the FLDS Church. They were in their late teens and early twenties. After Warren's revelation that all FLDS marriages were null and void, these children saw no future or family in the FLDS Church. With so many strange revelations coming out, they weren't the only ones questioning where the church was going.

I decided to see if my four kids and I could live with Sterling and Casey in Salt Lake City. I wanted to get my kids away from the Short Creek influence, and we could help with Sterling's recovery. Casey agreed to let us all move in. My kids kept their plans secret so Lyle wouldn't try to talk them out of it. One night, they snuck out and drove north. At the last moment, one daughter decided not to go.

When Constance joined us in Salt Lake, I now had six of my children with me. However, even though the children had left the church, they were still loyal to Warren. I tried tactfully discussing Warren with these kids, but they would run away. On the few occasions we exchanged words, it soon turned into fighting. Sterling finally informed me that if I didn't stop saying bad things about Warren, they would make me move out.

Shifting tactics, I began talking to my children about getting an education. For my entire life, I'd desperately wanted to go to college, to improve myself and become a better provider. But I'd been forbidden a college education. I wanted my children to have a better life than me. I cannot describe the guilt I still feel for perpetuating the lies I grew up with and instilling false doctrines into my children. However, even when I kept things positive and emphasized education, my children didn't trust me.

Except for my son Luke, my kids just wanted to party. They did little but hang out and drink with their new friends. One daughter would go party all night, come home sick, sleep all day, and then get up about four o'clock to go out again. When they held weekend parties at our house, I would leave.

I finally decided that if my children didn't want to be with me and do something with their lives, I would create a life of my own without them, mostly to show them it's possible. Today, I enjoy getting together with some of my twenty children and their children. Others remain in the FLDS Church, however, and I have no contact with them. I don't even know the names of several of my grandchildren.

My children are my world. I will move heaven and earth to return to the loving relationship we once had. It will not happen overnight, but it will happen.

Chapter Thirty-Two

True Love

IN 2011, I FILED TO GET EMERGENCY CUSTODY OF JESSICA'S THREE minor children, who were in hiding with the church. In an incredible breach of ethics, the FLDS attorney sent a personal letter to the judge saying he was too busy to work on the case right now, and so the judge did not rule. Then Jessica filed for divorce to delay the hearing, and my accident postponed it even more.

Jessica's attorney knew he'd always eventually lose his FLDS custody cases, but he did everything he could to stretch them out. He told Jessica to claim she'd left the church, which prevented me from saying my children were in immediate danger. However, Jessica never spoke out against Warren. I don't believe that, in her heart, she actually left the church. But it was an excellent delaying tactic. Eventually, she retracted the suit and refused to communicate with me.

In September 2012, I started thinking about relationships. I was still legally married to Jessica, but we'd been separated for five years and she'd filed for divorce, so I felt single. I'd always been faithful to the FLDS Church and lived by its marriage placement principle, but now I wanted to show my children that they could choose their own mate. It was not okay for Warren or any man to say, "I stand between you and God." I felt rejuvenated—now that I was free of all FLDS governing, I could date who I wanted.

I started a new job with the National Federation of Independent Businesses, selling memberships door to door. My ankle was still weak, but my strength improved every day. As I worked, I had to overcome my religious fears about communicating with women. If an FLDS man was caught alone with a female who wasn't his wife—including texting her—he was considered a sinner. Warren instructed that we could never look below a nonwife's chin or into her eyes. If we needed to talk to a woman, we stared at her forehead.

At first, I felt like I was doing something wrong whenever I talked to a woman. It was exciting, but I felt awkward and guarded, and the women could sense my discomfort. With practice, I learned how to talk and flirt with them. I started looking at women differently, thinking *wow*. A few women even asked me out. At age fifty-one, I went on my first date.

DATING MADE ME FEEL AMAZINGLY FREE, BUT IT WAS ALSO SCARY. ONE woman I met online said she was five-foot-six with a "medium build." We arranged to meet at a local sports bar. Imagine my surprise when a five-foot-two, two-hundred-eighty-pound woman with two-inch-thick makeup showed up. It was the deception that bothered me. This kind of thing happened several times, and often the woman would ask for another date. I thought, *If this is what dating is like, kill me now.*

With other women, I faced other obstacles. Smiling and leaning forward, a woman would ask, "So, tell me how many children you have."

"Uh, twenty."

"You are hilarious! Seriously, how many kids do you have?"

"Um . . . twenty."

The woman would get a puzzled look. "How is that even possible?"

"Well, I was a polygamist. But let's emphasize the word *was*."

The woman would soon find an excuse to cut our date short.

As much as I disliked disingenuous people, I started massaging my own personal information. Instead of introducing myself as Wallace Jeffs, I would say my name was Wally without giving my last name. If a woman asked, I would say I had eight children, which was true—I just didn't mention my other twelve. After a first date, if it seemed like things could move ahead, I'd immediately come clean about my situation. Needless to say, I didn't get a lot of second dates.

Eventually I met a nice Filipino lady. I told her everything, and it didn't seem to bother her. Our relationship was comfortable. Once, she invited me to watch a boxing match at her friend's house. I enjoyed the feeling of acceptance. But one evening, I had to cancel a date so I could attend an urgent business meeting. She completely flipped out, saying I'd made it up because I didn't really like her. I said we could go out the next evening, but she continued to be irrational. Confused, I decided to let her make the next move. She never called me again.

I began thinking maybe I could never seriously date anyone because I was too weird. The reality of who I'd been was too much for women. I wished I could be honest about my past and still find someone who could love me for who I'd become.

Then I met Katherine in passing at a restaurant. As we texted, she asked the inevitable question about how many kids I had. I answered eight, and I added that I needed to tell her more about it.

When we met for our first date, I was ready to tell Katherine everything, but she shied away. She wouldn't ask any questions about my past family situation—it was like she didn't want to know. She said she just wanted to get to know me for who I was today. She could find out the rest later.

We really hit it off, and we dated for several weeks. Finally, Katherine said she was ready to hear everything. I told her to Google me, and then we would talk.

The next day, she texted me: *WOW!*

Feeling nervous, I asked what she thought. She said it weirded her out, but she wanted to hear my explanation. The next time we got together, I laid it all out for her, who I'd been and who I was now.

To my relief, Katherine said she didn't care about my past. Things quickly became more serious, and we began spending all our time together. For the first time in my life, I was falling in love with a woman of my own choosing. It was the greatest feeling! I didn't have to ask anyone for permission to be with her. I didn't have to worry that the church would take her away from me.

Katherine had been married twice before. Her first husband died young, and an eighteen-year marriage had ended in divorce. Katherine knew I was still married. She asked me what my intentions were.

The next time I saw her, I brought a ring. I knelt down and asked, "Will you marry me after I'm divorced?" She said yes. She said I was the love of her life, the best man she'd ever known. For the first time ever, a woman loved me just for me, not because a prophet assigned her to me. This felt almost miraculous.

OVER THE NEXT SIX MONTHS, KATHERINE AND I SPENT EVERY MOMENT we could with each other. I met her children, and she met mine. I loved her youngest son who still lived with her, and my kids liked Katherine. I felt free of friction and lies. I honestly believed our relationship was what heaven would be like.

One morning while I was at work, Katherine and I were texting back and forth. At about eleven, however, she stopped responding. I continued to text, but she wouldn't reply. A dark pit formed in my gut. I knew something was wrong.

When I got off work, I texted Katherine that I was heading to her apartment and hoped she'd be home. I received the reply we all dread: *I'm here. We need to talk.* She told me to drive to her place but not to come up.

At Katherine's, I saw some people on her balcony who I didn't recognize. When Katherine came out, I could tell by her body language that it wasn't good. As I stood below, she told me she'd spent the day with her brother, her sister, and her boss, who was a friend of the family. The three of them had looked into my past, and they suspected I wanted to trap her in polygamy. They all agreed our relationship had to end.

"None of that is true," I said to Katherine, as the three stood silently by her side. "Why would you ruin your life because of them?"

"I know you're a good man," she said. "I don't believe them. But my family won't accept me if I stay with you."

"Are you going to live your life through them?"

"They've always been there for me. Please never contact me again."

Crying, Katherine ran back into her apartment.

THAT EVENING, I FELT THAT I NEEDED TO APOLOGIZE TO KATHERINE. I poured my feelings into an email. I said I was sorry if I'd put her in a compromising position with her family. There were no bad feelings, and I would always love her.

After sending my email, I couldn't sleep. I paced and tinkered around my house until the early morning hours.

Then, surprisingly, Katherine replied: *I love you. I can't live without you. You are the best man I've ever known. Please come back.*

So, I went back. I felt a bit gun-shy, but we enjoyed several more weeks of bliss.

One day, Katherine's sister friended me on Facebook. Feeling a little concerned, I accepted the request. The sister immediately private-messaged me. She claimed she was an open and caring person, but I was the worst man on Earth. I needed to leave her sister alone or suffer the consequences. Katherine's family would never accept me. They would do whatever they could to stop me from ruining their sister's life.

I called Katherine. She admitted she knew about the message. "They will never accept you," she said. "I can't see you again. You should go back to the FLDS and lead the people."

"I don't want to lead the people," I said. "I just want you."

She hung up. I never heard from her again.

At that point, I gave up on finding a relationship. The FLDS had always said the outside world would never accept us because we were too different—and for once, I had to agree with them. I tried to accept that I'd be a bachelor for the rest of my life.

As the weeks passed, I didn't eat or sleep much. My kids tried their best to buoy me up. About a month after the breakup, I started working at a car dealership in June 2013. I spent as much time there as I could. Many kind people listened to my problems. I was a fifty-one-year-old man facing what most people endured in their teens and twenties.

Weeks turned into years.

IN JULY 2016, FACEBOOK SUGGESTED I BECOME FRIENDS WITH A woman named Spring. When I saw how many connections we had in common, I sent her a friend request. Spring didn't respond immediately, but before long we were chatting online. Then we started speaking on the phone. I asked her on a date. Within moments of meeting her in person, I knew she was my soulmate.

We found it odd that, although we ran in the same networking circles, we hadn't recognized each other sooner. Spring had even been a guest speaker at a business function I'd attended. Just before she spoke, however, I'd stepped out to take a phone call, so I'd missed her. We wondered if divine intervention had put blinders on us so we didn't meet until the time was right.

When Spring first heard about my past polygamy, her inner reaction was, "Run like hell." But she realized I was a survivor. "I found it interesting that someone could live through such brainwashing and then awake to what's morally right," she says. "To fight against his own father, mother, and brother and follow his inner light of truth showed me how honorable and brave he is."

As a member of the mainstream LDS Church, Spring bore testimony to me of its truthfulness. When I started attending LDS meetings with her, I found the doctrine familiar and comfortable. My father, Rulon Jeffs, was originally LDS, and he'd taught me the LDS gospel. The FLDS believed essentially the same gospel, only with polygamy and a false prophet.

Rulon's first marriage had been with Zola Brown, daughter of high-ranking LDS apostle Hugh B. Brown. Little did the Browns know, Rulon's dad was living polygamy in secret. Eventually, he convinced Rulon to start attending polygamist meetings. In the 1940s, Rulon told Zola he was taking another wife. According to my dad, Elder Brown told him that if he'd stop seeking after polygamy, he would probably become an LDS apostle. He might even eventually become president of the LDS Church. However, Rulon wanted to embrace polygamy, so Zola divorced him and he lost their three children.

Years later, Rulon dreamed about dark clouds that eventually subsided. He decided this dream was about Zola. After Zola's husband died in 2002, Rulon sent me and my father-in-law, Adrian Morgan, to ask Zola if she would marry Rulon again. She wouldn't let us in, so Rulon sent several of his young wives. Zola met with them but refused to consider remarrying Rulon.

THREE MONTHS AFTER WE MET, I PROPOSED TO SPRING. JESSICA agreed to sign the divorce papers if I relinquished my rights to our underage children. Otherwise, Jessica threatened, the kids would be drawn into a battle. For their sake, I agreed. Spring and I were married on February 8, 2017.

As I continued experiencing the LDS Church, I felt good about it. I'd never liked polygamy—it didn't resonate with me, and I'd never sought it. I liked how the LDS Church had proof of priesthood succession. I believe that God is order, and the LDS Church provided order. I preferred this to baseless FLDS stories about how Wilford Woodruff was a false prophet and committed polygamist John W. Woolley was the true successor.

After several months of thorough vetting, I was baptized into the LDS Church in January 2017. I had to meet not only with our local stake president and mission president but also with a senior official at LDS headquarters in Salt Lake City. The church wanted to make sure I completely disavowed polygamy and would not preach any false doctrine.

People often ask me if I'm bitter that God has asked me to endure so much. My life has been difficult, but it's made me a better man. In the FLDS, I felt no love from God—he was a being to be feared. Now, I have a deeper relationship with Heavenly Father. I can feel his love, as well as Spring's.

It has definitely been worth it.

Chapter Thirty-Three

It's Not Over Yet

EVEN THOUGH WARREN JEFFS WILL NEVER AGAIN BE A FREE MAN, HE continues to run the FLDS Church and act as prophet. His sentence has turned him into a martyr. His loyal followers seem more willing than ever to heed his call. At the same time, many FLDS still believe that Rulon Jeffs will eventually be renewed, take his rightful place as prophet, and lead the people to utopia.

Meanwhile, Warren has plenty of opportunities to communicate with the FLDS people. He's authorized to email, and he can use the prison phone once a week for fifteen minutes. Every Sunday, up to ten direct family members can visit, including mother, brothers, sisters, sons, daughters, and wives. He sends out written revelations with family members and his attorneys. Technically, the lawyers are only allowed to take out documents pertinent to Warren's case. The prison has caught them sneaking out revelations but has never reprimanded them.

Before and after his 2011 Texas trial, Warren wrote letters to world leaders such as U.S. president Barack Obama, Russian president Vladimir Putin, Mexican president Enrique Peña Nieto, and Canadian prime minister Stephen Harper. He wrote to every U.S. congressman, governor, and legislator, and he sent a copy of his letter to every U.S. library. Among other ramblings, Warren stated: "Follow me, or the world will be destroyed."

To spread Warren's writings, Lyle bought a huge printing press because no commercial printer could keep up. They put the press in a special building in Short Creek, surrounded by a fifteen-foot fence with guards stationed at all hours. They took truckloads of mail to the local post office.

At one point, Warren received a revelation that Mount Olympus above Salt Lake City would crack open and come crashing down. According to Warren, the mountain was full of water. Once it broke open, a flood would destroy the Salt Lake Valley. Another time, Warren commanded the people to store two thousand pounds of whole-kernel wheat per person. The streets of the Crick became crowded with forklifts moving pallets of wheat from house to house.

With Warren absent, no new marriages were taking place. About a year after my lawsuit, my moles informed me that Warren had also declared all existing celestial marriages null and void. Married couples could no longer have sex—they had to sleep in separate rooms or, if that wasn't possible, put books between themselves. Until they proved they could live the celestial law, they couldn't hug, kiss, or even hold hands.

A few months later, I learned Warren's reason, and it sickened me. The Lord had found only fifteen men worthy enough to father children. These men, through a special ordinance, became the only ones who could impregnate women. The husband was required to stay in the bedroom and supervise the act of impregnation.

FROM PRISON, WARREN TRIED TO MAINTAIN CONTROL OF THE Church's YFZ Ranch in Texas. In 2011, he instructed the people to build an amphitheater at the ranch. Seating up to five thousand people, the structure would feature a statue of Warren wearing long robes, like Christ. In one hand, he would hold a book. His other hand would hold a child by the hand. Growing up FLDS, I'd always been taught that making something in the likeness of ourselves was evil.

This amphitheater was to serve as a gathering place after the final destruction. During this desolation, the Church's true people would be lifted up and saved. After the desolation, the faithful FLDS would gather with the returning people of Enoch in the amphitheater, and Warren would instruct them. However, construction abruptly stopped about halfway through, and the statue was never made.

In 2013, Warren instructed the people to build a tower one hundred and fifty feet high at the ranch. With two cranes and probably $1 million worth of materials, the people constructed a concrete tower with two-foot-thick walls. No one knew what it was for, but it seemed capable of surviving a nuclear bomb. The day the tower was completed, Warren received a revelation to tear it down, and so the people did.

After Warren revealed that Texas was no longer a chosen place, people started moving to Pringle, South Dakota. I think the Church intends Pringle to become the new Short Creek, complete with a temple. In 2014, the state of Texas seized the YFZ property to cover the cost of the raid and subsequent trial. More recently, several FLDS leaders, including Lyle Jeffs and Seth Jeffs, were arrested for food-stamp fraud and money laundering. Lyle Jeffs, Warren's loyal mouthpiece, was subsequently banished from the church.

With all the lawsuits and upheavals, I wouldn't be surprised to see the FLDS Church crumble and fall apart. I can only hope.

Acknowledgements

WALLACE, SHAUNA, AND SHERRY WOULD LIKE TO THANK CHRIS BIGElow at Zarahemla Books for his belief in this story as well as his gifted editing. This book would not have been possible without his support and vision. Thanks too to Jason Robinson for his talent in creating the amazing cover.

WALLACE JEFFS: I WANT TO THANK SHAUNA PACKER AND SHERRY TAYlor for believing in me enough to take the time to write my story. It has been an emotional and difficult journey, but so very worth the effort.

I wish to thank all of my twenty-eight children for their love and support. I wrote this book to show them how much I love each and every one of them. And, for my beautiful wife Spring, who has given me the confidence, love, and support in order for me to find the courage to write this book and has shown me how important family truly is.

Thank you to Sam Brower for putting in long hours of research and time to help me achieve a free life for myself and my kids.

I would like to thank the Utah and Washington County Sheriff's Departments, the FBI, and the Utah Attorney General's Office for their willingness to put many months of time, effort, and expertise into assisting me with the rescue of my children and bringing them to a safe place.

I would like to thank Roger Hoole and his wife Sharon for their professional insight through this tough situation and their never-wavering friendship and encouragement.

Finally, I wish to thank my youngest children for their continued smiles and hugs when times were tough.

SHAUNA PACKER: I would like to thank Sherry Taylor for her kindness and trust in thinking about me when this project was presented to her. Also, Wallace Jeffs for his bravery in telling his story. It has been a true pleasure to work on this project with both of you.

Kudos to the Point Writers for their friendship, brilliant insight, and tough love as needed over the years. I am blessed to have the viewpoints and advice of such gifted wordsmiths. Best of all, your stories and characters live large in my head. Thanks to Terri Barton, Sarah Beard, Sabine Berlin, Ami Chopine, Paul Eckheart, Alyson Parry, Chris Weston, Kylee Wilkins, and Garrett Winn.

Thanks to Angela Hallstrom for making the introduction to Chris Bigelow during a very difficult time in your life. You really are an angel on earth.

I feel such gratitude for all my wonderful clients who I have worked with throughout the years; it is such a pleasure to be a part of your lives and projects. Particularly, I have loved all the fabulous stories I have had the honor of reading and helping you to nurture. You inspire me!

Finally, a warm thank you to my family for always standing behind me. It is possible to do difficult things when you know you have a safety net under you.

SHERRY TAYLOR: I'd like to thank Wallace Jeffs for his faith and trust in asking me to help him tell his story and for his courage to bring such a sensitive topic to light. Also, Shauna Packer for her willingness to help pull this all together. Your research, organization, and computer skills far exceed my own. It has been so much fun working with you both on this incredible project.

I'd also like to thank my family for their love and support. You truly hold me up with your love and encouragement so I can reach new heights that I never dreamed were possible. And my friends, whose excitement for this project always brought a smile to my face. You guys are the best!

About the Authors

WALLACE JEFFS WAS BORN THE THIRTIETH CHILD OF RULON JEFFS, polygamous prophet of the Fundamentalist Church of Jesus Christ of Latter-Day Saints (FLDS). Wallace is half-brother to imprisoned FLDS prophet Warren Jeffs. Raised as a devout FLDS member, Wallace was eventually excommunicated for defying Warren. After the FLDS prophet kidnapped Wallace's children, Wallace worked with the FBI and other authorities to ensure his brother could never hurt another young girl. Now he helps people leave the FLDS community and advocates for human rights and the protection of children. Father of twenty children and stepfather of eight, Wallace lives in Salt Lake City, Utah.

SHAUNA PACKER HAS BEEN A PROFESSIONAL CORPORATE AND FREE-lance writer, researcher, and content editor for over twelve years. She is a multi-award-winning fiction and nonfiction author. Shauna has been published in several anthologies, including *Angels to Bear You Up*, *Utah Voices: A Literary Annual*, and *Mother's Messages in a Bottle*. She resides in Salt Lake City, Utah.

SHERRY TAYLOR HAS PUBLISHED HER POETRY IN THE NATIONAL Library of Poetry's book *The Voice Within*. She has three anecdotes published in the anthology *Mormon Mishaps and Mischief: Hilarious Stories for Saints*. Sherry is the author of a young adult fantasy series called the Ceramia Trilogy. She lives in Salt Lake City, Utah.

www.ingramcontent.com/pod-product-compliance
Lightning Source LLC
Chambersburg PA
CBHW020419010526
44118CB00010B/322